AT THE END OF YOUR TETHER

CREATED AND WRITTEN BY:

ADAM SMITH

ILLUSTRATED BY:

V.V. GLASS

COLORED BY:

HILARY JENKINS

LETTERED BY:

JIM CAMPBELL

COVER BY:

DEENA SO'OTEH

DESIGNED BY:

MIKE REDDY & ANDWORLD DESIGN

EDITED BY:

JASMINE AMIRI

Published by Oni-Lion Forge Publishing Group, LLC

James Lucas Jones, president & publisher • **Sarah Gaydos,** editor in chief
Charlie Chu, e.v.p. of creative & business development • **Brad Rooks,**
director of operations • **Amber O'Neill,** special projects manager
Harris Fish, events manager • **Margot Wood,** director of marketing & sales
Jeremy Atkins, director of brand communications • **Devin Funches,** sales &
marketing manager • **Tara Lehmann,** marketing & publicity associate
Troy Look, director of design & production • **Kate Z. Stone,** senior graphic
designer • **Sonja Synak,** graphic designer • **Hilary Thompson,** graphic
designer • **Angie Knowles,** digital prepress lead • **Shawna Gore,** senior
editor • **Robin Herrera,** senior editor • **Amanda Meadows,** senior editor
Jasmine Amiri, editor • **Grace Bornhoft,** editor • **Zack Soto,** editor • **Steve
Ellis,** director of games • **Ben Eisner,** game developer • **Michelle Nguyen,**
executive assistant • **Jung Lee,** logistics coordinator
Joe Nozemack, publisher emeritus

1319 SE Martin Luther King, Jr. Blvd.
Suite 240
Portland, OR 97214

onipress.com
facebook.com/onipress
twitter.com/onipress
onipress.tumblr.com
instagram.com/onipress

First Edition: February 2020
ISBN 978-1-62010-731-7
eISBN 978-1-62010-726-3

Library of Congress Control Number: 2019945818

1 2 3 4 5 6 7 8 9 10

FOREWORD

I was, at first, very much not going to write this foreword.

My editor Jasmine was putting the trade together and told me I could do this. Or alternatively, a dedication page, thanking all the folks who made *At the End of Your Tether* a real, functioning comic, instead of just loose notes and hope. I was leaning that direction because honestly, it felt off writing an introduction to a story that I wrote. It felt like whistling along to a song instead of just listening.

I also wasn't sure if I had anything to add to Ludo and Arlo's story that I hadn't already said in the hundred-and-twenty pages beautifully illustrated and brought to life by V.V., Hilary & Jim. So, I thought about who to thank, wrote some names down, and then ended the list with Arlo and Ludo.

Now, I know this sounds pretentious, but I genuinely love those two. 'Love' is not a word I toss around much outside of maybe ten people, coffee, bikes, and comix. But I looked at their names on that list, and there was enough distance between writing the scripts after my bar shifts, that it struck me that I sincerely *missed* these two. I thought again about writing a foreword and I realized that while I may not have anything new to say about their experience together, (as that's something I like to let float around like a lost kite) I suppose I could tell you what Arlo and Ludo mean to me.

As a person, I'm trying to be better. I don't think I'm awful by any stretch of the word, but as I get older, I hope that I'm more than what I was the day before. When I think back to the things I've written, the things I'm pitching now, or the real-life folk I love; they're all steadfast on trying. Watching these two kids screw up, make mistakes, and *try* over the extent of their story was something I needed in my life at that particular moment in time.

And I love them for helping me through that moment. I love them because of the way they loved one another. Maybe in ways that made them selfish, or screw-ups at times. But I think that's what life is, at least to me. It's thinking about the day before, and what can be done today to be better.

I hope that comes across in *At the End of Your Tether*. I hope you see Arlo and Ludo try. I hope it comes across in the way V.V. flawlessly illustrated Benny's head on Myriam's shoulder. I hope you see it in the sunsets painted by Hilary, and hear it in the way Jim perfectly lettered the cadence and tone, turning simple texts on a screen into genuine voices coming out of living characters. I hope this book feels like a hug by the time you read the last page. You have Jasmine to thank for that, as she put the whole team together and wrangled some pretty unruly scripts into the story she knew I wanted to tell.

That's what I hope.

But, I'm trying to be better. By the end of typing up this foreword, I think I'm a little more alright with the idea of whistling along if it makes you smile. That's something I didn't believe yesterday, and I think I'm better off for it.

-Adam Smith

CHAPTER ONE

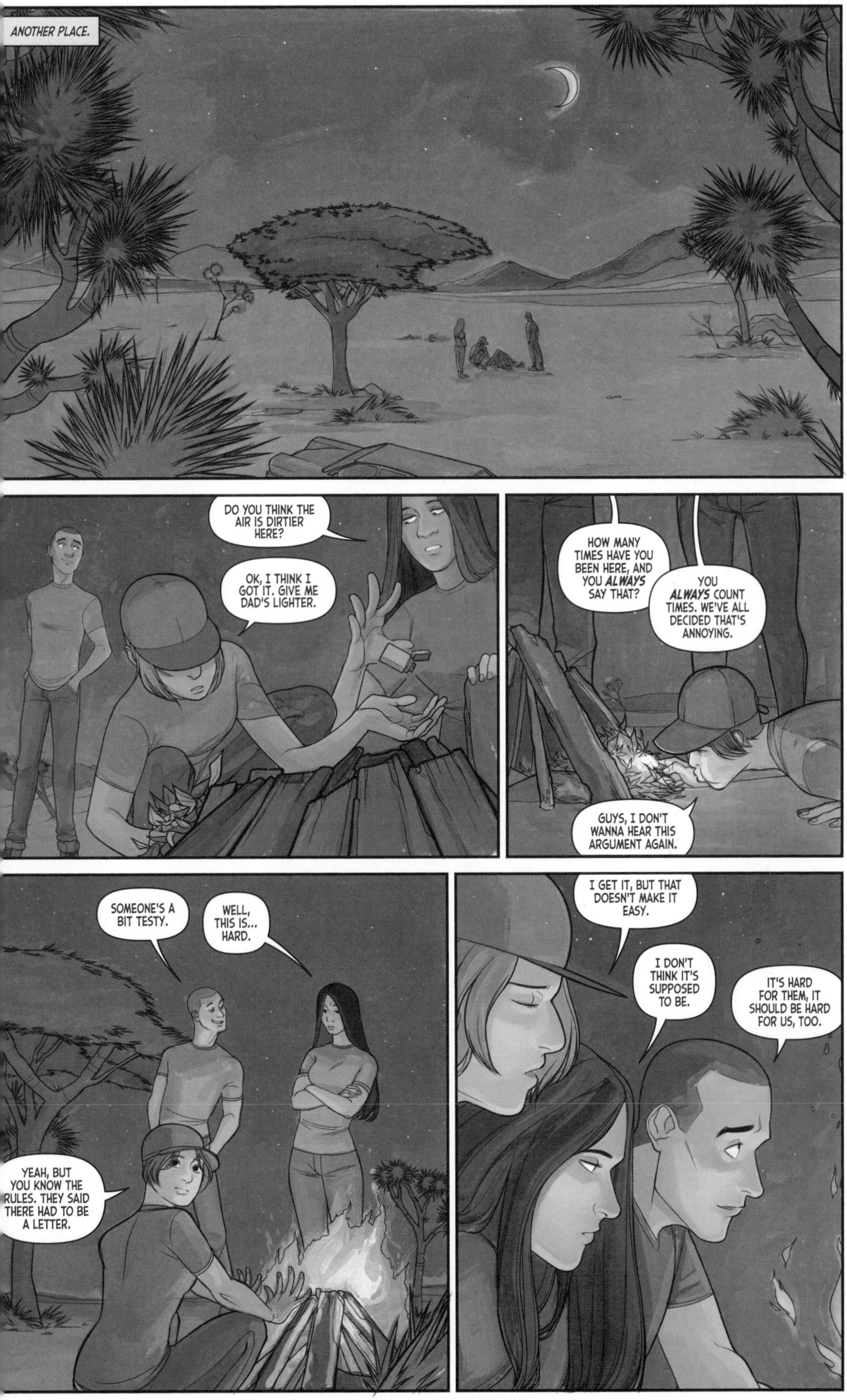
ANOTHER PLACE.
DO YOU THINK THE AIR IS DIRTIER HERE?
OK, I THINK I GOT IT. GIVE ME DAD'S LIGHTER.
HOW MANY TIMES HAVE YOU BEEN HERE, AND YOU *ALWAYS* SAY THAT?
YOU *ALWAYS* COUNT TIMES. WE'VE ALL DECIDED THAT'S ANNOYING.
GUYS, I DON'T WANNA HEAR THIS ARGUMENT AGAIN.
SOMEONE'S A BIT TESTY.
WELL, THIS IS... HARD.
YEAH, BUT YOU KNOW THE RULES. THEY SAID THERE HAD TO BE A LETTER.
I GET IT, BUT THAT DOESN'T MAKE IT EASY.
I DON'T THINK IT'S SUPPOSED TO BE.
IT'S HARD FOR THEM, IT SHOULD BE HARD FOR US, TOO.

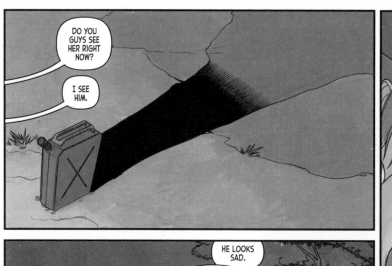

DO YOU GUYS SEE HER RIGHT NOW?

I SEE HIM.

IT'S OKAY, WE'LL COME BACK LATER.

YEAH, I UNDERSTAND.

HE LOOKS SAD.

LOOK AT HIM. NOW, LISTEN TO WHAT HE'S SAYING.

DID YOU BRING THE THING?

YOU DID.

SORRY GUYS, I'M JUST OUT OF IT.

DON'T BE SORRY, IT'S HAPPENED BEFORE AND IT'LL HAPPEN AGAIN. YOU'RE OKAY.

THANKS, GUYS.

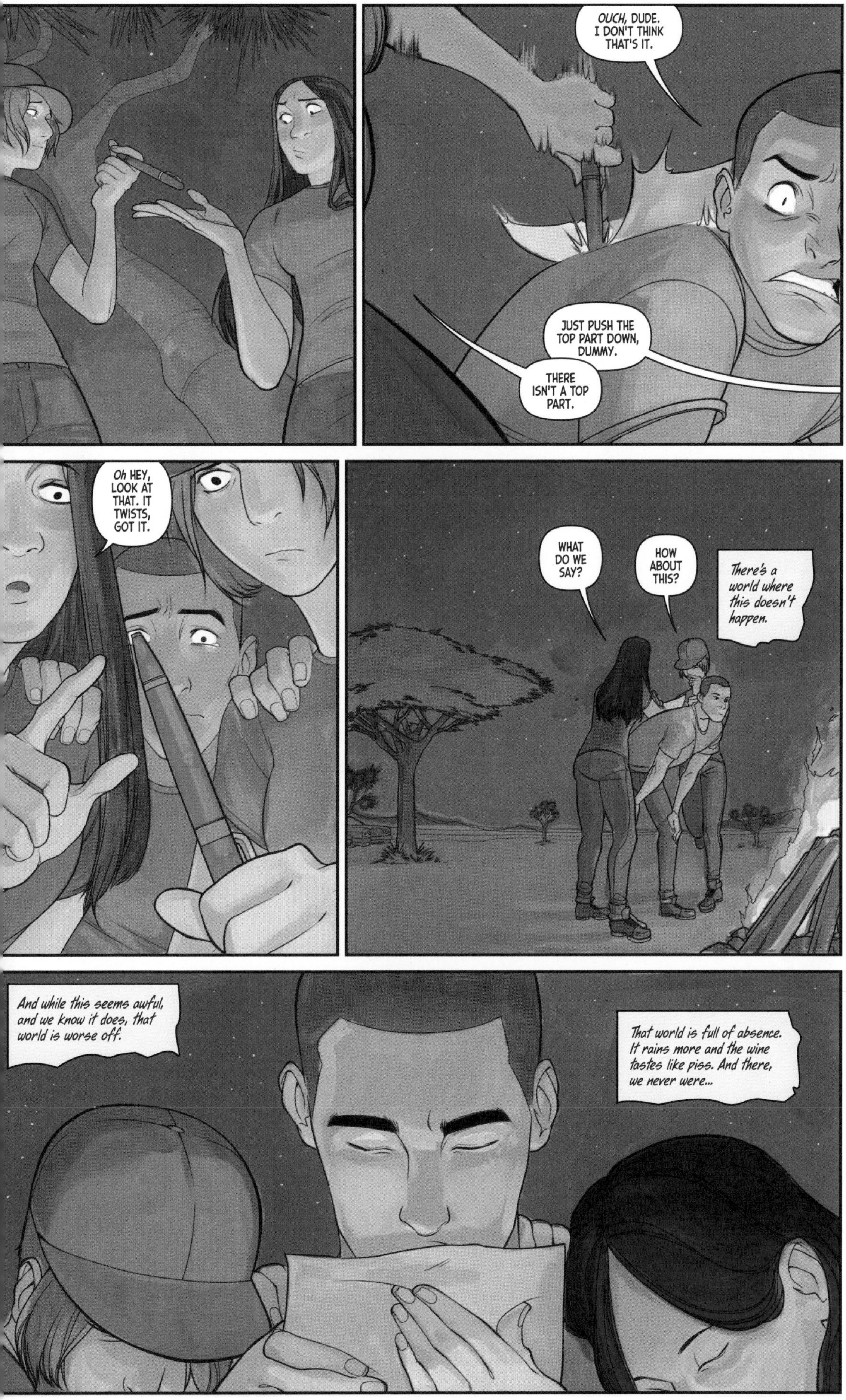
OUCH, DUDE. I DON'T THINK THAT'S IT.
JUST PUSH THE TOP PART DOWN, DUMMY.
THERE ISN'T A TOP PART.
Oh HEY, LOOK AT THAT. IT TWISTS, GOT IT.
WHAT DO WE SAY?
HOW ABOUT THIS?
There's a world where this doesn't happen.
And while this seems awful, and we know it does, that world is worse off.
That world is full of absence. It rains more and the wine tastes like piss. And there, we never were...

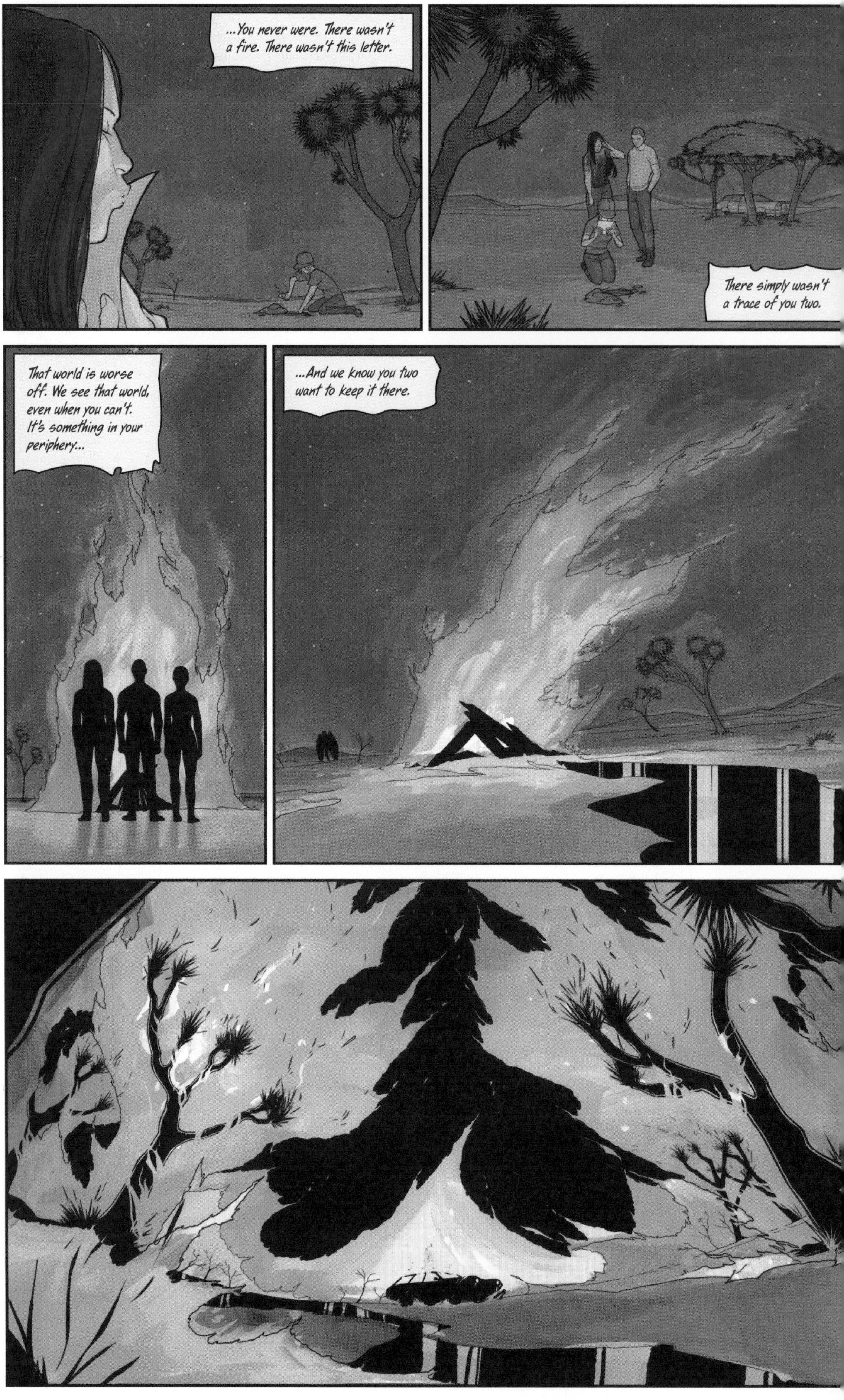
...You never were. There wasn't a fire. There wasn't this letter.
There simply wasn't a trace of you two.
That world is worse off. We see that world, even when you can't. It's something in your periphery...
...And we know you two want to keep it there.

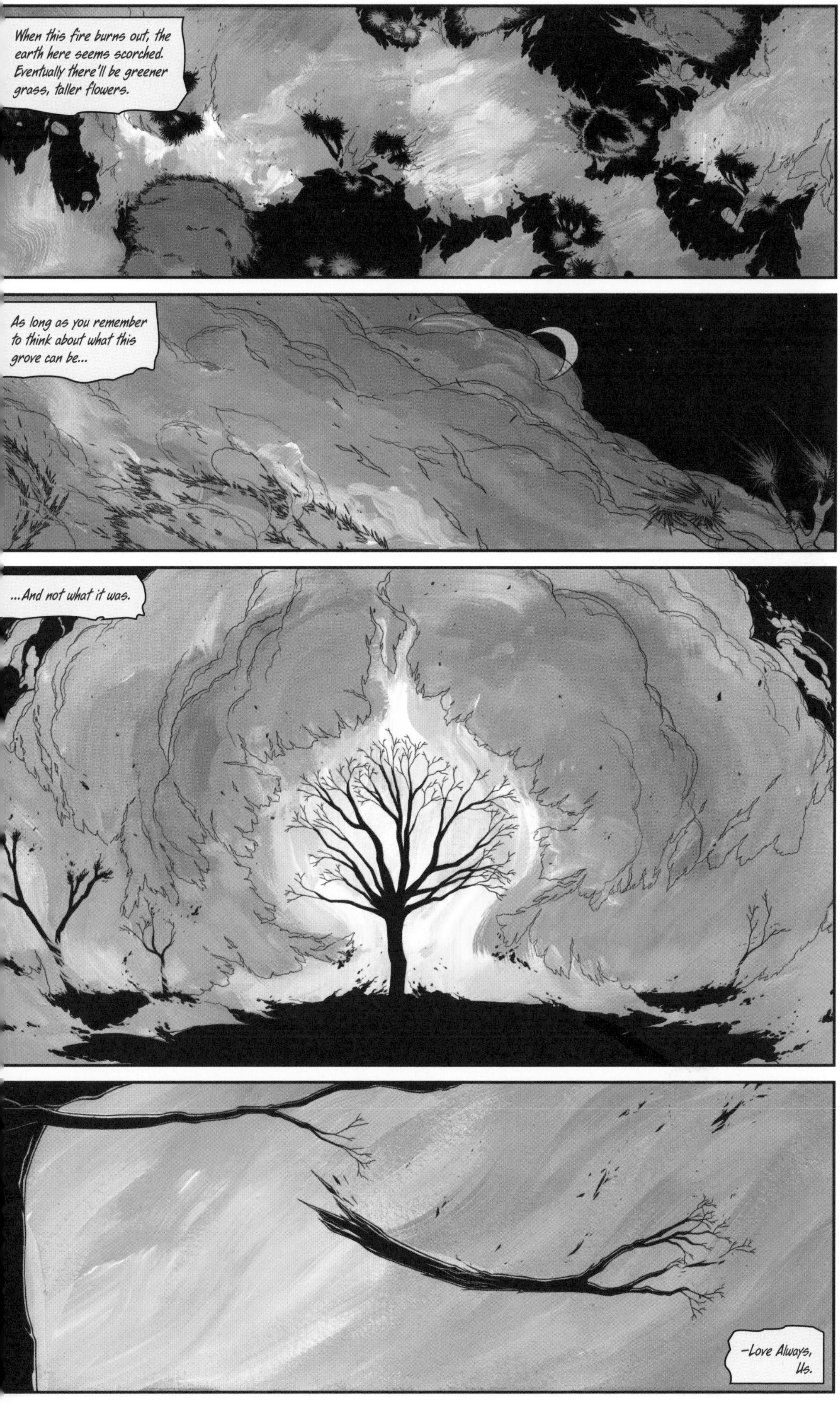
When this fire burns out, the earth here seems scorched. Eventually there'll be greener grass, taller flowers.
As long as you remember to think about what this grove can be...
...And not what it was.
–Love Always,
Us.

Part I:
Another Place,
Another Time

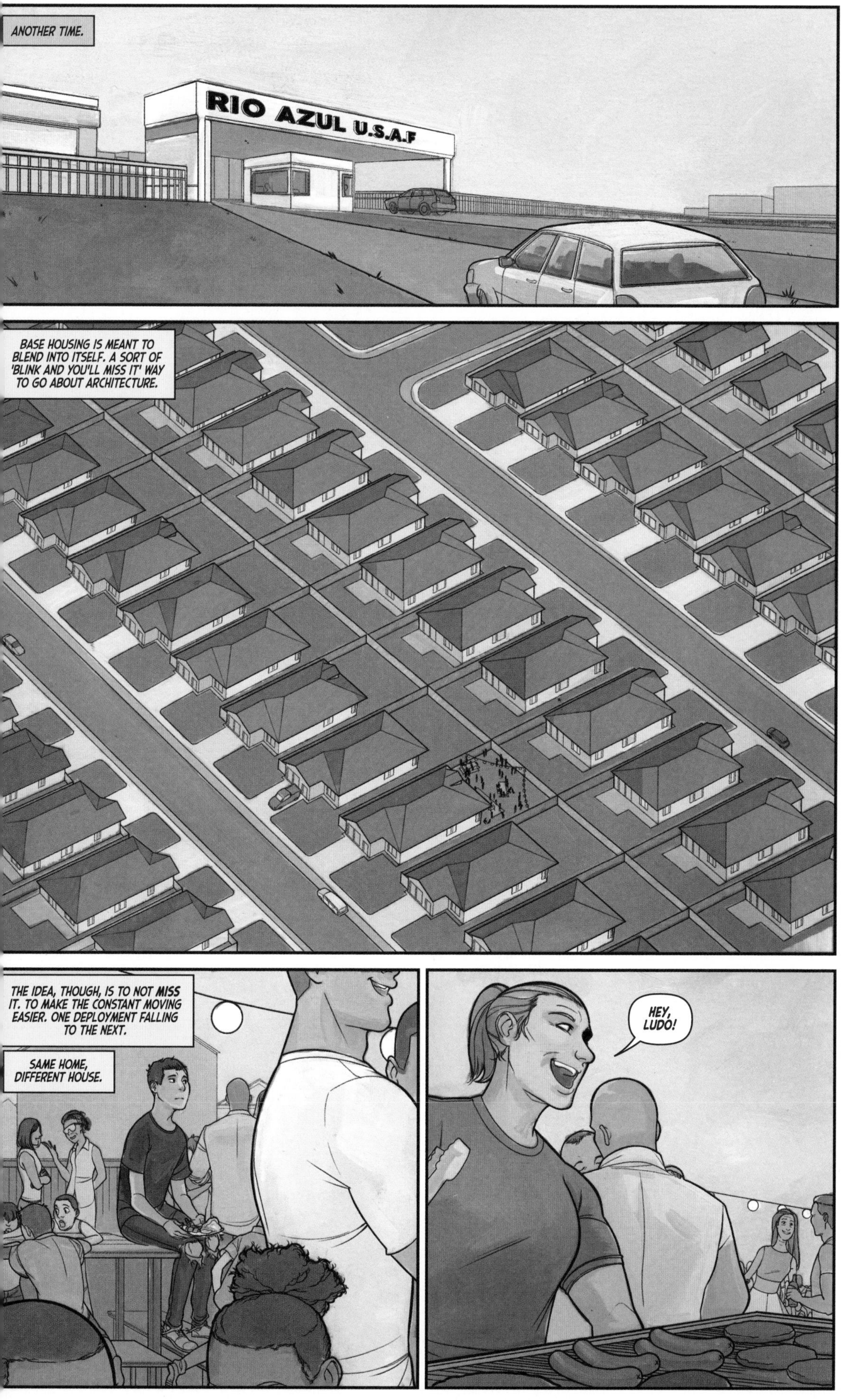
ANOTHER TIME.
RIO AZUL U.S.A.F
BASE HOUSING IS MEANT TO BLEND INTO ITSELF. A SORT OF 'BLINK AND YOU'LL MISS IT' WAY TO GO ABOUT ARCHITECTURE.
THE IDEA, THOUGH, IS TO NOT MISS IT. TO MAKE THE CONSTANT MOVING EASIER. ONE DEPLOYMENT FALLING TO THE NEXT.
SAME HOME, DIFFERENT HOUSE.
HEY, LUDO!

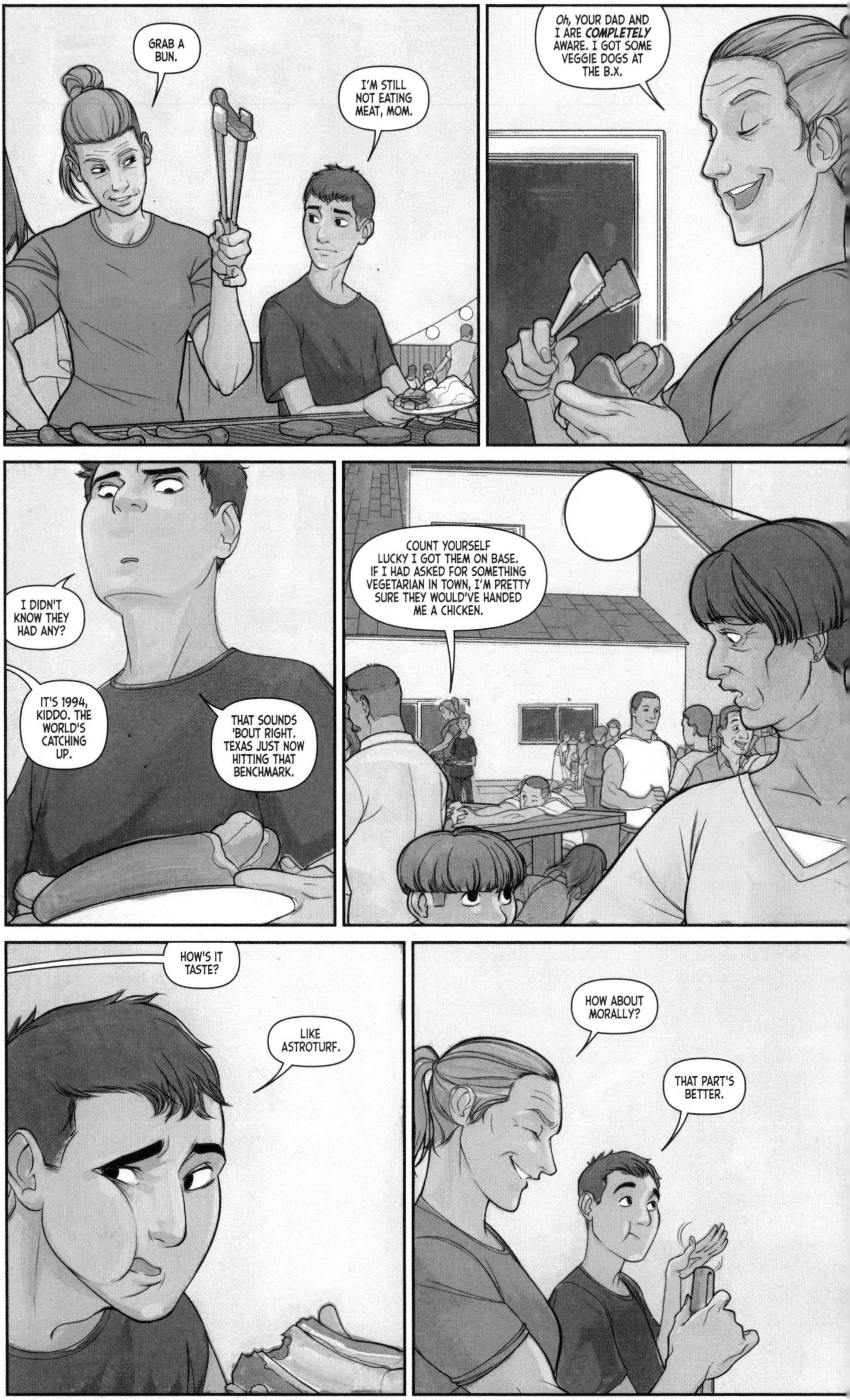
GRAB A BUN.
I'M STILL NOT EATING MEAT, MOM.
Oh, YOUR DAD AND I ARE ***COMPLETELY*** AWARE. I GOT SOME VEGGIE DOGS AT THE B.X.
I DIDN'T KNOW THEY HAD ANY?
IT'S 1994, KIDDO. THE WORLD'S CATCHING UP.
THAT SOUNDS 'BOUT RIGHT. TEXAS JUST NOW HITTING THAT BENCHMARK.
COUNT YOURSELF LUCKY I GOT THEM ON BASE. IF I HAD ASKED FOR SOMETHING VEGETARIAN IN TOWN, I'M PRETTY SURE THEY WOULD'VE HANDED ME A CHICKEN.
HOW'S IT TASTE?
LIKE ASTROTURF.
HOW ABOUT MORALLY?
THAT PART'S BETTER.

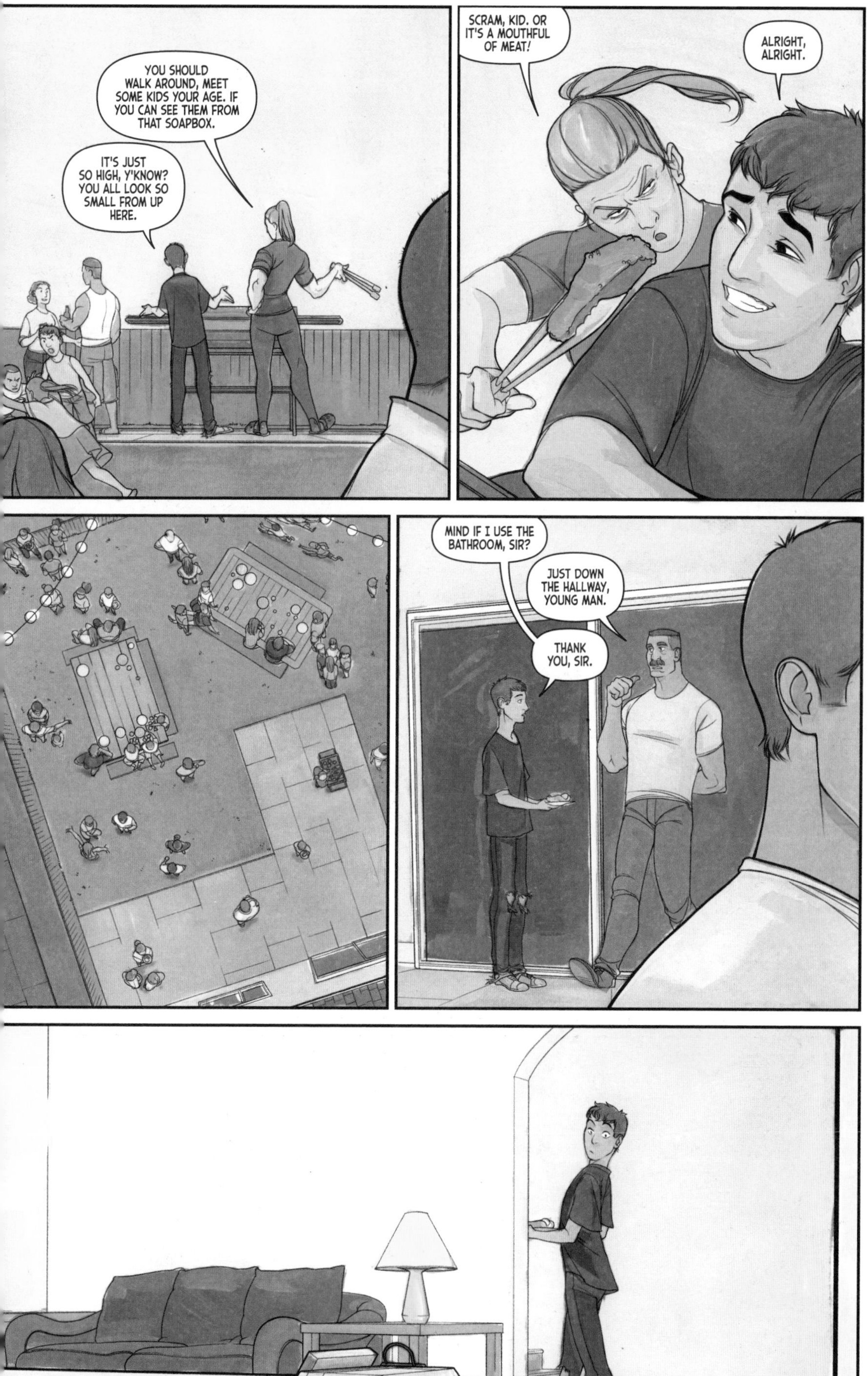
YOU SHOULD WALK AROUND, MEET SOME KIDS YOUR AGE. IF YOU CAN SEE THEM FROM THAT SOAPBOX.
IT'S JUST SO HIGH, Y'KNOW? YOU ALL LOOK SO SMALL FROM UP HERE.
SCRAM, KID. OR IT'S A MOUTHFUL OF MEAT!
ALRIGHT, ALRIGHT.
MIND IF I USE THE BATHROOM, SIR?
JUST DOWN THE HALLWAY, YOUNG MAN.
THANK YOU, SIR.

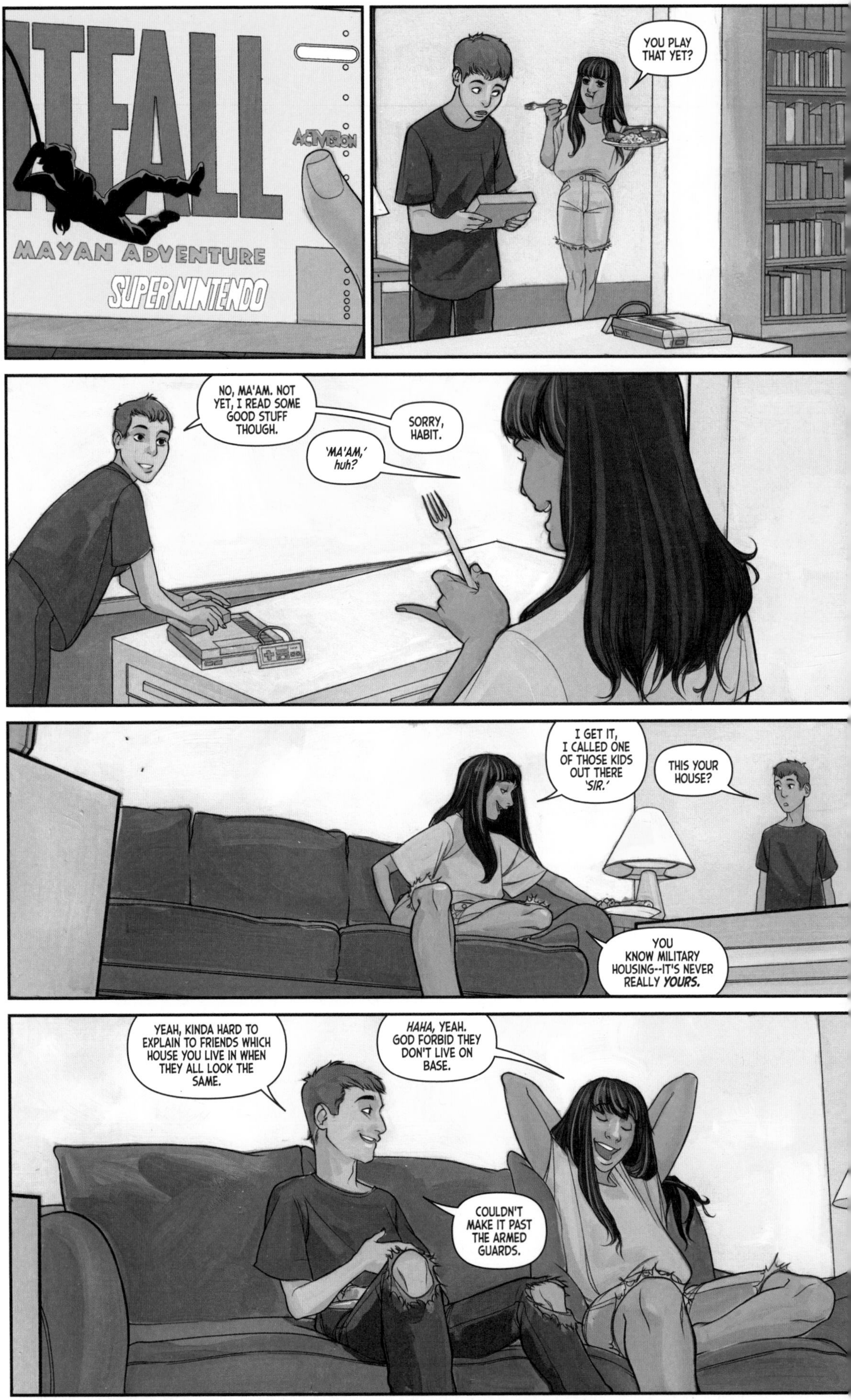
ITFALL
ACTIVISION
MAYAN ADVENTURE
SUPER NINTENDO
YOU PLAY THAT YET?
NO, MA'AM. NOT YET, I READ SOME GOOD STUFF THOUGH.
SORRY, HABIT.
'MA'AM,' huh?
I GET IT, I CALLED ONE OF THOSE KIDS OUT THERE *'SIR.'*
THIS YOUR HOUSE?
YOU KNOW MILITARY HOUSING--IT'S NEVER REALLY ***YOURS.***
YEAH, KINDA HARD TO EXPLAIN TO FRIENDS WHICH HOUSE YOU LIVE IN WHEN THEY ALL LOOK THE SAME.
HAHA, YEAH. GOD FORBID THEY DON'T LIVE ON BASE.
COULDN'T MAKE IT PAST THE ARMED GUARDS.

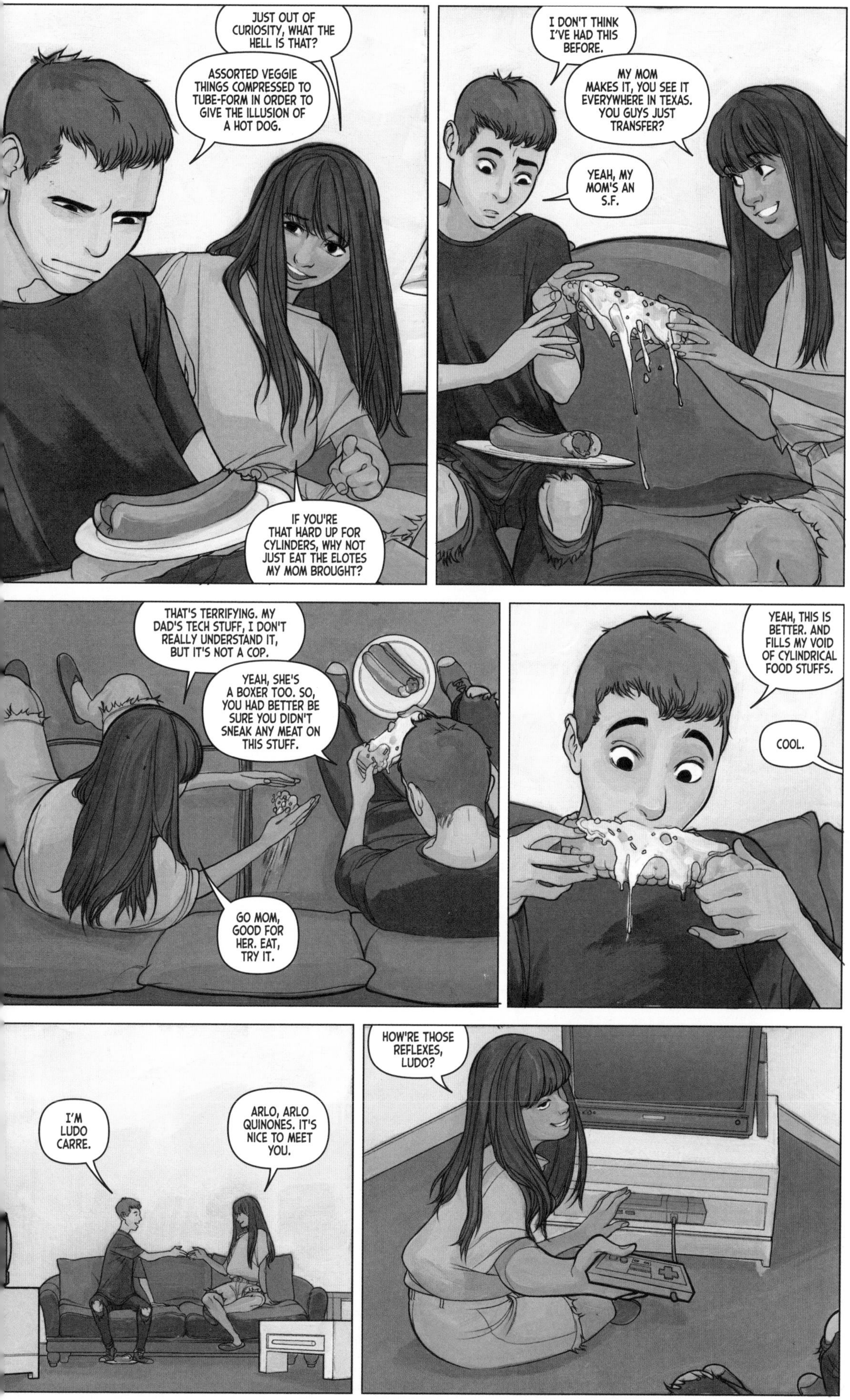
JUST OUT OF CURIOSITY, WHAT THE HELL IS THAT?
ASSORTED VEGGIE THINGS COMPRESSED TO TUBE-FORM IN ORDER TO GIVE THE ILLUSION OF A HOT DOG.
IF YOU'RE THAT HARD UP FOR CYLINDERS, WHY NOT JUST EAT THE ELOTES MY MOM BROUGHT?
I DON'T THINK I'VE HAD THIS BEFORE.
MY MOM MAKES IT, YOU SEE IT EVERYWHERE IN TEXAS. YOU GUYS JUST TRANSFER?
YEAH, MY MOM'S AN S.F.
THAT'S TERRIFYING. MY DAD'S TECH STUFF, I DON'T REALLY UNDERSTAND IT, BUT IT'S NOT A COP.
YEAH, SHE'S A BOXER TOO. SO, YOU HAD BETTER BE SURE YOU DIDN'T SNEAK ANY MEAT ON THIS STUFF.
GO MOM, GOOD FOR HER. EAT, TRY IT.
YEAH, THIS IS BETTER. AND FILLS MY VOID OF CYLINDRICAL FOOD STUFFS.
COOL.
I'M LUDO CARRE.
ARLO, ARLO QUINONES. IT'S NICE TO MEET YOU.
HOW'RE THOSE REFLEXES, LUDO?

NOW.

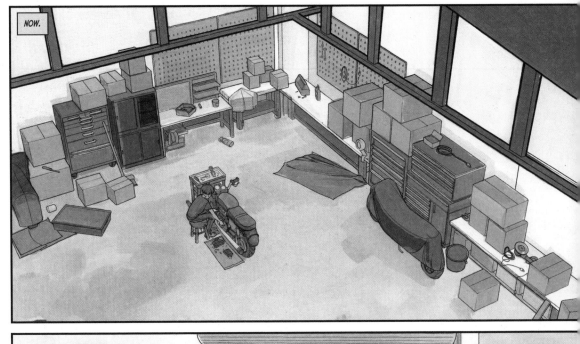

THIS IS IT, BACK HERE.

Oh MAN, LOOK AT THAT.

YOU DID GOOD WORK ON THIS'UN, BENNY.

CAN'T TAKE ALL THE CREDIT. MY BOY LUDO HERE HELPED ME OUT.

GOOD TO MEET YOU, SIR.

HOW MUCH YOU ASKIN' ON THIS?

I DON'T KNOW. IT'S GOT A REBUILT ENGINE, LUDO WELDED THE EXHAUST HIMSELF, ALL NEW ELECTRIC, FAT TIRES, SO MUCH MORE, TOO. GOTTA BE AT LEAST SEVEN GRAND PLUS--

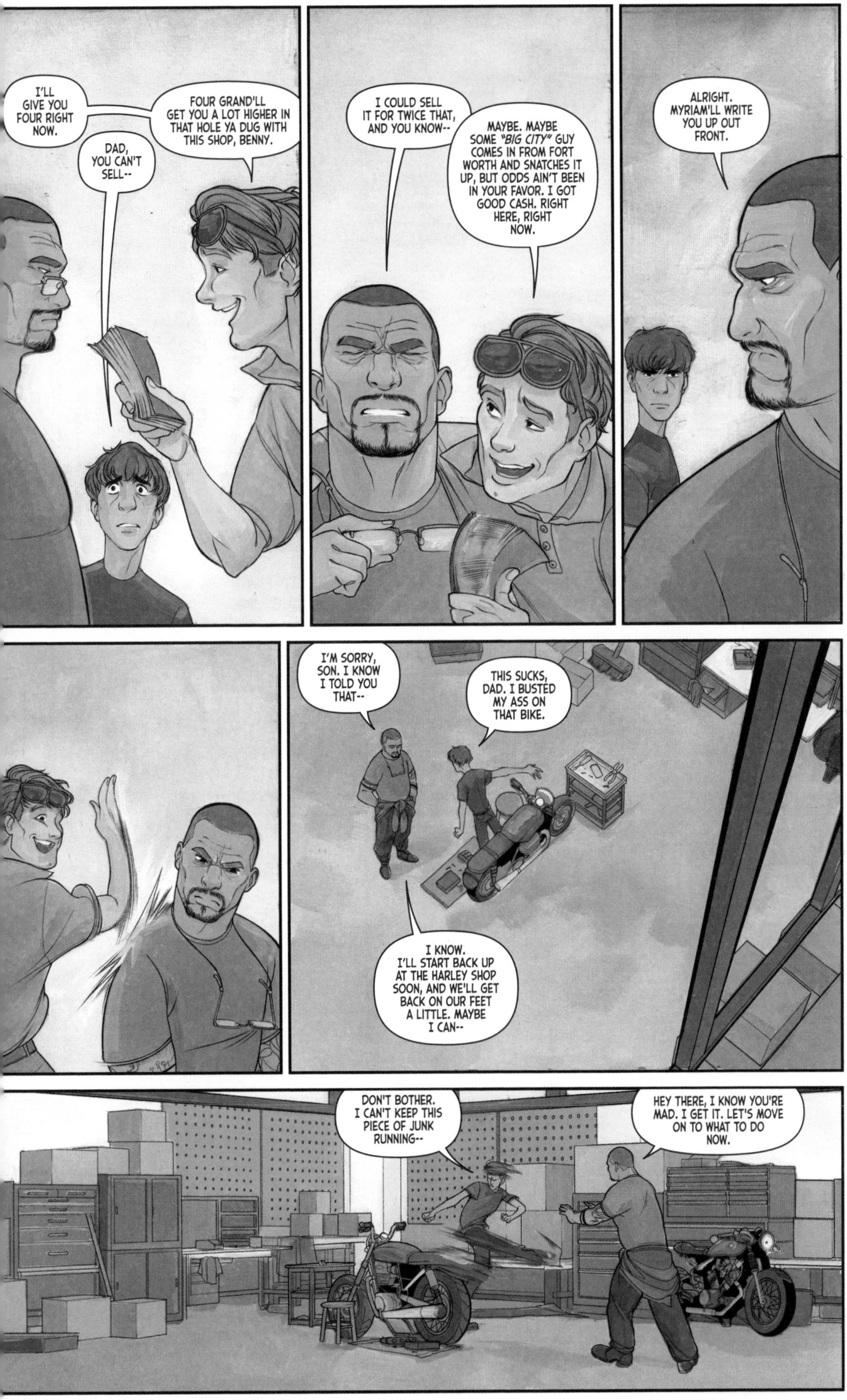
I'LL GIVE YOU FOUR RIGHT NOW.
FOUR GRAND'LL GET YOU A LOT HIGHER IN THAT HOLE YA DUG WITH THIS SHOP, BENNY.
DAD, YOU CAN'T SELL--
I COULD SELL IT FOR TWICE THAT, AND YOU KNOW--
MAYBE. MAYBE SOME "BIG CITY" GUY COMES IN FROM FORT WORTH AND SNATCHES IT UP, BUT ODDS AIN'T BEEN IN YOUR FAVOR. I GOT GOOD CASH. RIGHT HERE, RIGHT NOW.
ALRIGHT. MYRIAM'LL WRITE YOU UP OUT FRONT.
I'M SORRY, SON. I KNOW I TOLD YOU THAT--
THIS SUCKS, DAD. I BUSTED MY ASS ON THAT BIKE.
I KNOW. I'LL START BACK UP AT THE HARLEY SHOP SOON, AND WE'LL GET BACK ON OUR FEET A LITTLE. MAYBE I CAN--
DON'T BOTHER. I CAN'T KEEP THIS PIECE OF JUNK RUNNING--
HEY THERE, I KNOW YOU'RE MAD. I GET IT. LET'S MOVE ON TO WHAT TO DO NOW.

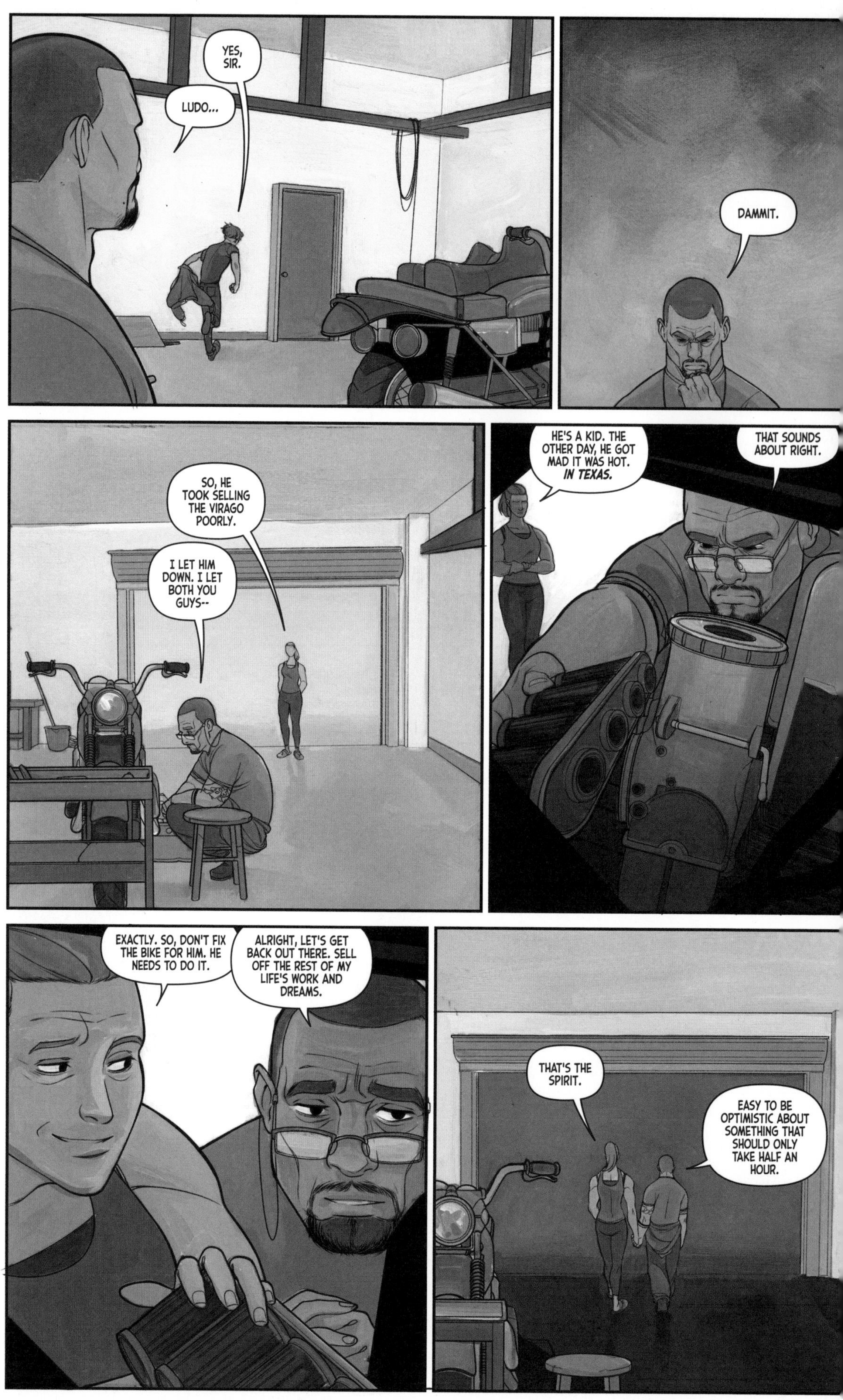
LUDO...
YES, SIR.
DAMMIT.
SO, HE TOOK SELLING THE VIRAGO POORLY.
I LET HIM DOWN. I LET BOTH YOU GUYS--
HE'S A KID. THE OTHER DAY, HE GOT MAD IT WAS HOT. *IN TEXAS.*
THAT SOUNDS ABOUT RIGHT.
EXACTLY. SO, DON'T FIX THE BIKE FOR HIM. HE NEEDS TO DO IT.
ALRIGHT, LET'S GET BACK OUT THERE. SELL OFF THE REST OF MY LIFE'S WORK AND DREAMS.
THAT'S THE SPIRIT.
EASY TO BE OPTIMISTIC ABOUT SOMETHING THAT SHOULD ONLY TAKE HALF AN HOUR.

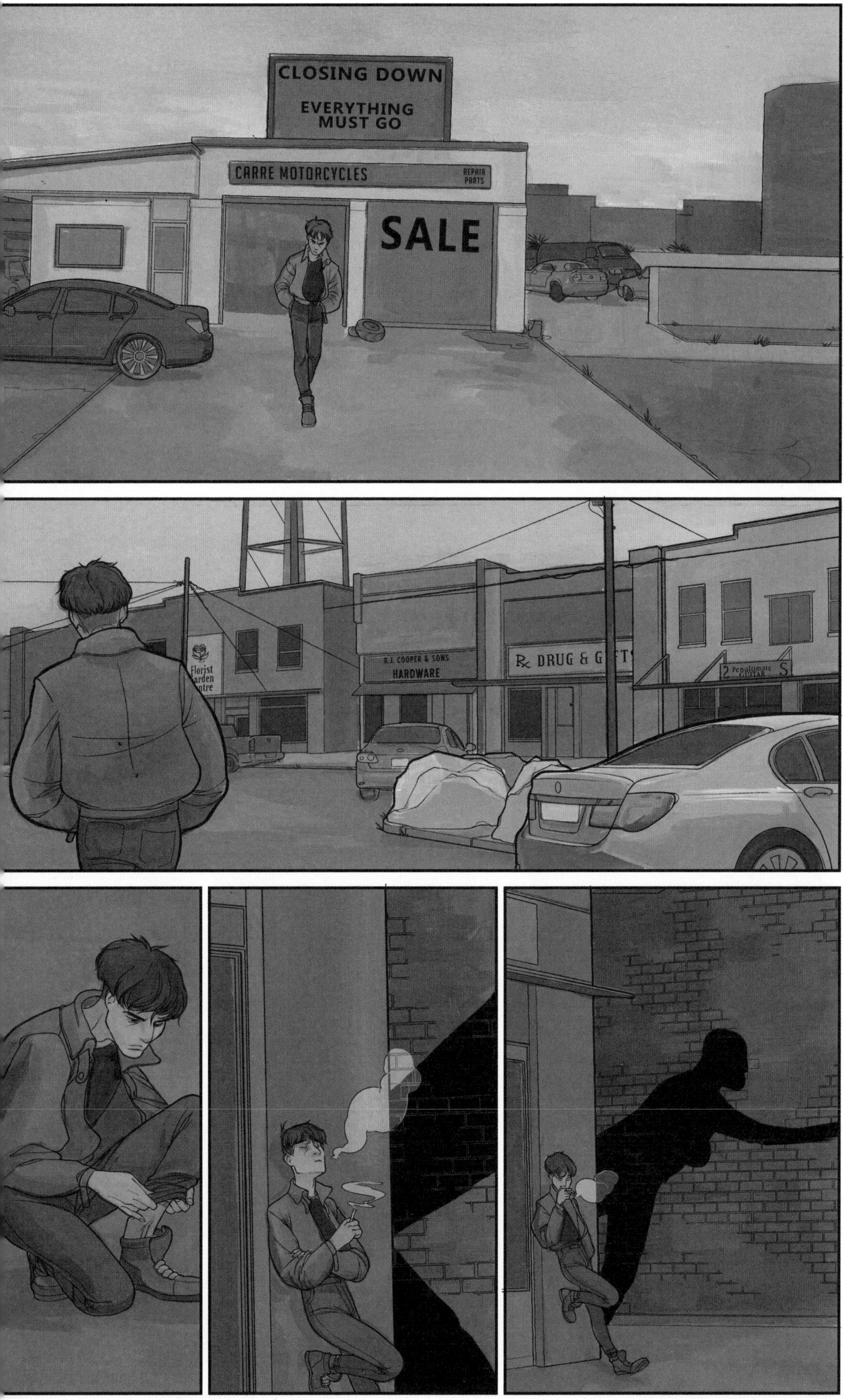
CLOSING DOWN
EVERYTHING MUST GO
CARRE MOTORCYCLES
REPAIR PARTS
SALE
Florist
R.J. COOPER & SONS
HARDWARE
Penultimate GUITAR

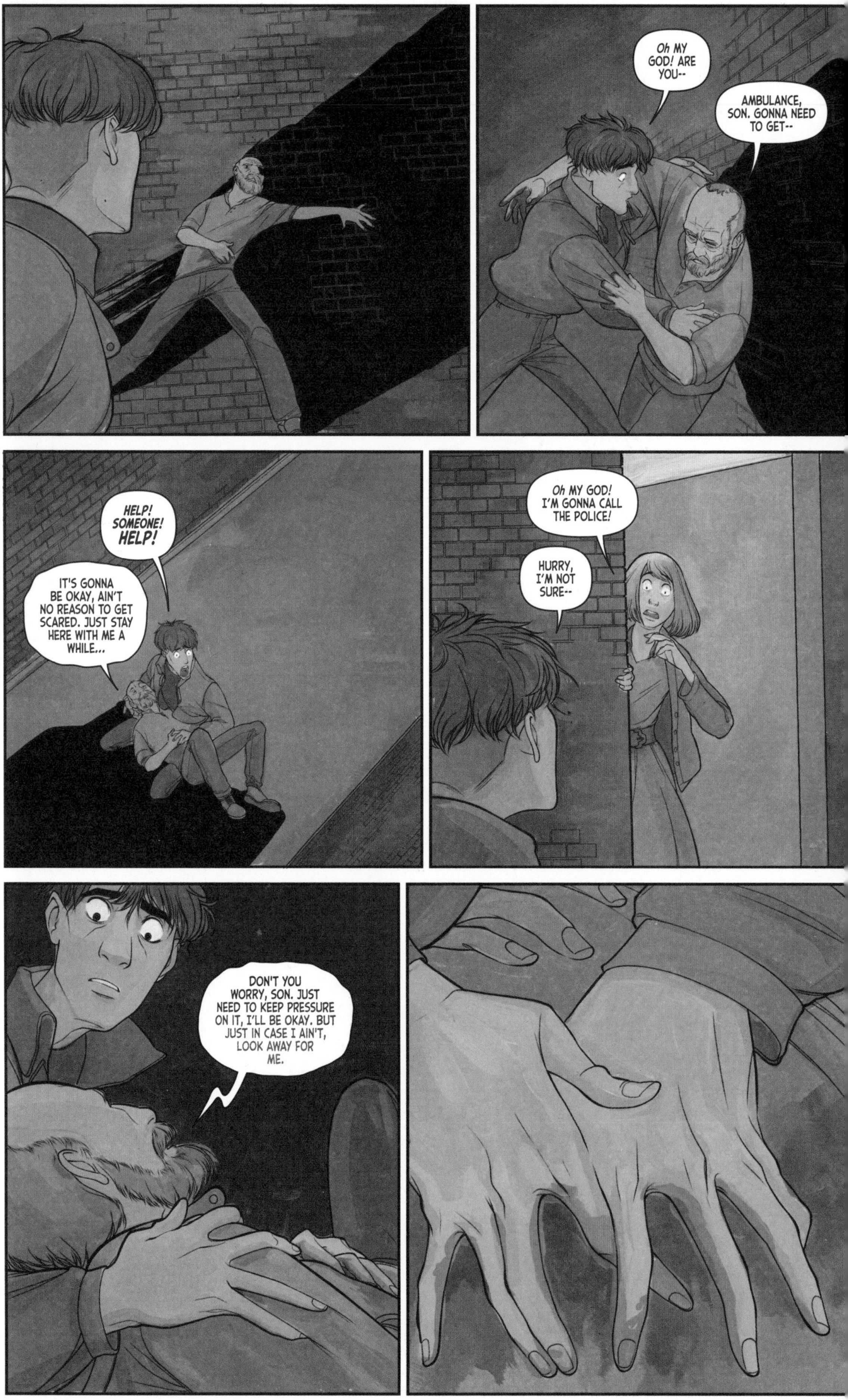
Oh MY GOD! ARE YOU--
AMBULANCE, SON. GONNA NEED TO GET--
HELP! SOMEONE! HELP!
IT'S GONNA BE OKAY, AIN'T NO REASON TO GET SCARED. JUST STAY HERE WITH ME A WHILE...
Oh MY GOD! I'M GONNA CALL THE POLICE!
HURRY, I'M NOT SURE--
DON'T YOU WORRY, SON. JUST NEED TO KEEP PRESSURE ON IT, I'LL BE OKAY. BUT JUST IN CASE I AIN'T, LOOK AWAY FOR ME.

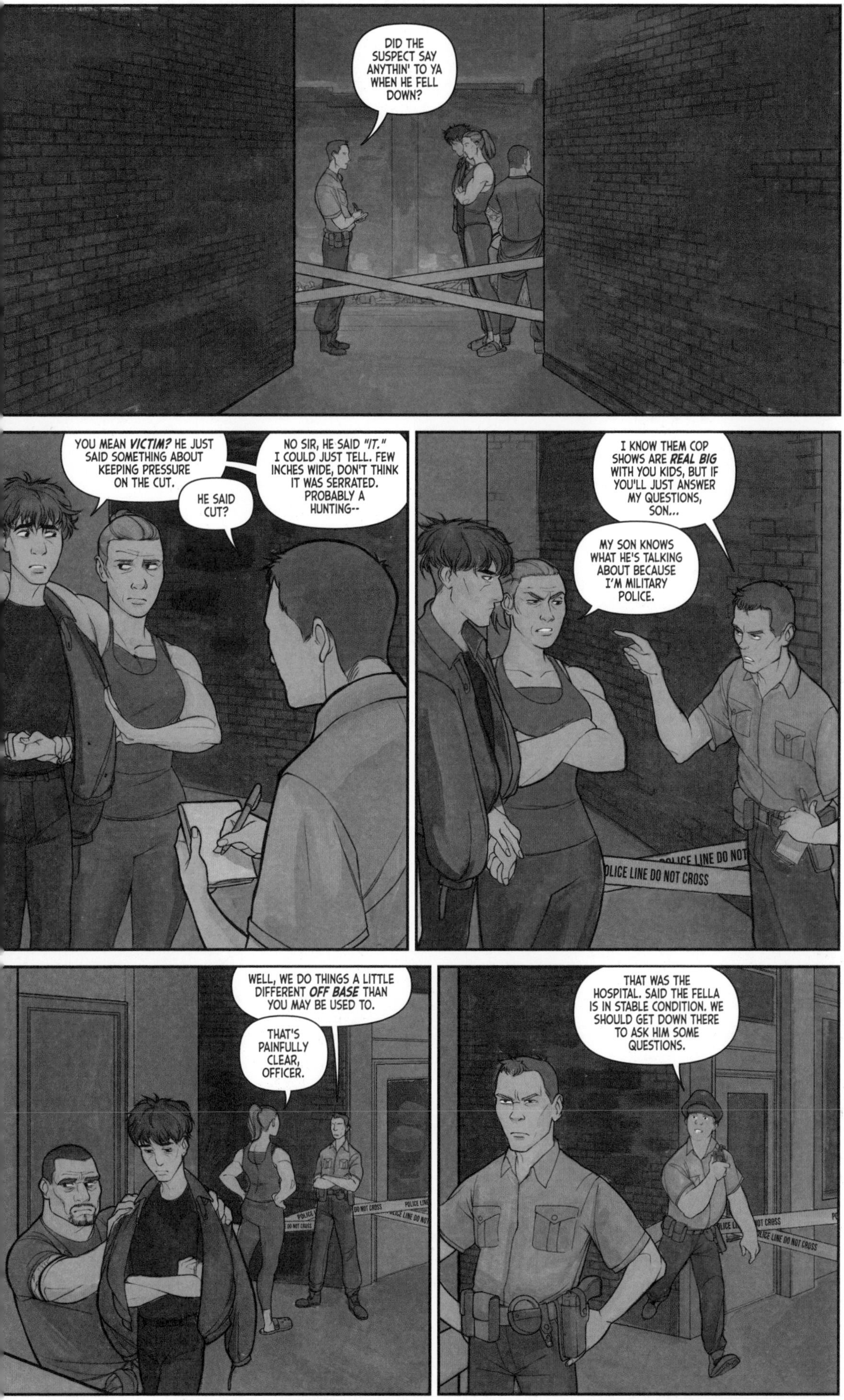
DID THE SUSPECT SAY ANYTHIN' TO YA WHEN HE FELL DOWN?
YOU MEAN *VICTIM?* HE JUST SAID SOMETHING ABOUT KEEPING PRESSURE ON THE CUT.
HE SAID CUT?
NO SIR, HE SAID *"IT."* I COULD JUST TELL. FEW INCHES WIDE, DON'T THINK IT WAS SERRATED. PROBABLY A HUNTING--
I KNOW THEM COP SHOWS ARE *REAL BIG* WITH YOU KIDS, BUT IF YOU'LL JUST ANSWER MY QUESTIONS, SON...
MY SON KNOWS WHAT HE'S TALKING ABOUT BECAUSE I'M MILITARY POLICE.
POLICE LINE DO NOT
POLICE LINE DO NOT CROSS
WELL, WE DO THINGS A LITTLE DIFFERENT *OFF BASE* THAN YOU MAY BE USED TO.
THAT'S PAINFULLY CLEAR, OFFICER.
THAT WAS THE HOSPITAL. SAID THE FELLA IS IN STABLE CONDITION. WE SHOULD GET DOWN THERE TO ASK HIM SOME QUESTIONS.

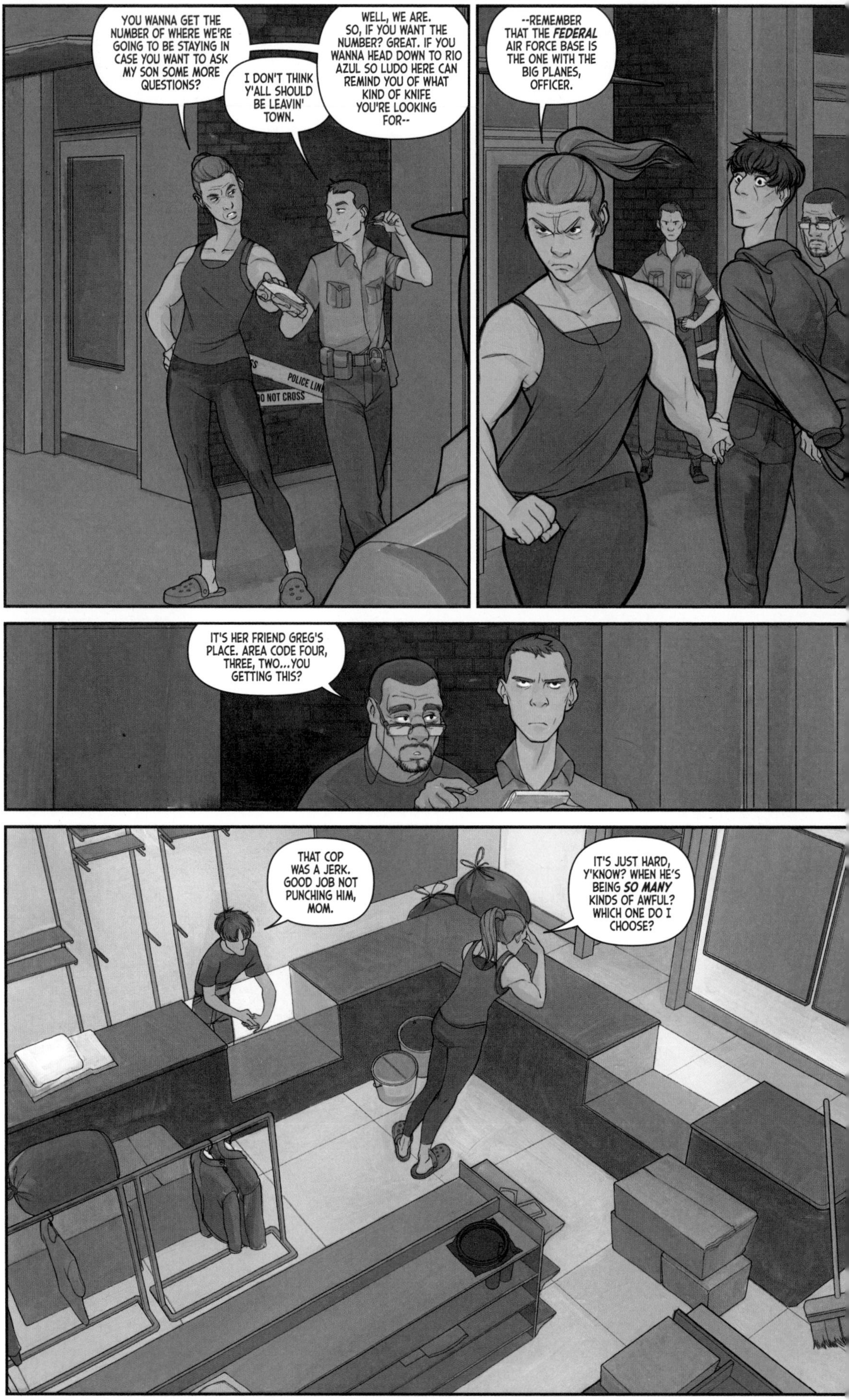
YOU WANNA GET THE NUMBER OF WHERE WE'RE GOING TO BE STAYING IN CASE YOU WANT TO ASK MY SON SOME MORE QUESTIONS?
I DON'T THINK Y'ALL SHOULD BE LEAVIN' TOWN.
WELL, WE ARE. SO, IF YOU WANT THE NUMBER? GREAT. IF YOU WANNA HEAD DOWN TO RIO AZUL SO LUDO HERE CAN REMIND YOU OF WHAT KIND OF KNIFE YOU'RE LOOKING FOR--
POLICE LINE
DO NOT CROSS
--REMEMBER THAT THE *FEDERAL* AIR FORCE BASE IS THE ONE WITH THE BIG PLANES, OFFICER.
IT'S HER FRIEND GREG'S PLACE. AREA CODE FOUR, THREE, TWO...YOU GETTING THIS?
THAT COP WAS A JERK. GOOD JOB NOT PUNCHING HIM, MOM.
IT'S JUST HARD, Y'KNOW? WHEN HE'S BEING *SO MANY* KINDS OF AWFUL? WHICH ONE DO I CHOOSE?

SPEAKING OF GOOD JOB, WAY TO NOTICE THE DETAILS, KIDDO.

THEY WERE KINDA RIGHT THERE...

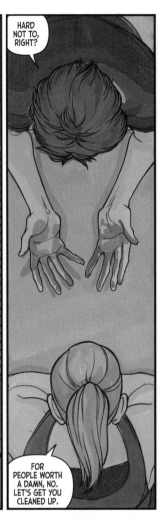

HARD NOT TO, RIGHT?

FOR PEOPLE WORTH A DAMN, NO. LET'S GET YOU CLEANED UP.

HERE YOU GO, BOY.

YOU OKAY, LUDO?
YEAH, I MEAN THE GUY'S GONNA LIVE, SO...IT'S WEIRD, BUT, I DON'T KNOW? WHAT DO YOU GUYS THINK HAPPENED TO HIM?
MAN THAT AGE, MY FIRST GUESS WOULD BE SOMEONE CLOSE TO HIM.
WELL, THAT'S ON THE LOCAL YOKELS, NOW. WE'RE JUST WORRIED ABOUT YOU. ARE YOU OKAY?
YEAH, YEAH. I'M FINE. I'M JUST GLAD I WAS THERE, I GUESS.
US TOO.
YOU DID A GOOD THING, YOU ALWAYS DO.

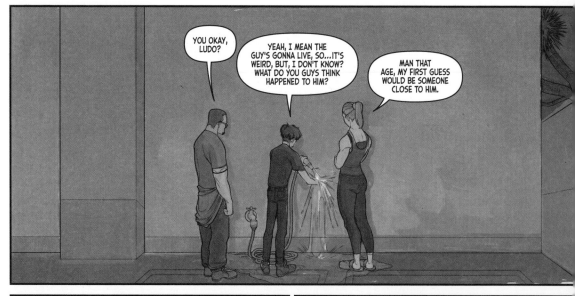

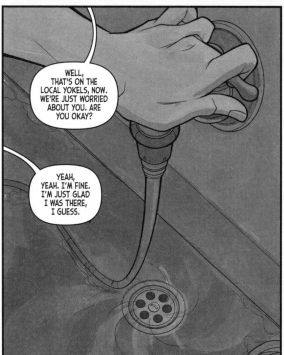

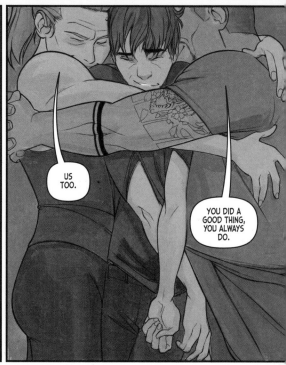

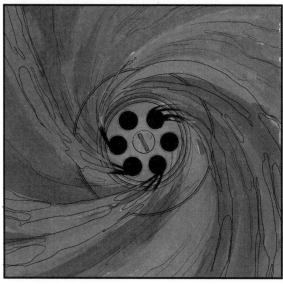

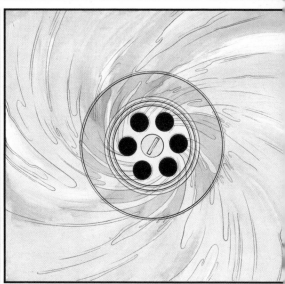

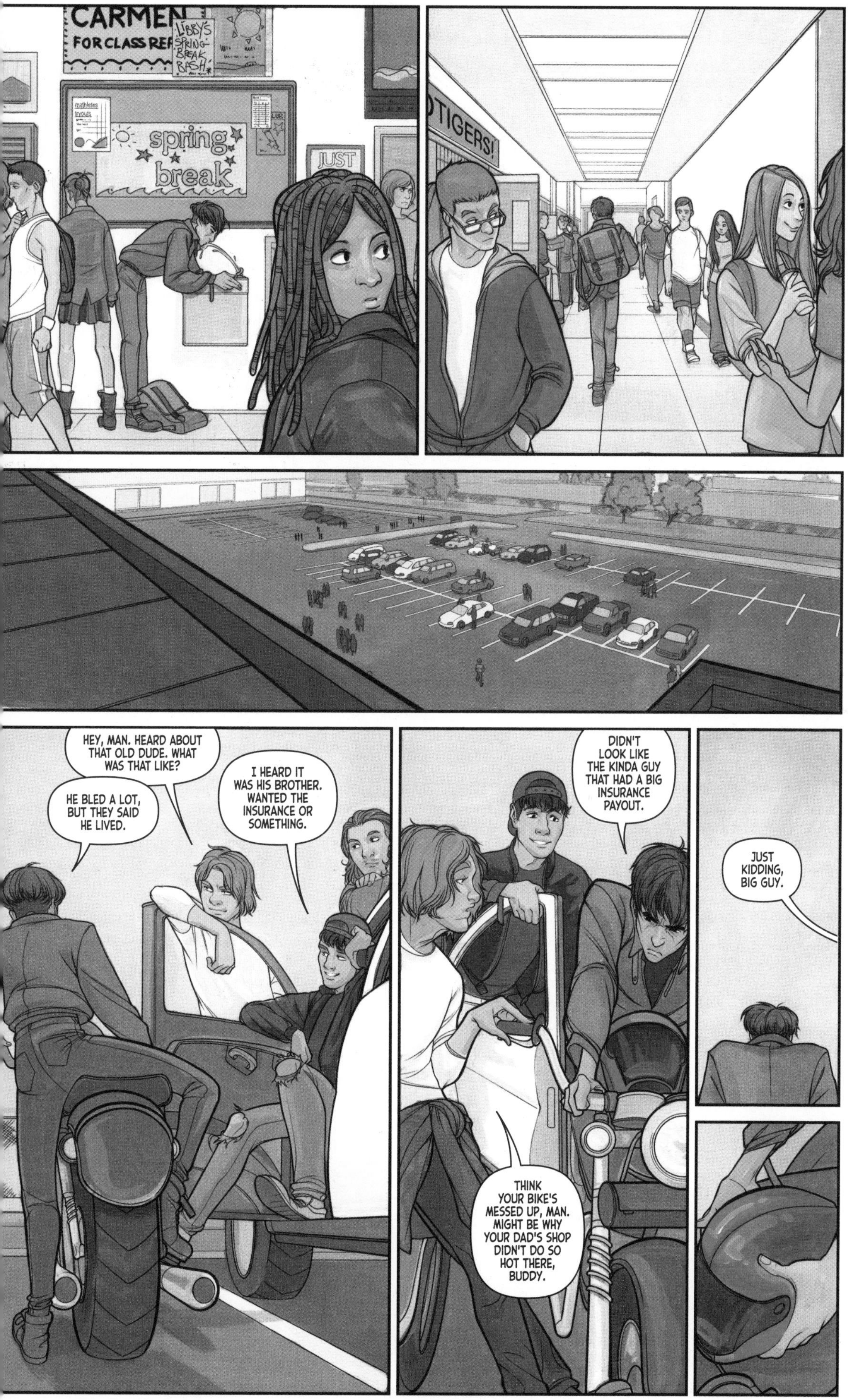
CARMEN
LIBBY'S SPRING-BREAK BASH
spring break
JUST
TIGERS!
HEY, MAN. HEARD ABOUT THAT OLD DUDE. WHAT WAS THAT LIKE?
HE BLED A LOT, BUT THEY SAID HE LIVED.
I HEARD IT WAS HIS BROTHER. WANTED THE INSURANCE OR SOMETHING.
DIDN'T LOOK LIKE THE KINDA GUY THAT HAD A BIG INSURANCE PAYOUT.
THINK YOUR BIKE'S MESSED UP, MAN. MIGHT BE WHY YOUR DAD'S SHOP DIDN'T DO SO HOT THERE, BUDDY.
JUST KIDDING, BIG GUY.

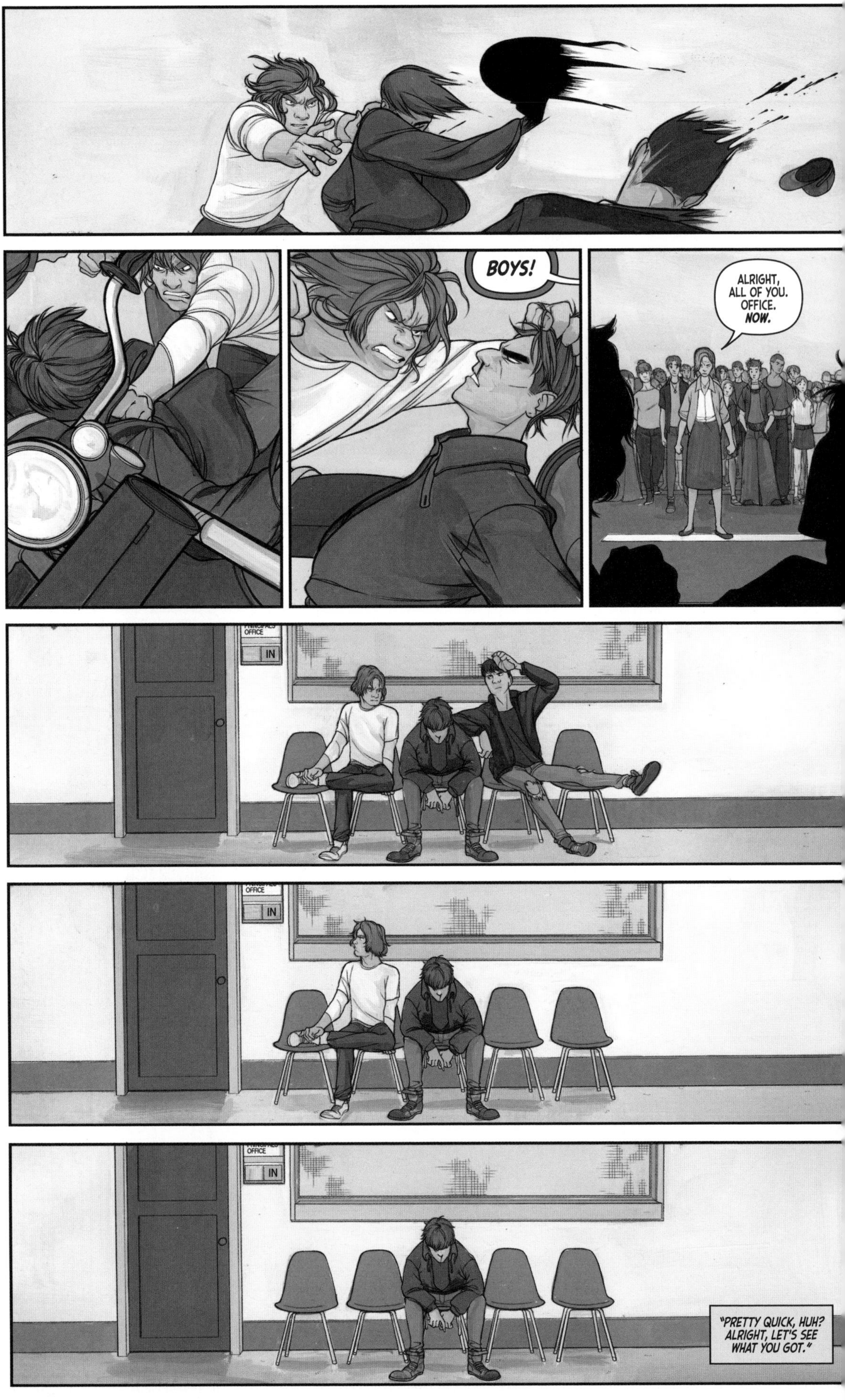
BOYS!
ALRIGHT, ALL OF YOU. OFFICE. NOW.
OFFICE
IN
"PRETTY QUICK, HUH? ALRIGHT, LET'S SEE WHAT YOU GOT."

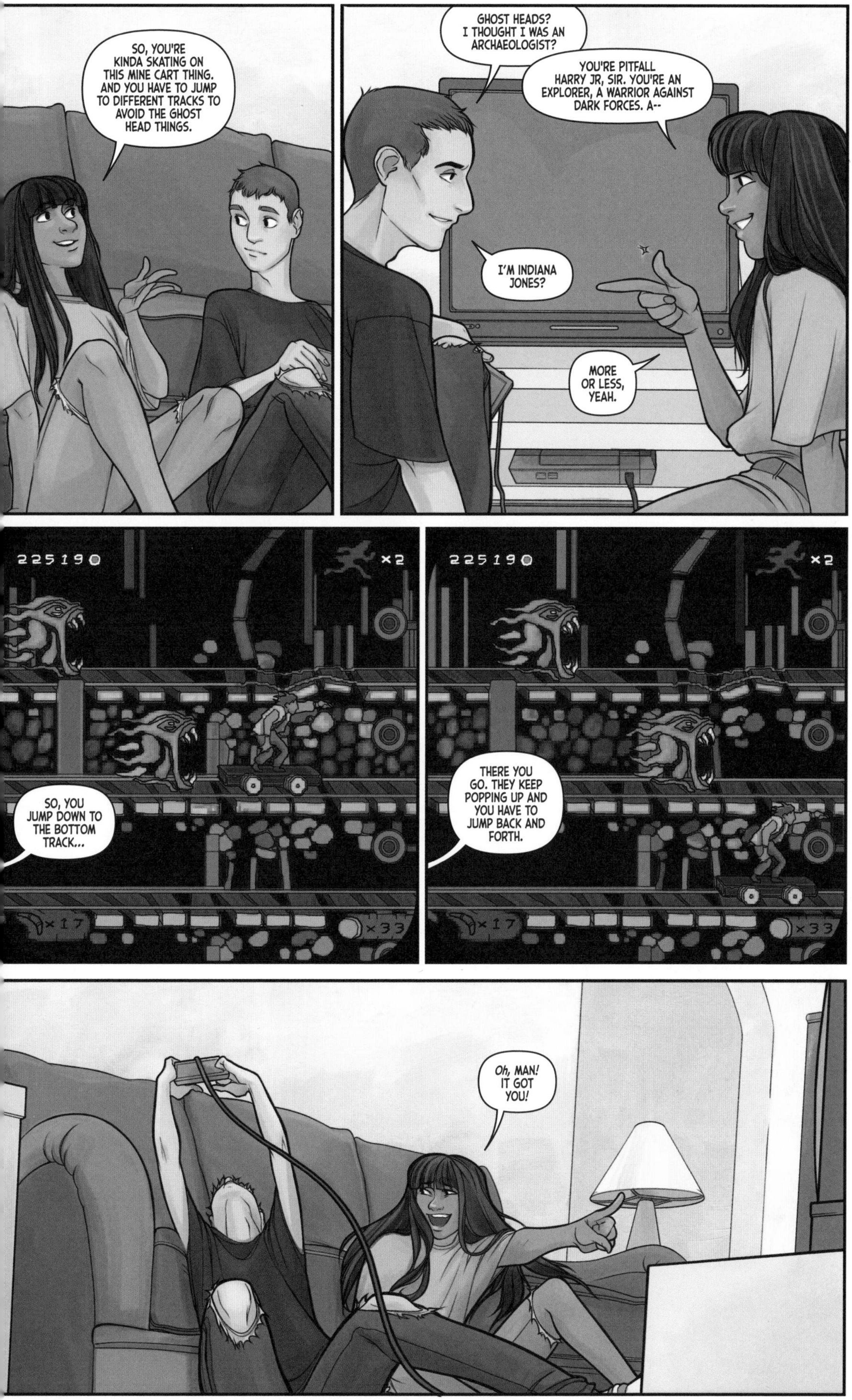
SO, YOU'RE KINDA SKATING ON THIS MINE CART THING. AND YOU HAVE TO JUMP TO DIFFERENT TRACKS TO AVOID THE GHOST HEAD THINGS.
GHOST HEADS? I THOUGHT I WAS AN ARCHAEOLOGIST?
YOU'RE PITFALL HARRY JR, SIR. YOU'RE AN EXPLORER, A WARRIOR AGAINST DARK FORCES. A--
I'M INDIANA JONES?
MORE OR LESS, YEAH.
225190
×2
SO, YOU JUMP DOWN TO THE BOTTOM TRACK...
×17
×33
225190
×2
THERE YOU GO. THEY KEEP POPPING UP AND YOU HAVE TO JUMP BACK AND FORTH.
×17
×33
Oh, MAN! IT GOT YOU!

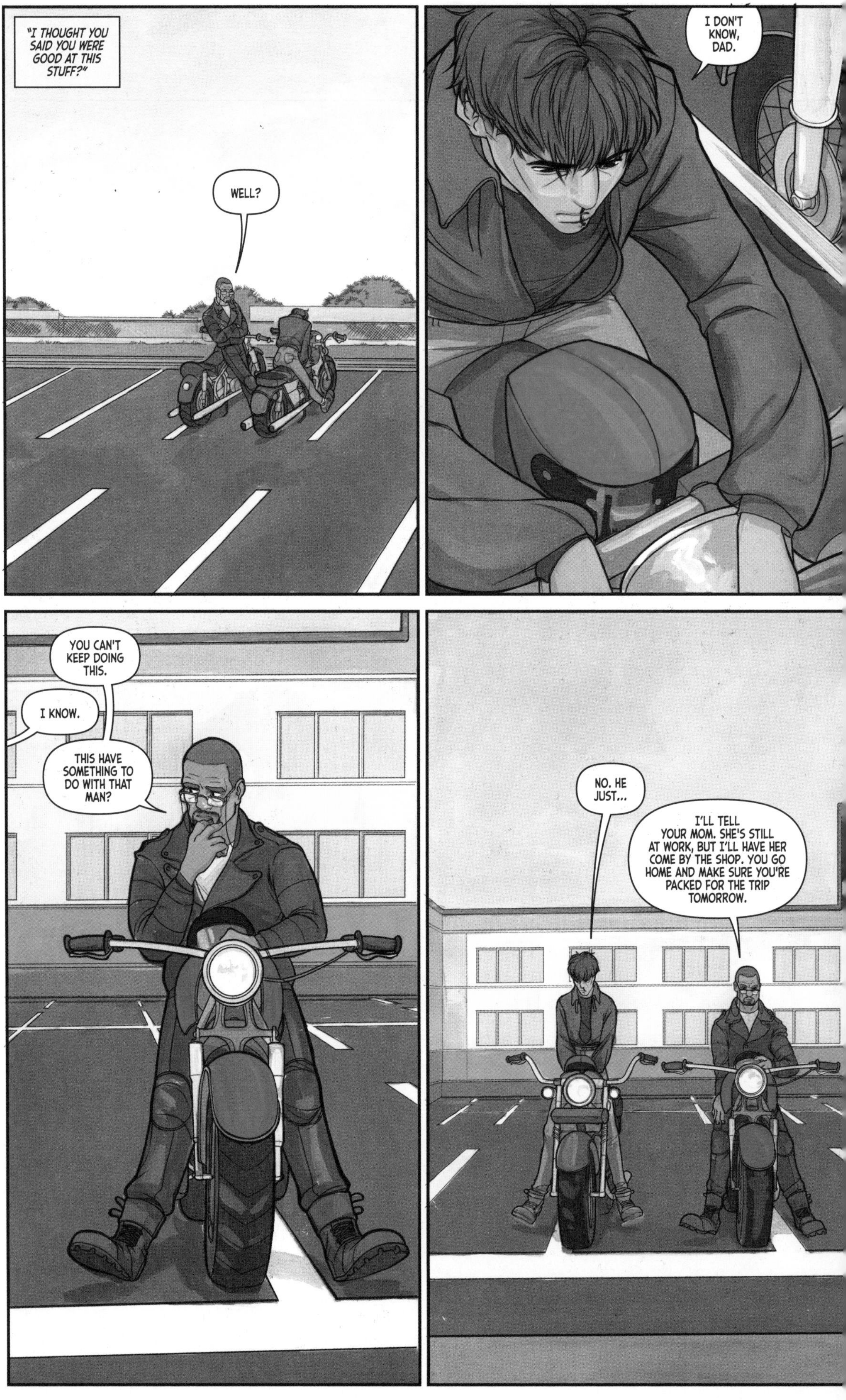
"I THOUGHT YOU SAID YOU WERE GOOD AT THIS STUFF?"
WELL?
I DON'T KNOW, DAD.
YOU CAN'T KEEP DOING THIS.
I KNOW.
THIS HAVE SOMETHING TO DO WITH THAT MAN?
NO. HE JUST...
I'LL TELL YOUR MOM. SHE'S STILL AT WORK, BUT I'LL HAVE HER COME BY THE SHOP. YOU GO HOME AND MAKE SURE YOU'RE PACKED FOR THE TRIP TOMORROW.

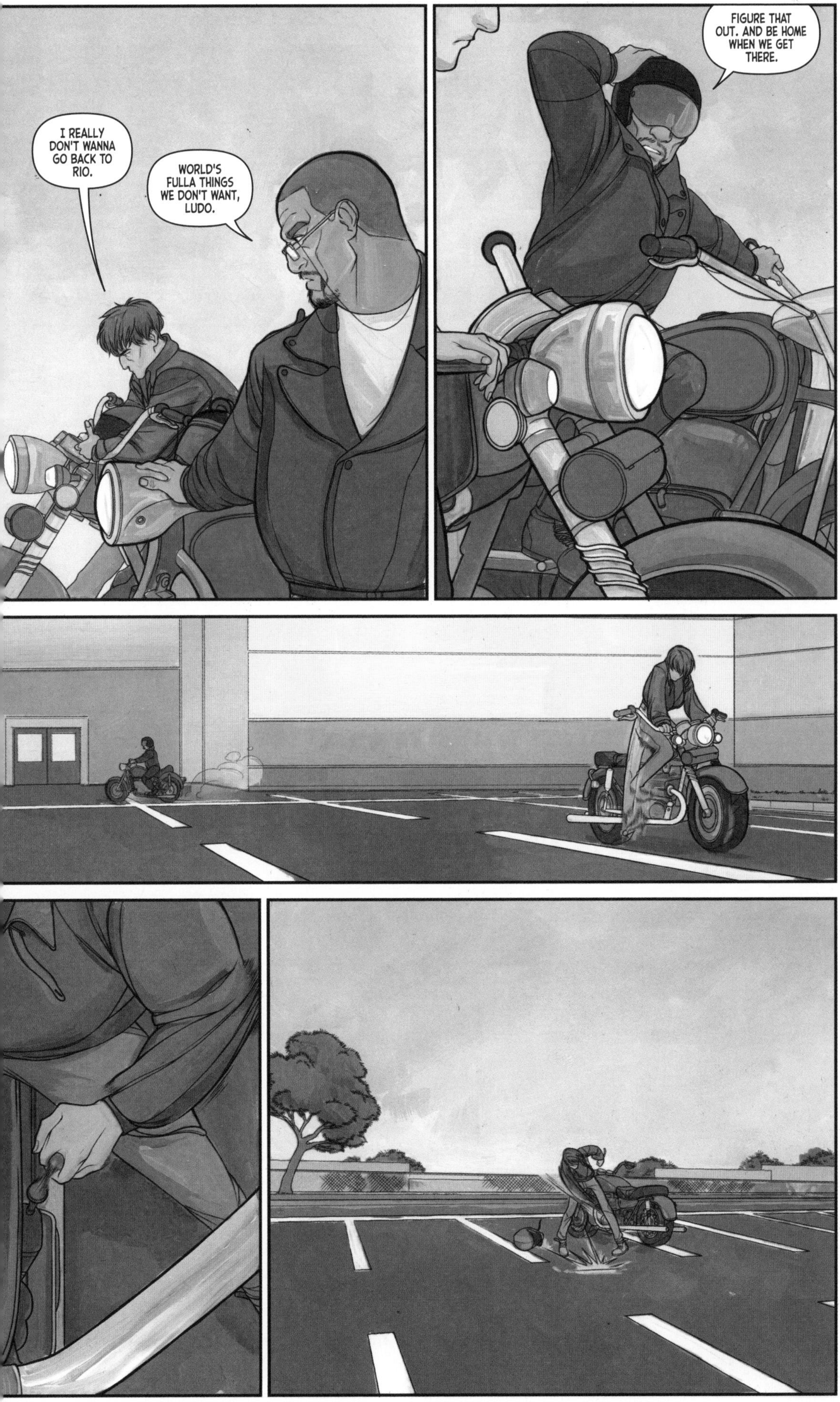
I REALLY DON'T WANNA GO BACK TO RIO.
WORLD'S FULLA THINGS WE DON'T WANT, LUDO.
FIGURE THAT OUT. AND BE HOME WHEN WE GET THERE.

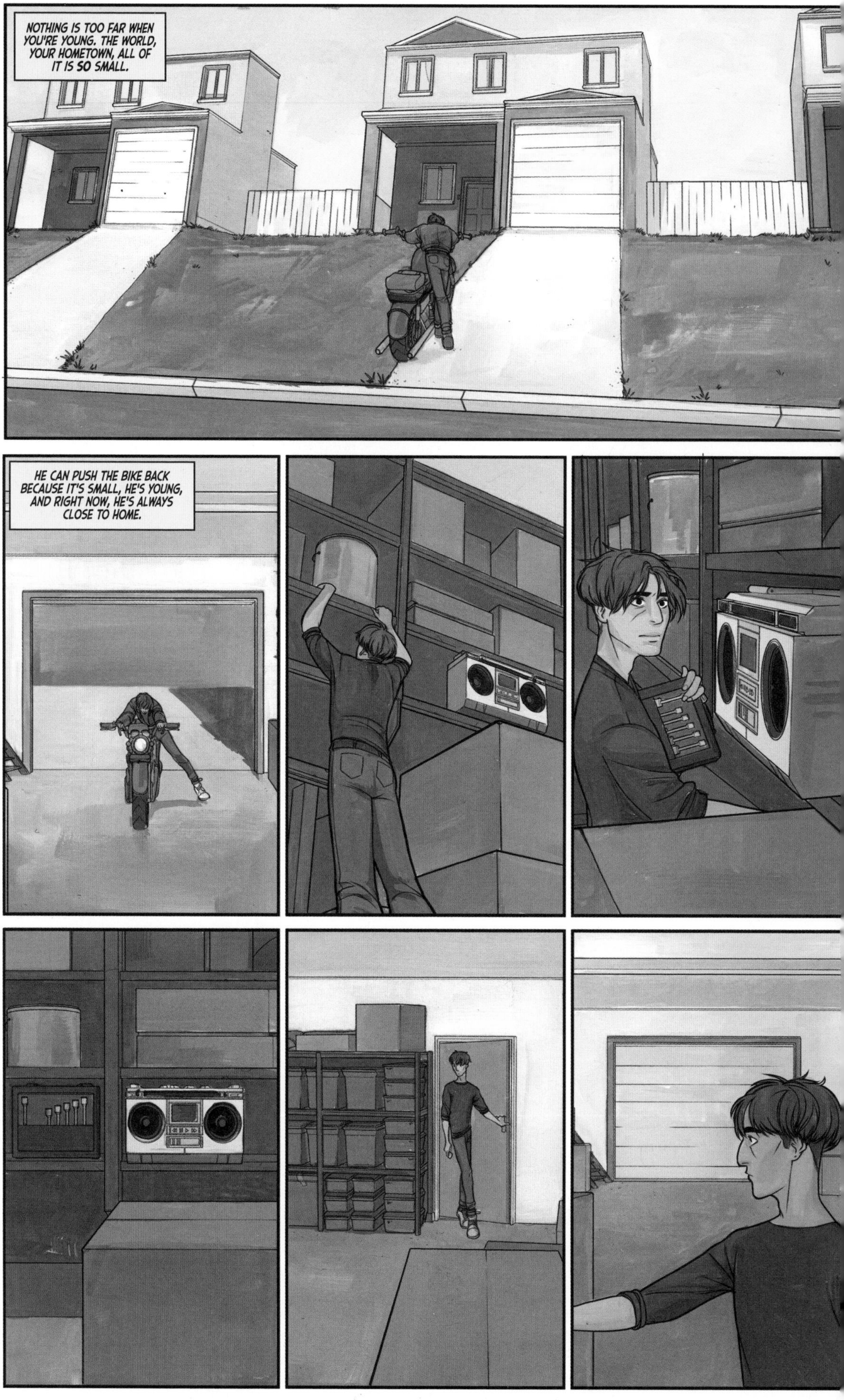
NOTHING IS TOO FAR WHEN YOU'RE YOUNG. THE WORLD, YOUR HOMETOWN, ALL OF IT IS SO SMALL.
HE CAN PUSH THE BIKE BACK BECAUSE IT'S SMALL, HE'S YOUNG, AND RIGHT NOW, HE'S ALWAYS CLOSE TO HOME.

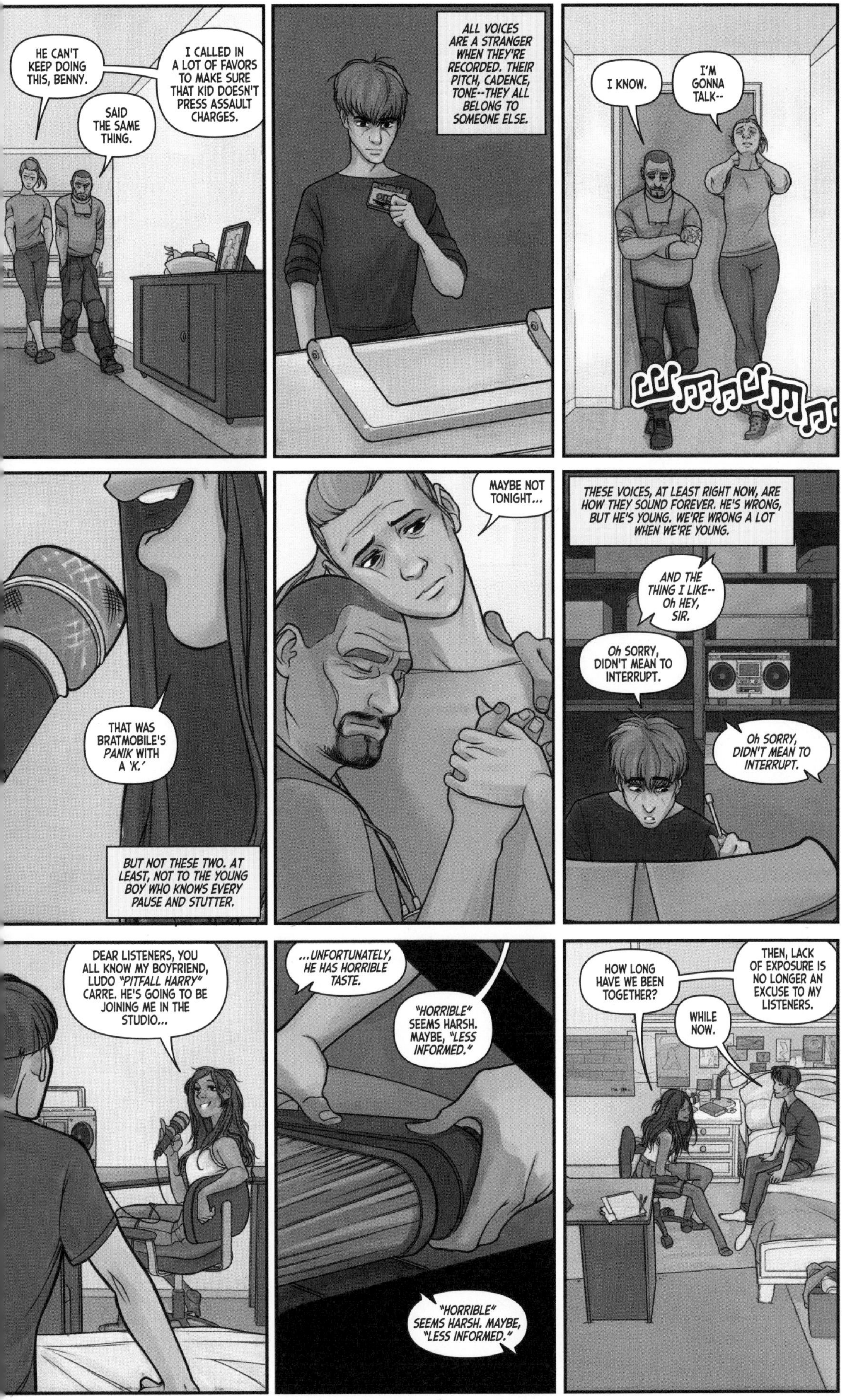
HE CAN'T KEEP DOING THIS, BENNY.
I CALLED IN A LOT OF FAVORS TO MAKE SURE THAT KID DOESN'T PRESS ASSAULT CHARGES.
SAID THE SAME THING.
ALL VOICES ARE A STRANGER WHEN THEY'RE RECORDED. THEIR PITCH, CADENCE, TONE--THEY ALL BELONG TO SOMEONE ELSE.
I KNOW.
I'M GONNA TALK--
THAT WAS BRATMOBILE'S *PANIK* WITH A 'K.'
BUT NOT THESE TWO. AT LEAST, NOT TO THE YOUNG BOY WHO KNOWS EVERY PAUSE AND STUTTER.
MAYBE NOT TONIGHT...
THESE VOICES, AT LEAST RIGHT NOW, ARE HOW THEY SOUND FOREVER. HE'S WRONG, BUT HE'S YOUNG. WE'RE WRONG A LOT WHEN WE'RE YOUNG.
AND THE THING I LIKE-- Oh HEY, SIR.
Oh SORRY, DIDN'T MEAN TO INTERRUPT.
Oh SORRY, DIDN'T MEAN TO INTERRUPT.
DEAR LISTENERS, YOU ALL KNOW MY BOYFRIEND, LUDO *"PITFALL HARRY"* CARRE. HE'S GOING TO BE JOINING ME IN THE STUDIO...
...UNFORTUNATELY, HE HAS HORRIBLE TASTE.
"HORRIBLE" SEEMS HARSH. MAYBE, "LESS INFORMED."
"HORRIBLE" SEEMS HARSH. MAYBE, "LESS INFORMED."
HOW LONG HAVE WE BEEN TOGETHER?
WHILE NOW.
THEN, LACK OF EXPOSURE IS NO LONGER AN EXCUSE TO MY LISTENERS.

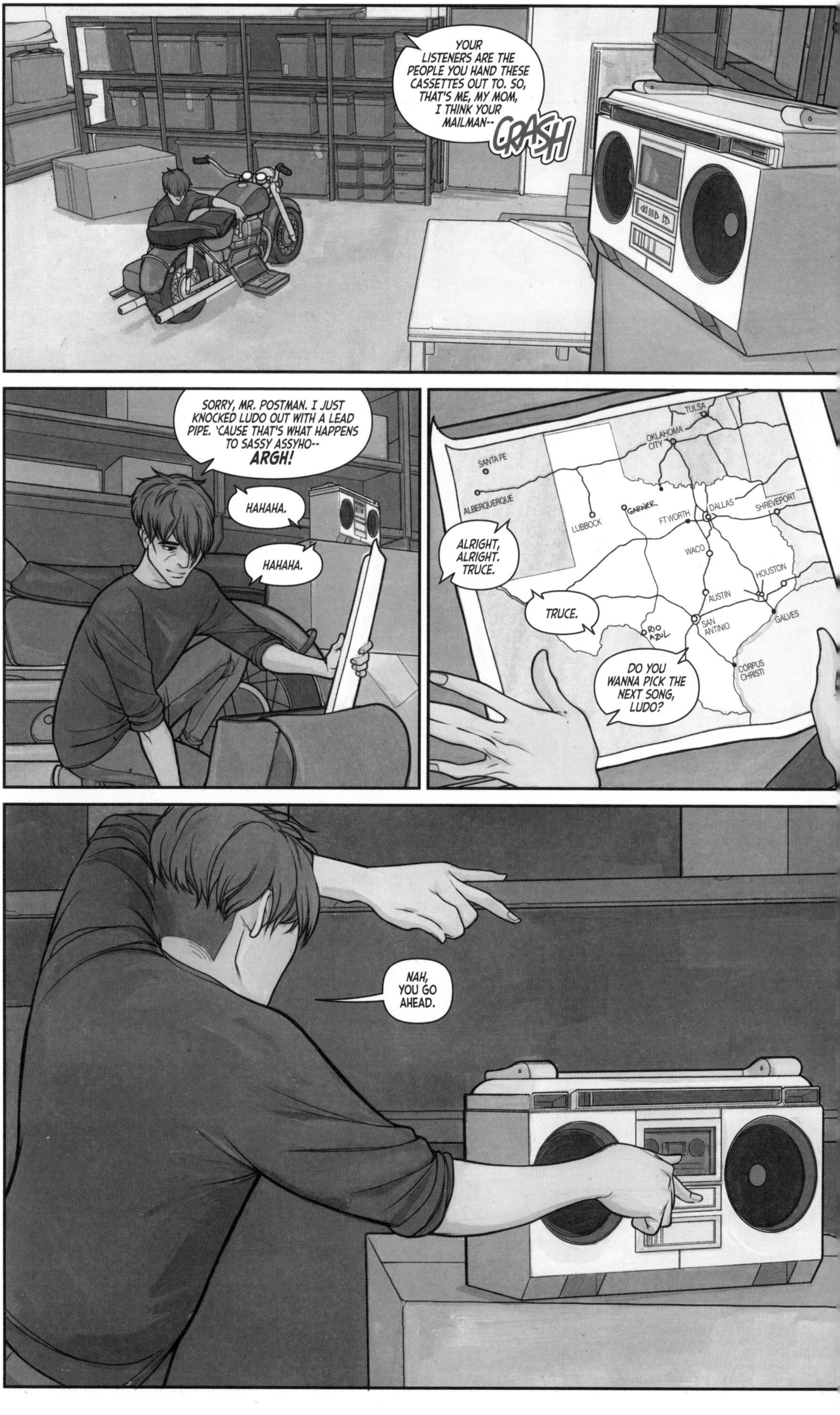
YOUR LISTENERS ARE THE PEOPLE YOU HAND THESE CASSETTES OUT TO. SO, THAT'S ME, MY MOM, I THINK YOUR MAILMAN--
CRASH
SORRY, MR. POSTMAN. I JUST KNOCKED LUDO OUT WITH A LEAD PIPE. 'CAUSE THAT'S WHAT HAPPENS TO SASSY ASSYHO-- ARGH!
HAHAHA.
HAHAHA.
TULSA
OKLAHOMA CITY
SANTA FE
ALBERQUERQUE
GARNER
LUBBOCK
FT WORTH
DALLAS
SHREVEPORT
WACO
HOUSTON
AUSTIN
RIO AZUL
SAN ANTINIO
GALVES
CORPUS CHRISTI
ALRIGHT, ALRIGHT. TRUCE.
TRUCE.
DO YOU WANNA PICK THE NEXT SONG, LUDO?
NAH, YOU GO AHEAD.

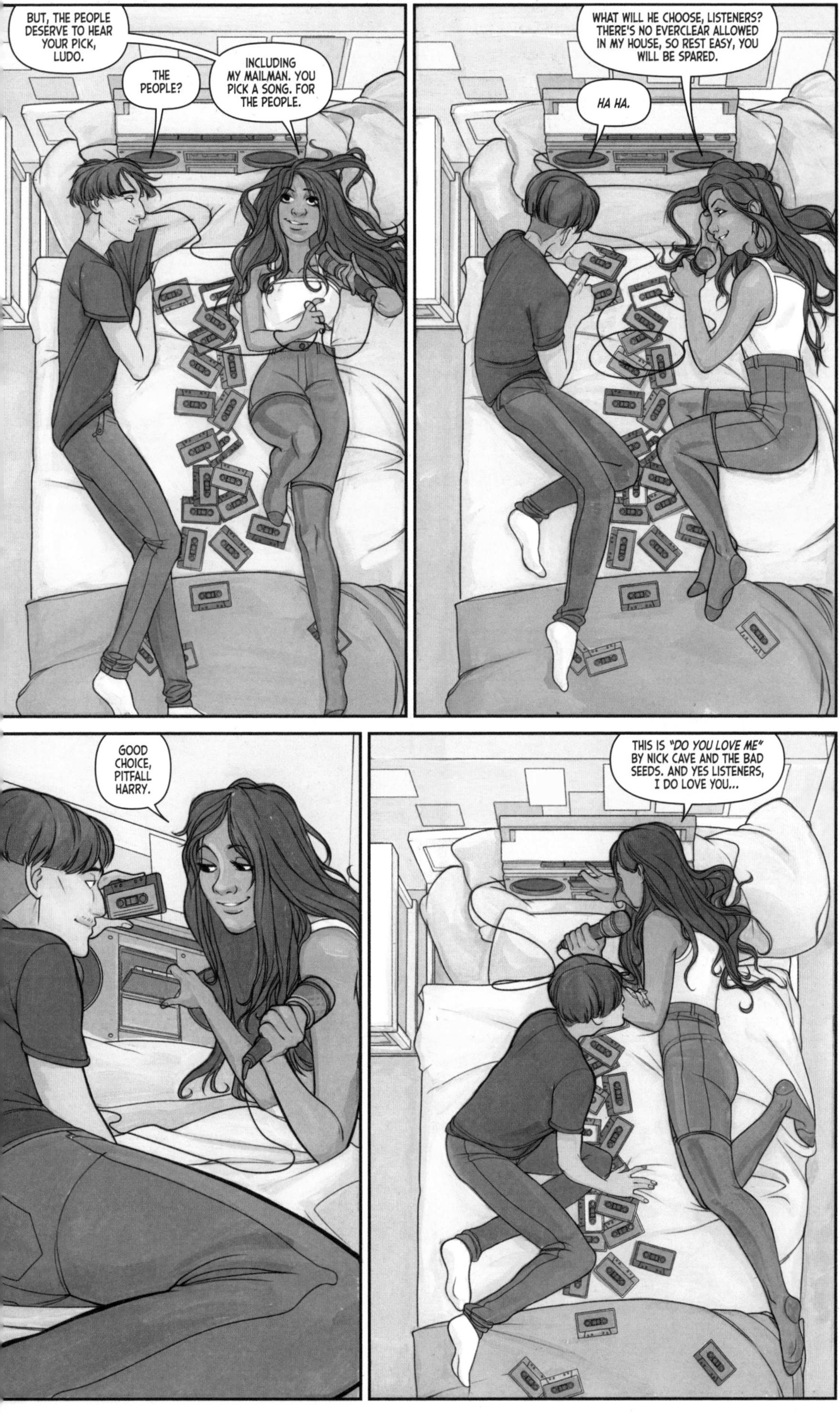
BUT, THE PEOPLE DESERVE TO HEAR YOUR PICK, LUDO.
THE PEOPLE?
INCLUDING MY MAILMAN. YOU PICK A SONG. FOR THE PEOPLE.
WHAT WILL HE CHOOSE, LISTENERS? THERE'S NO EVERCLEAR ALLOWED IN MY HOUSE, SO REST EASY, YOU WILL BE SPARED.
HA HA.
GOOD CHOICE, PITFALL HARRY.
THIS IS "DO YOU LOVE ME" BY NICK CAVE AND THE BAD SEEDS. AND YES LISTENERS, I DO LOVE YOU...

...AND *YOU*, LUDO.

I LOVE YOU, TOO.

YOU THINK WE SHOULD LET NICK CAVE KEEP PLAYING, OR LET THE PEOPLE HEAR WHAT'S ABOUT TO HAPPEN?

DEPENDS IF YOU'RE STILL GONNA LET MY MOM HEAR IT.

NICK CAVE IT IS.

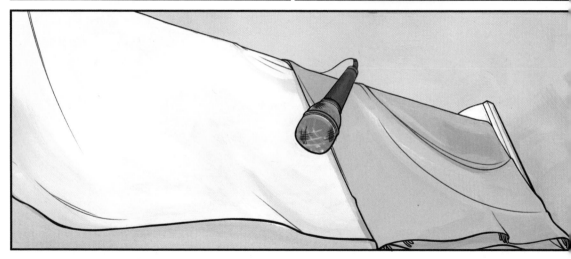

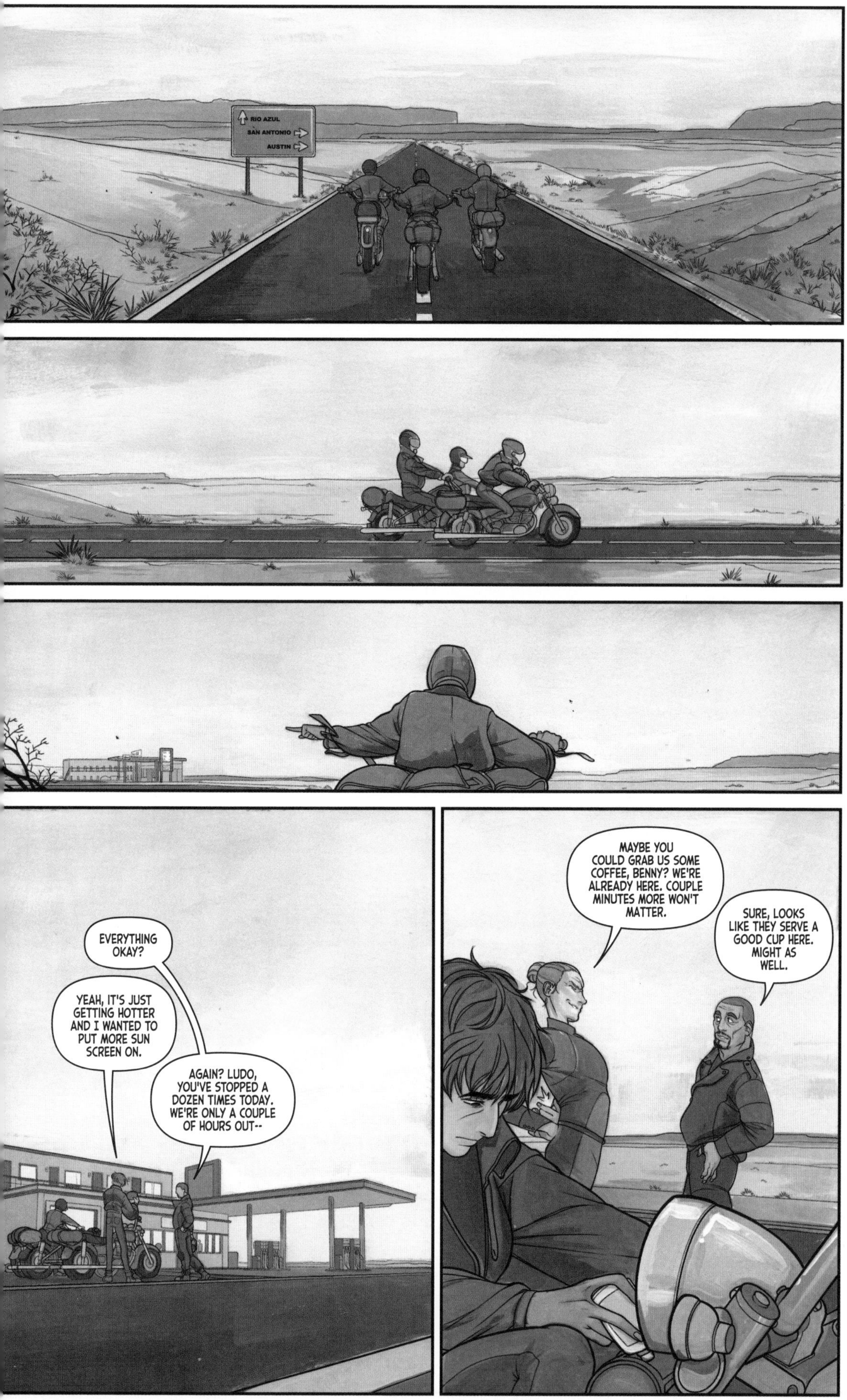
RIO AZUL
SAN ANTONIO
AUSTIN
EVERYTHING OKAY?
YEAH, IT'S JUST GETTING HOTTER AND I WANTED TO PUT MORE SUN SCREEN ON.
AGAIN? LUDO, YOU'VE STOPPED A DOZEN TIMES TODAY. WE'RE ONLY A COUPLE OF HOURS OUT--
MAYBE YOU COULD GRAB US SOME COFFEE, BENNY? WE'RE ALREADY HERE. COUPLE MINUTES MORE WON'T MATTER.
SURE, LOOKS LIKE THEY SERVE A GOOD CUP HERE. MIGHT AS WELL.

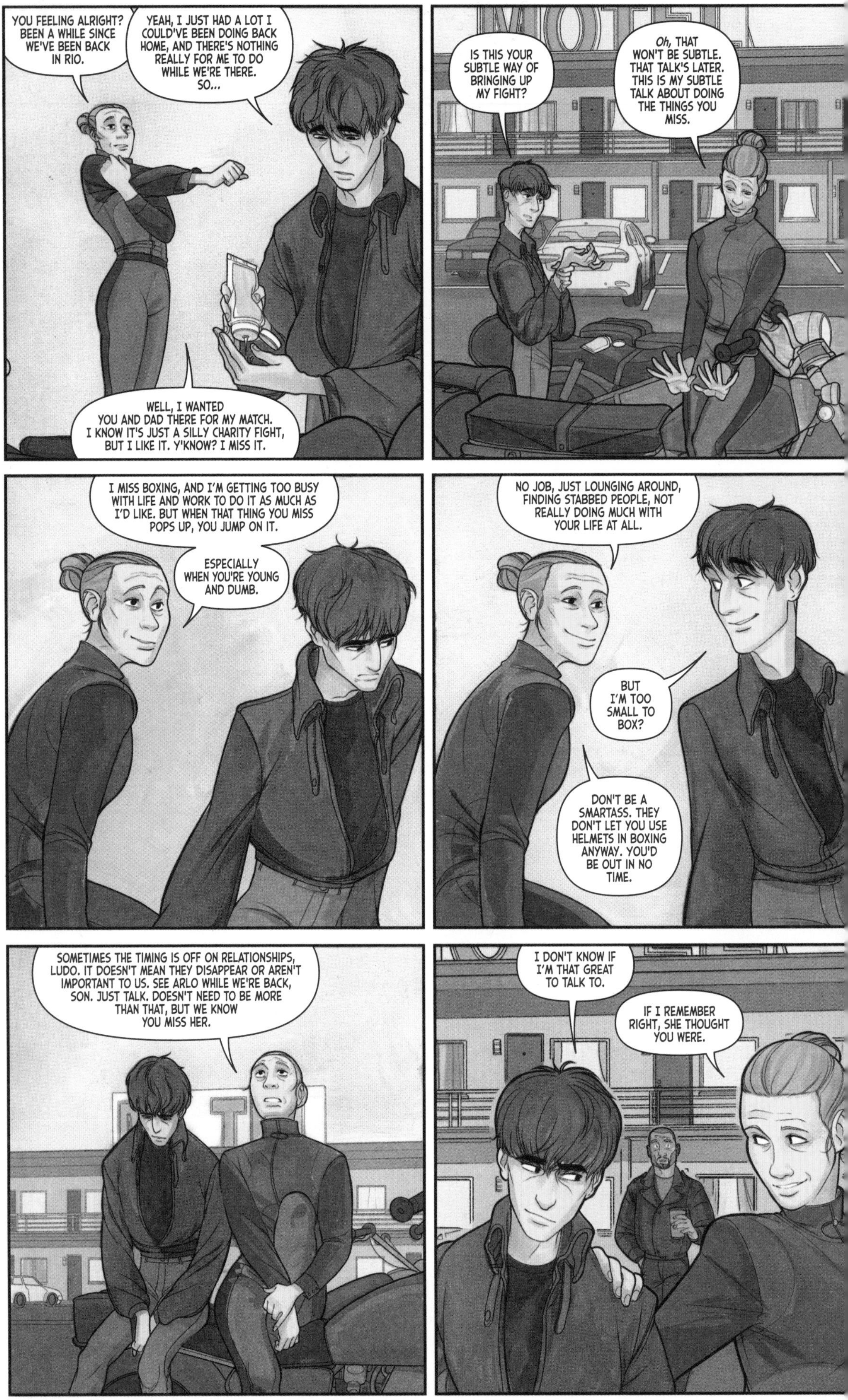
YOU FEELING ALRIGHT? BEEN A WHILE SINCE WE'VE BEEN BACK IN RIO.
YEAH, I JUST HAD A LOT I COULD'VE BEEN DOING BACK HOME, AND THERE'S NOTHING REALLY FOR ME TO DO WHILE WE'RE THERE. SO...
WELL, I WANTED YOU AND DAD THERE FOR MY MATCH. I KNOW IT'S JUST A SILLY CHARITY FIGHT, BUT I LIKE IT. Y'KNOW? I MISS IT.
IS THIS YOUR SUBTLE WAY OF BRINGING UP MY FIGHT?
Oh, THAT WON'T BE SUBTLE. THAT TALK'S LATER. THIS IS MY SUBTLE TALK ABOUT DOING THE THINGS YOU MISS.
I MISS BOXING, AND I'M GETTING TOO BUSY WITH LIFE AND WORK TO DO IT AS MUCH AS I'D LIKE. BUT WHEN THAT THING YOU MISS POPS UP, YOU JUMP ON IT.
ESPECIALLY WHEN YOU'RE YOUNG AND DUMB.
NO JOB, JUST LOUNGING AROUND, FINDING STABBED PEOPLE, NOT REALLY DOING MUCH WITH YOUR LIFE AT ALL.
BUT I'M TOO SMALL TO BOX?
DON'T BE A SMARTASS. THEY DON'T LET YOU USE HELMETS IN BOXING ANYWAY. YOU'D BE OUT IN NO TIME.
SOMETIMES THE TIMING IS OFF ON RELATIONSHIPS, LUDO. IT DOESN'T MEAN THEY DISAPPEAR OR AREN'T IMPORTANT TO US. SEE ARLO WHILE WE'RE BACK, SON. JUST TALK. DOESN'T NEED TO BE MORE THAN THAT, BUT WE KNOW YOU MISS HER.
I DON'T KNOW IF I'M THAT GREAT TO TALK TO.
IF I REMEMBER RIGHT, SHE THOUGHT YOU WERE.

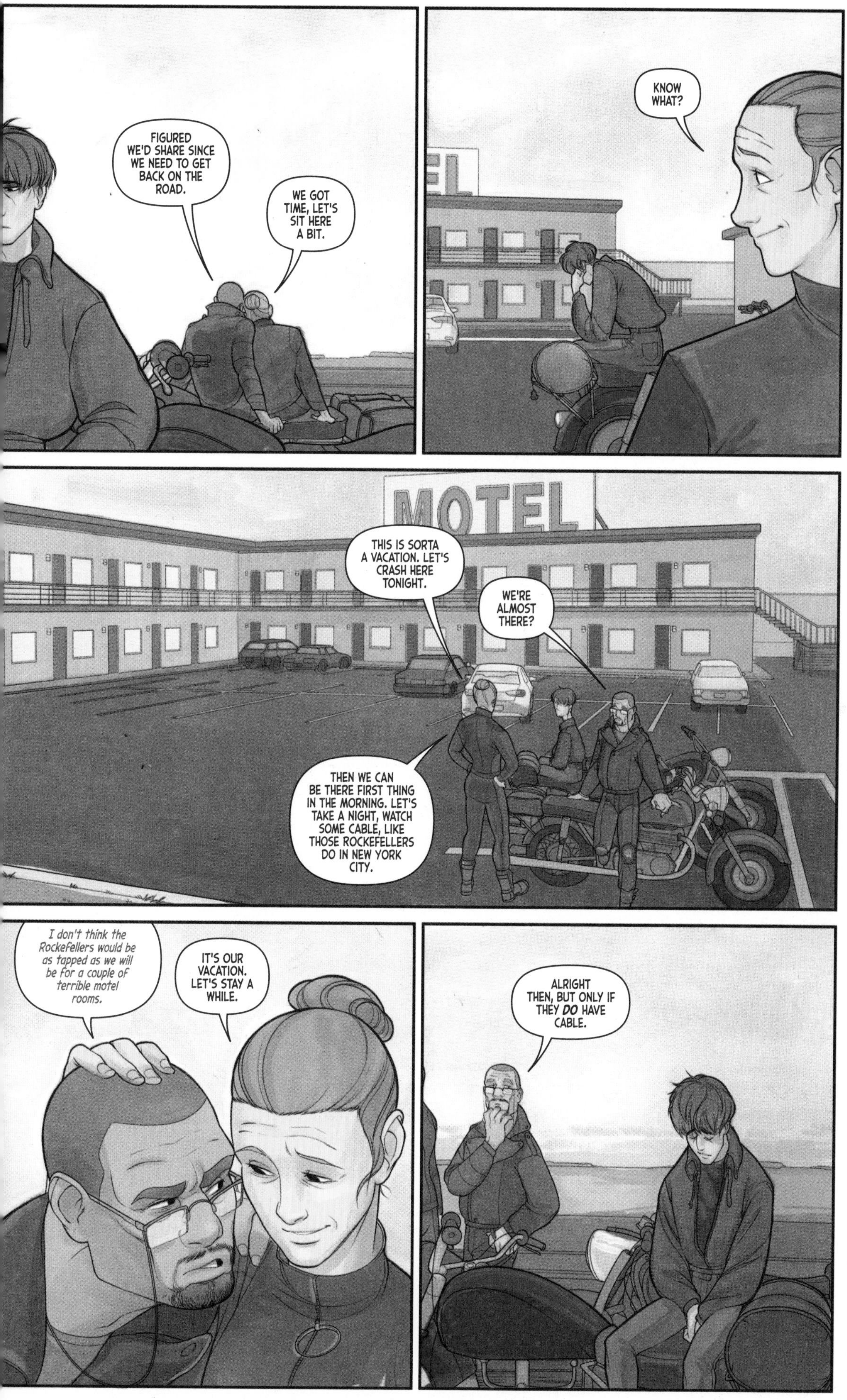
FIGURED WE'D SHARE SINCE WE NEED TO GET BACK ON THE ROAD.
WE GOT TIME, LET'S SIT HERE A BIT.
KNOW WHAT?
MOTEL
THIS IS SORTA A VACATION. LET'S CRASH HERE TONIGHT.
WE'RE ALMOST THERE?
THEN WE CAN BE THERE FIRST THING IN THE MORNING. LET'S TAKE A NIGHT, WATCH SOME CABLE, LIKE THOSE ROCKEFELLERS DO IN NEW YORK CITY.
I don't think the Rockefellers would be as tapped as we will be for a couple of terrible motel rooms.
IT'S OUR VACATION. LET'S STAY A WHILE.
ALRIGHT THEN, BUT ONLY IF THEY ***DO*** HAVE CABLE.

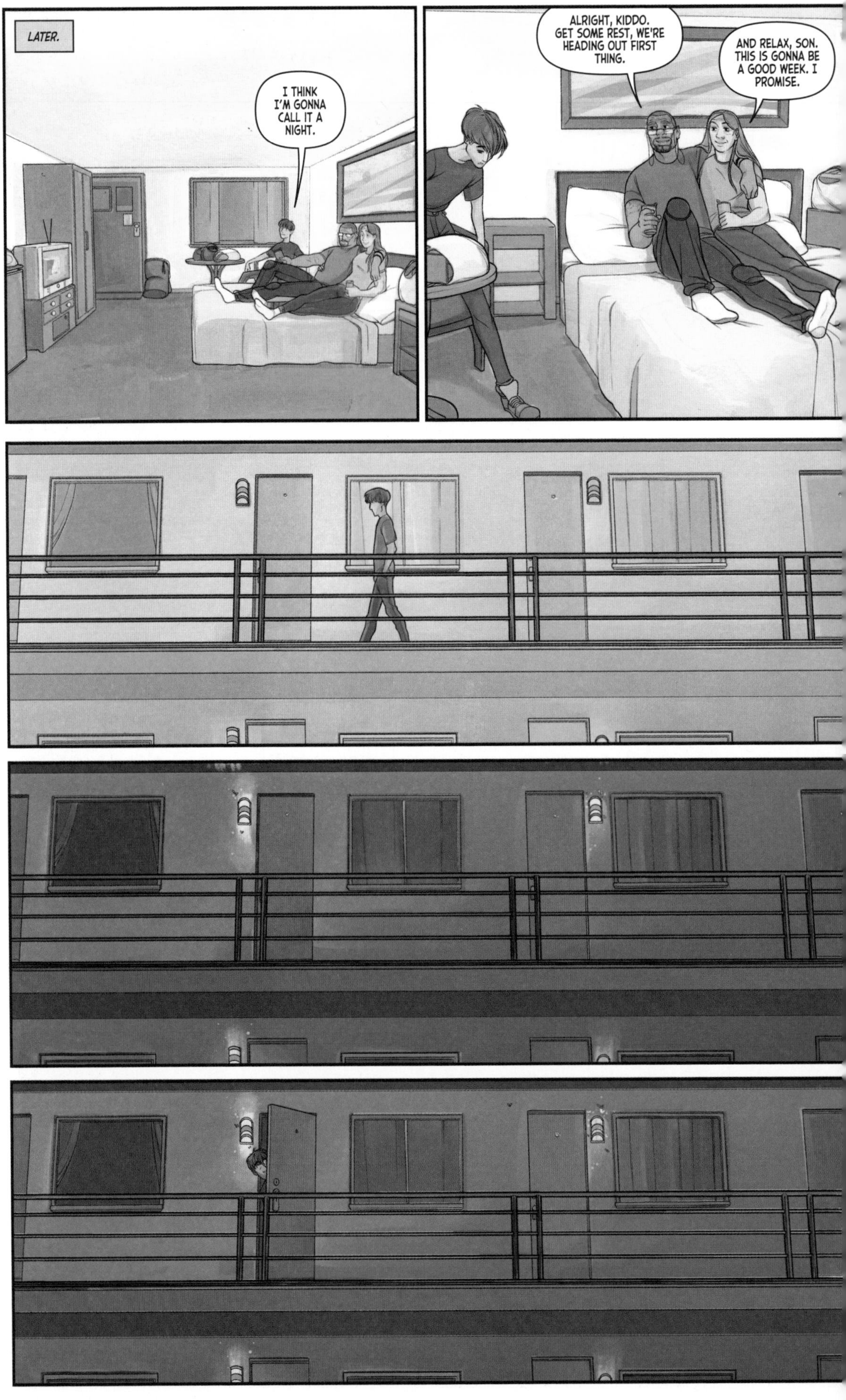
LATER.
I THINK I'M GONNA CALL IT A NIGHT.
ALRIGHT, KIDDO. GET SOME REST, WE'RE HEADING OUT FIRST THING.
AND RELAX, SON. THIS IS GONNA BE A GOOD WEEK. I PROMISE.

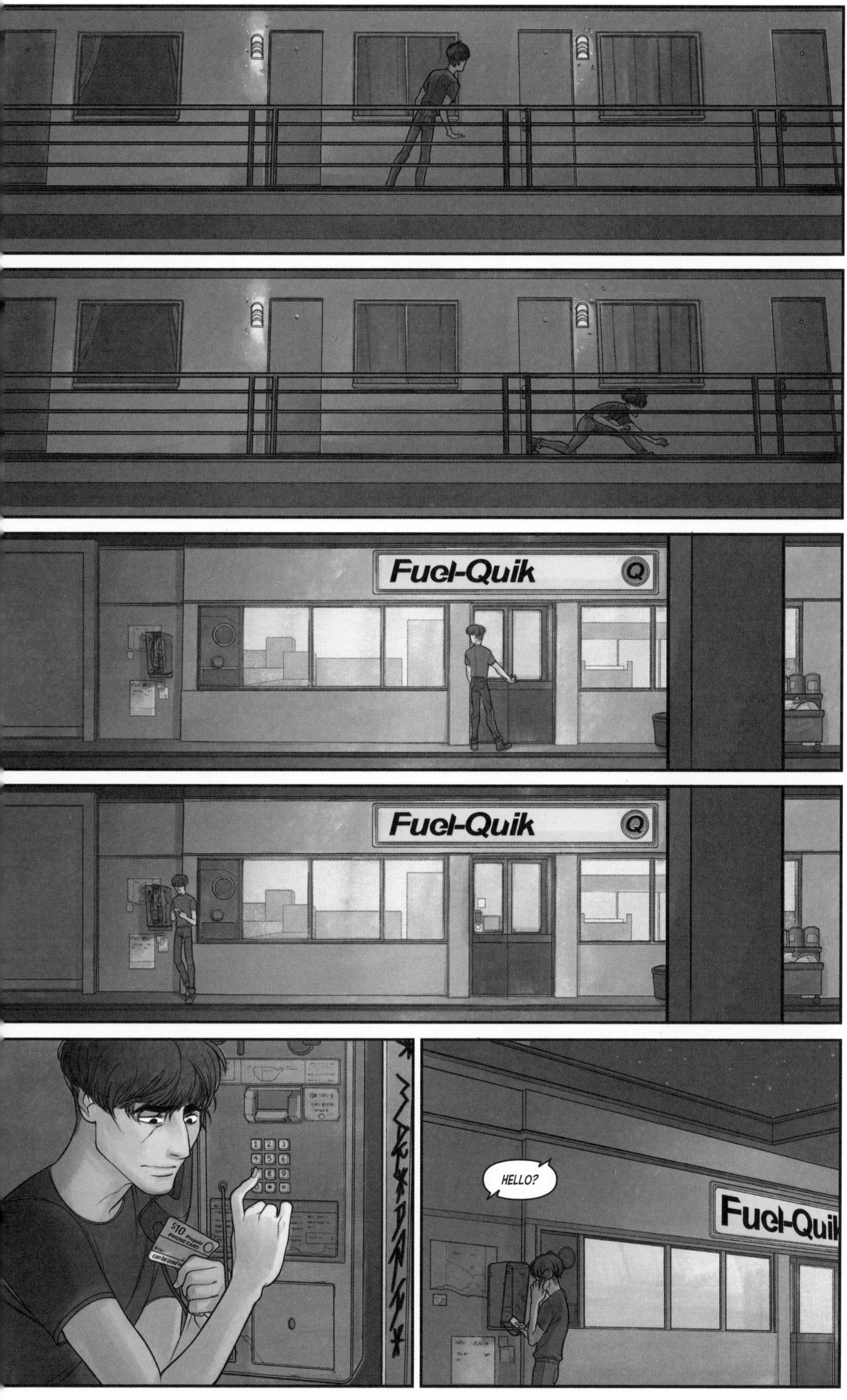
Fuel-Quik
Q
Fuel-Quik
Q
$10 Prepaid PHONE CARD
HELLO?
Fuel-Quik

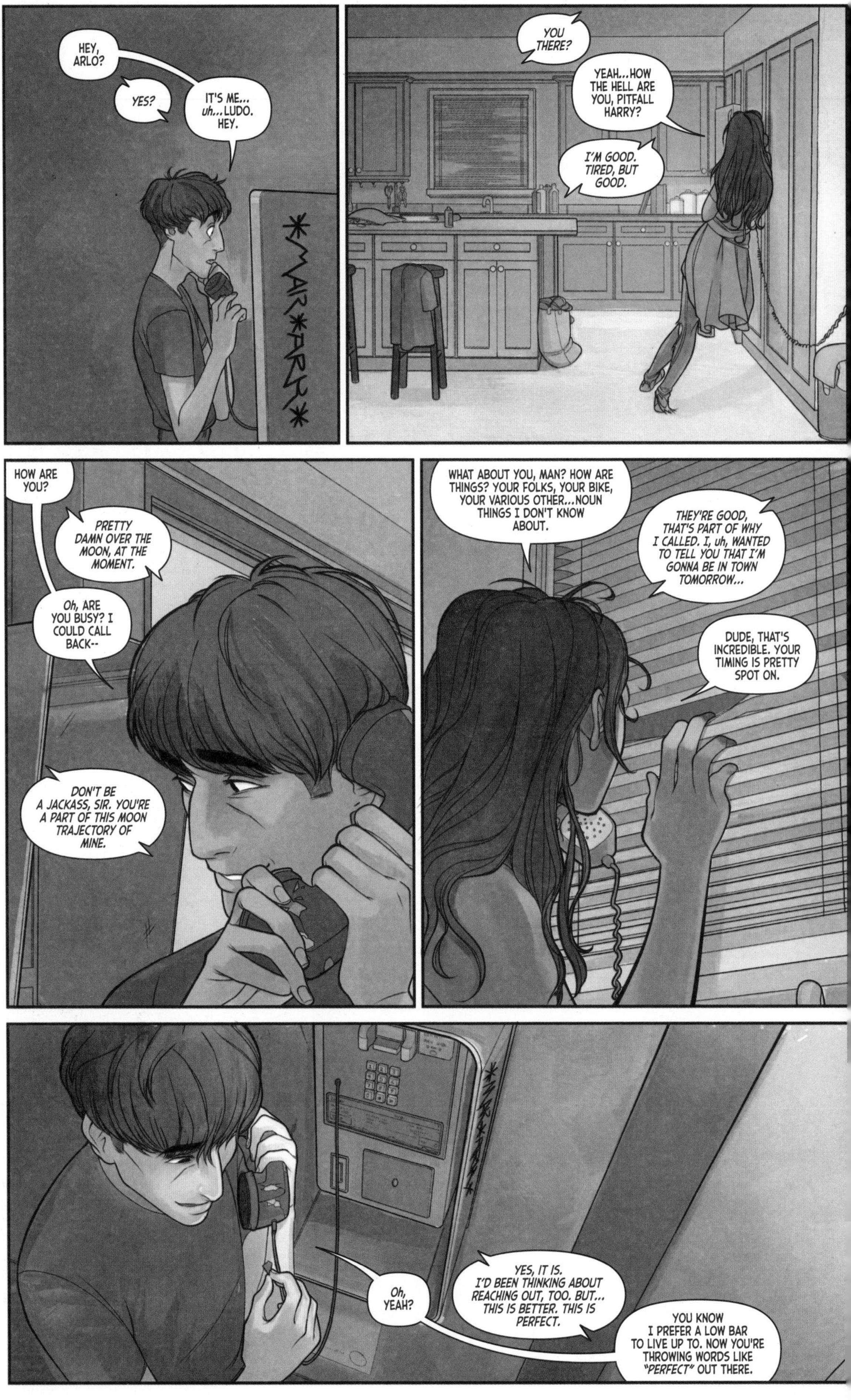
HEY, ARLO?
YES?
IT'S ME... uh... LUDO. HEY.
YOU THERE?
YEAH...HOW THE HELL ARE YOU, PITFALL HARRY?
I'M GOOD. TIRED, BUT GOOD.
HOW ARE YOU?
PRETTY DAMN OVER THE MOON, AT THE MOMENT.
Oh, ARE YOU BUSY? I COULD CALL BACK--
DON'T BE A JACKASS, SIR. YOU'RE A PART OF THIS MOON TRAJECTORY OF MINE.
WHAT ABOUT YOU, MAN? HOW ARE THINGS? YOUR FOLKS, YOUR BIKE, YOUR VARIOUS OTHER...NOUN THINGS I DON'T KNOW ABOUT.
THEY'RE GOOD, THAT'S PART OF WHY I CALLED. I, uh, WANTED TO TELL YOU THAT I'M GONNA BE IN TOWN TOMORROW...
DUDE, THAT'S INCREDIBLE. YOUR TIMING IS PRETTY SPOT ON.
Oh, YEAH?
YES, IT IS. I'D BEEN THINKING ABOUT REACHING OUT, TOO. BUT... THIS IS BETTER. THIS IS PERFECT.
YOU KNOW I PREFER A LOW BAR TO LIVE UP TO. NOW YOU'RE THROWING WORDS LIKE "PERFECT" OUT THERE.

WELL, YOU SOUND KINDA NERVOUS, SO I THOUGHT I'D HELP. HAD I KNOWN COMPLIMENTS WERE YOUR WEAKNESS--

YOU ABSOLUTELY SHOULD'VE KNOWN THAT.

LET ME SHIFT GEARS HERE, THEN. SURE, SHOW UP, THAT'S COOL I GUESS, EITHER WAY, IT'S WHATEVER.

THANKS, THAT'S BETTER. YOU DON'T SEEM NERVOUS...AT ALL?

BECAUSE I'M NOT. I'M EXCITED TO SEE YOU. YOU SHOULD GET EXCITED, LUDO. THIS IS EXCITING.

I AM.

GOOD. I KNOW THIS SUCKS, BUT I HAVE TO GET OFF--

YEAH, FOR SURE. SORRY TO CALL SO--

DON'T BE SORRY. BE EXCITED. BUT I DO HAVE TO GET OFF NOW, THOUGH.

OF COURSE. BYE, ARLO.

SEE YOU SOON, LUDO.

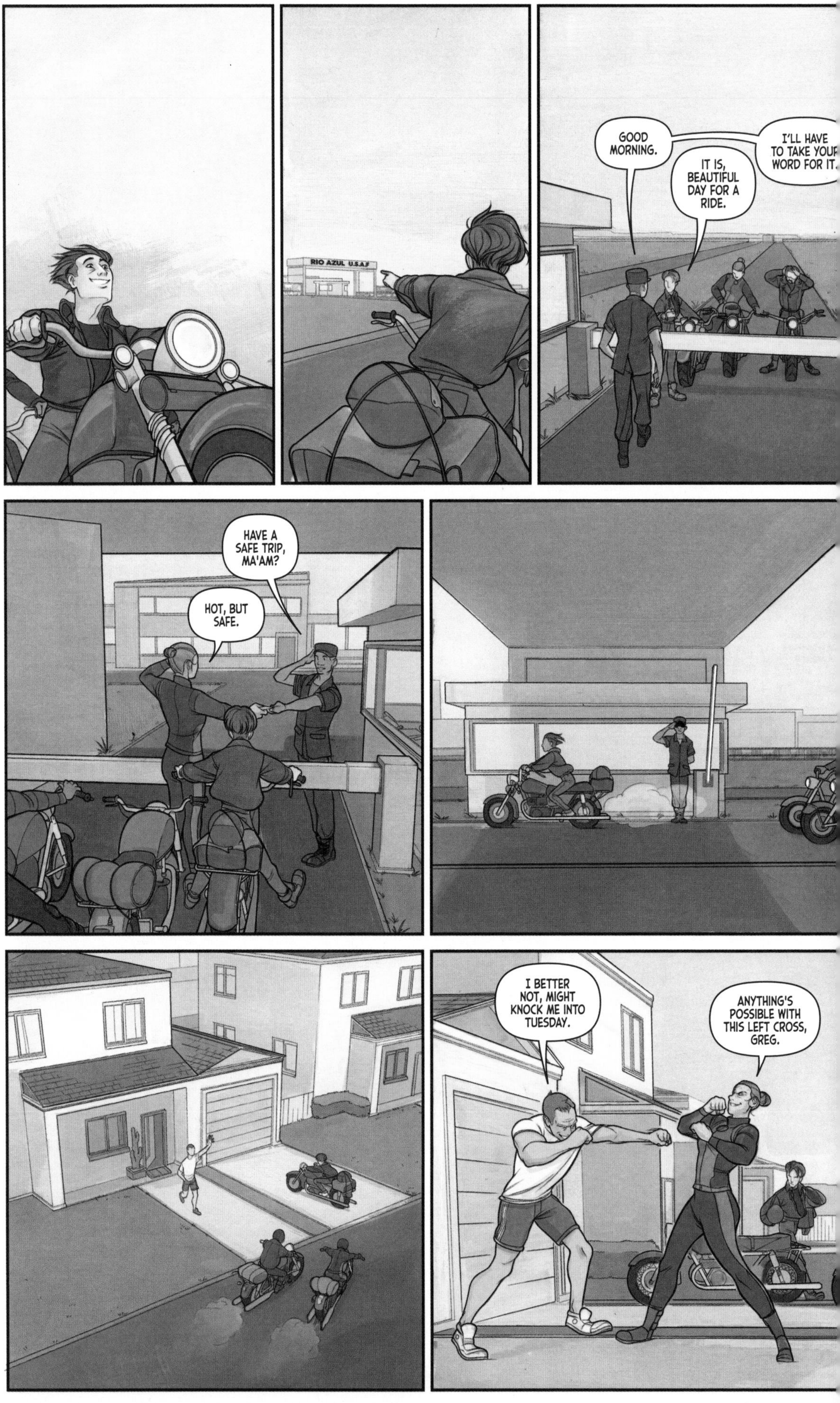
RIO AZUL U.S.A.F
GOOD MORNING.
IT IS, BEAUTIFUL DAY FOR A RIDE.
I'LL HAVE TO TAKE YOUR WORD FOR IT.
HAVE A SAFE TRIP, MA'AM?
HOT, BUT SAFE.
I BETTER NOT, MIGHT KNOCK ME INTO TUESDAY.
ANYTHING'S POSSIBLE WITH THIS LEFT CROSS, GREG.

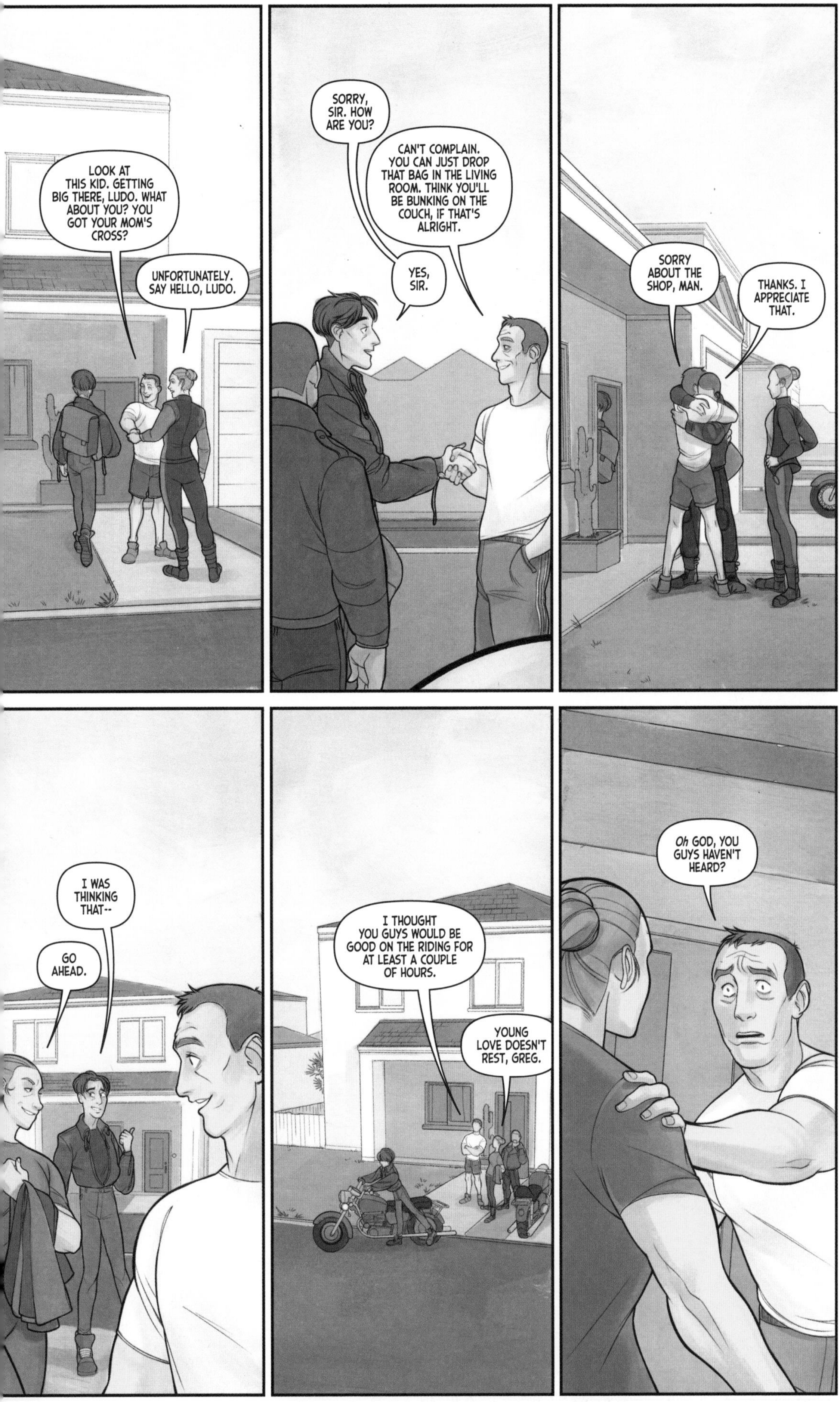
LOOK AT THIS KID. GETTING BIG THERE, LUDO. WHAT ABOUT YOU? YOU GOT YOUR MOM'S CROSS?
UNFORTUNATELY. SAY HELLO, LUDO.
SORRY, SIR. HOW ARE YOU?
CAN'T COMPLAIN. YOU CAN JUST DROP THAT BAG IN THE LIVING ROOM. THINK YOU'LL BE BUNKING ON THE COUCH, IF THAT'S ALRIGHT.
YES, SIR.
SORRY ABOUT THE SHOP, MAN.
THANKS. I APPRECIATE THAT.
I WAS THINKING THAT--
GO AHEAD.
I THOUGHT YOU GUYS WOULD BE GOOD ON THE RIDING FOR AT LEAST A COUPLE OF HOURS.
YOUNG LOVE DOESN'T REST, GREG.
Oh GOD, YOU GUYS HAVEN'T HEARD?

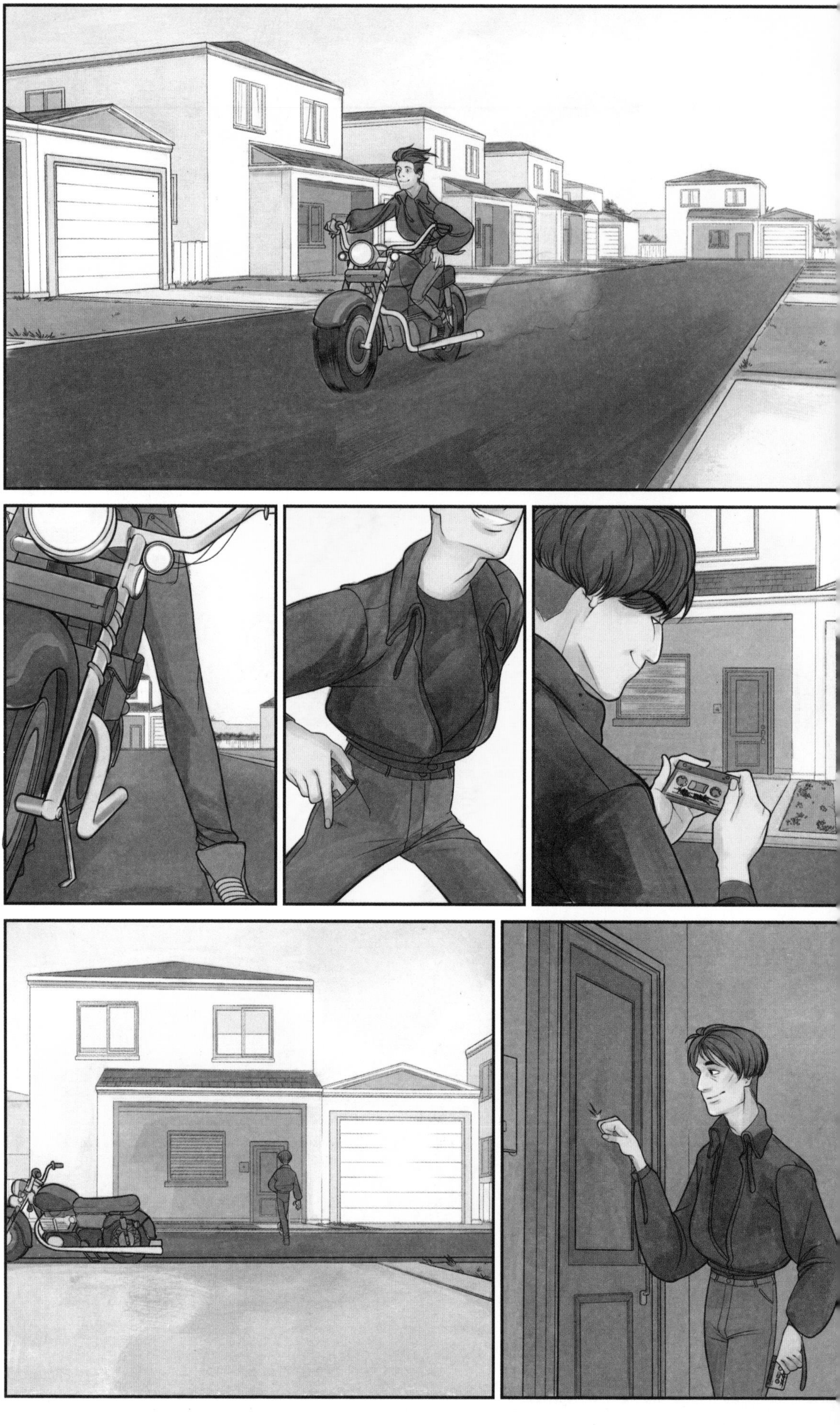

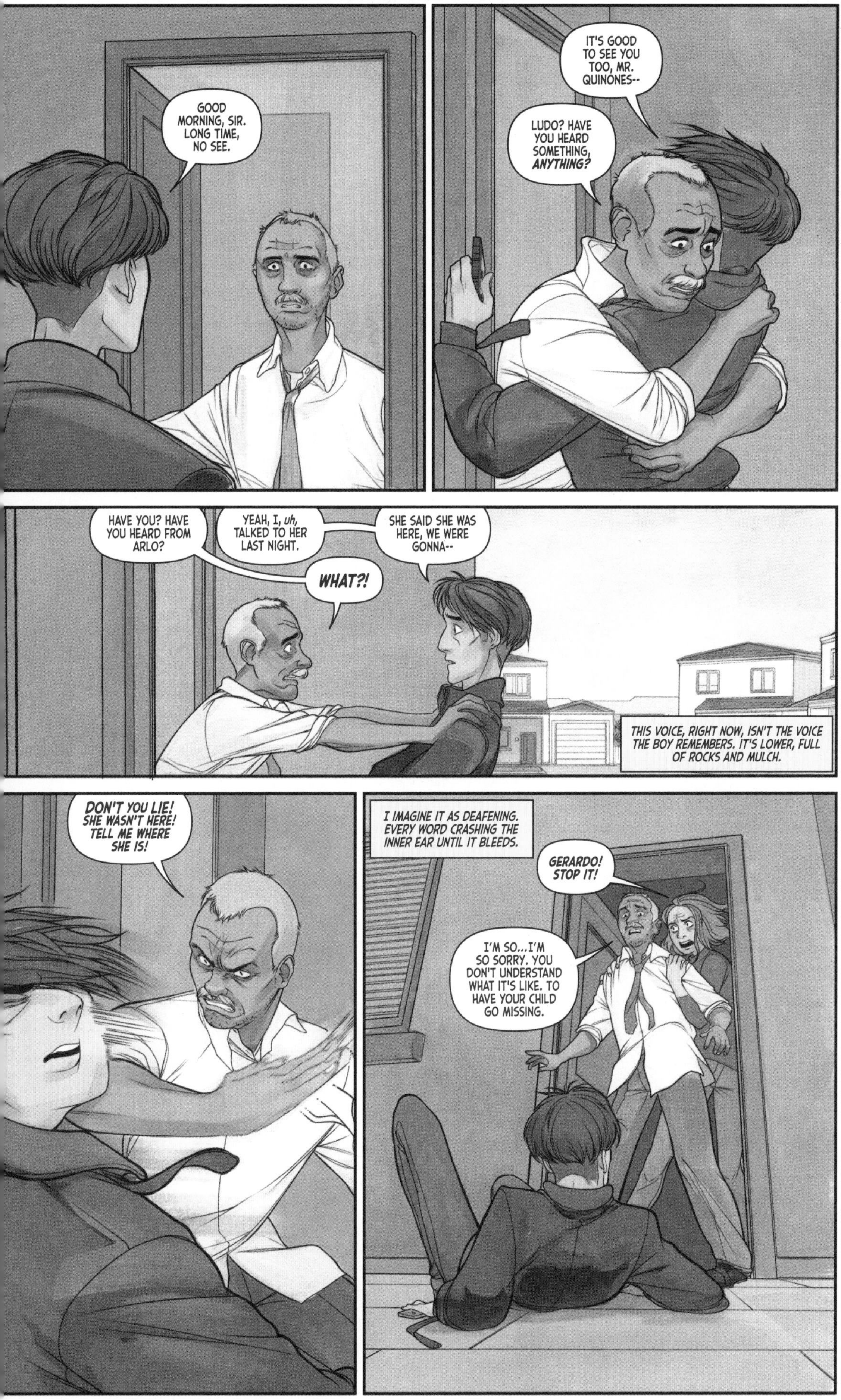
GOOD MORNING, SIR. LONG TIME, NO SEE.
IT'S GOOD TO SEE YOU TOO, MR. QUINONES--
LUDO? HAVE YOU HEARD SOMETHING, *ANYTHING?*
HAVE YOU? HAVE YOU HEARD FROM ARLO?
YEAH, I, *uh,* TALKED TO HER LAST NIGHT.
SHE SAID SHE WAS HERE, WE WERE GONNA--
WHAT?!
THIS VOICE, RIGHT NOW, ISN'T THE VOICE THE BOY REMEMBERS. IT'S LOWER, FULL OF ROCKS AND MULCH.
DON'T YOU LIE! SHE WASN'T HERE! TELL ME WHERE SHE IS!
I IMAGINE IT AS DEAFENING. EVERY WORD CRASHING THE INNER EAR UNTIL IT BLEEDS.
GERARDO! STOP IT!
I'M SO...I'M SO SORRY. YOU DON'T UNDERSTAND WHAT IT'S LIKE. TO HAVE YOUR CHILD GO MISSING.

THE WORD COMES OUT LIKE LIGHT INSTEAD OF SOUND AS SOON AS HE SAYS IT.

MISSING?

NO ONE HAS SEEN OR HEARD FROM ARLO IN TWO WEEKS. JUST VANISHED...

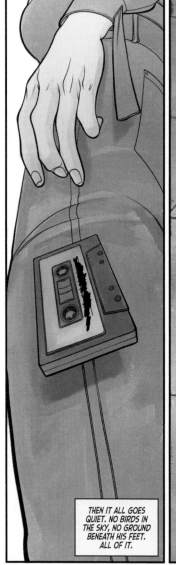

THEN IT ALL GOES QUIET. NO BIRDS IN THE SKY, NO GROUND BENEATH HIS FEET. ALL OF IT.

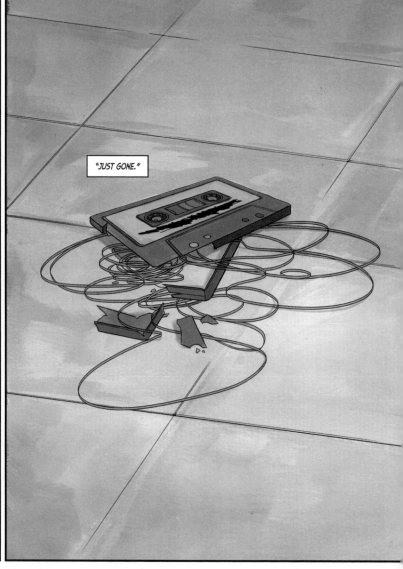

"JUST GONE."

CHAPTER TWO

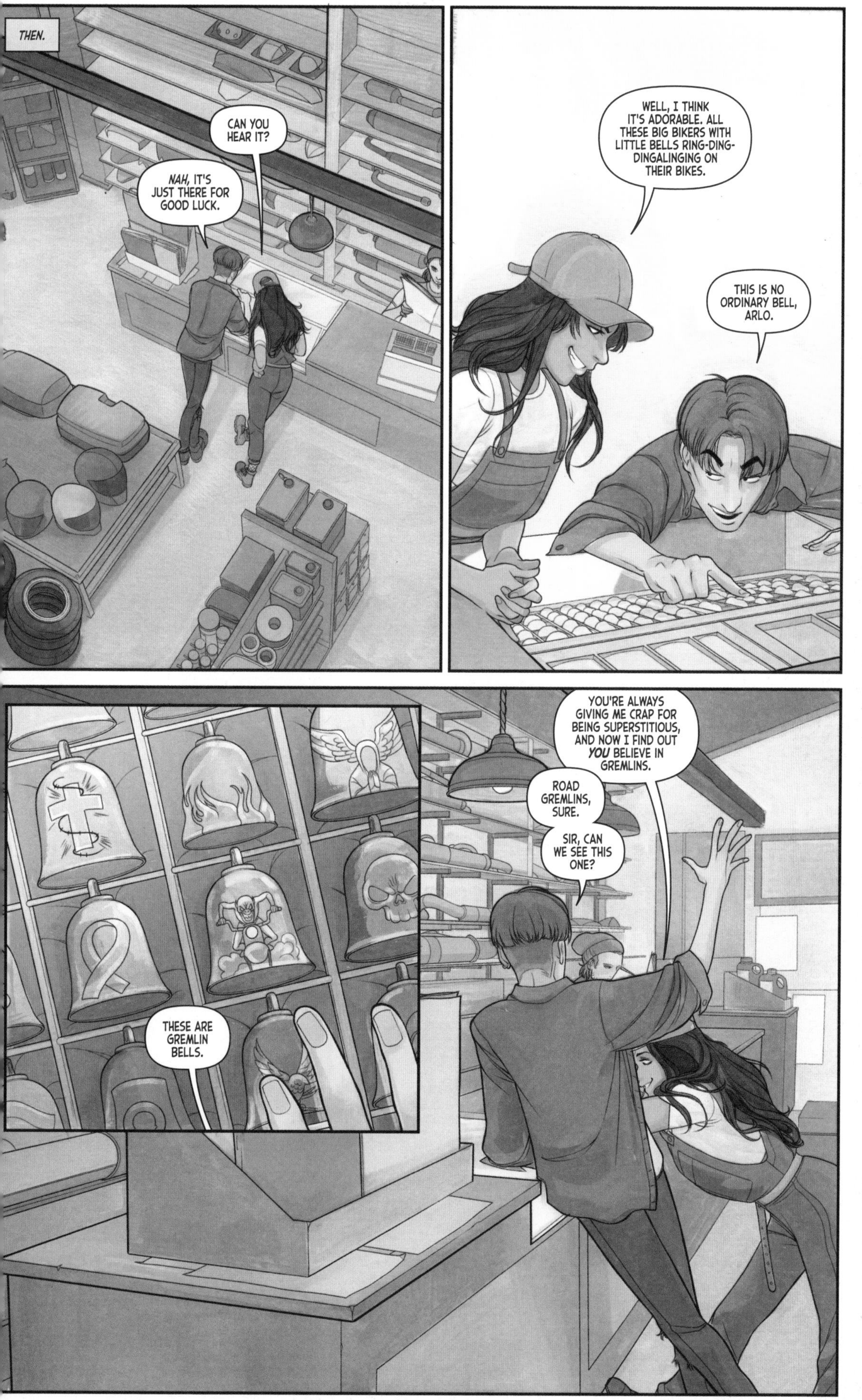

THEN.
CAN YOU HEAR IT?
NAH, IT'S JUST THERE FOR GOOD LUCK.
WELL, I THINK IT'S ADORABLE. ALL THESE BIG BIKERS WITH LITTLE BELLS RING-DING-DINGALINGING ON THEIR BIKES.
THIS IS NO ORDINARY BELL, ARLO.
THESE ARE GREMLIN BELLS.
YOU'RE ALWAYS GIVING ME CRAP FOR BEING SUPERSTITIOUS, AND NOW I FIND OUT ***YOU*** BELIEVE IN GREMLINS.
ROAD GREMLINS, SURE.
SIR, CAN WE SEE THIS ONE?

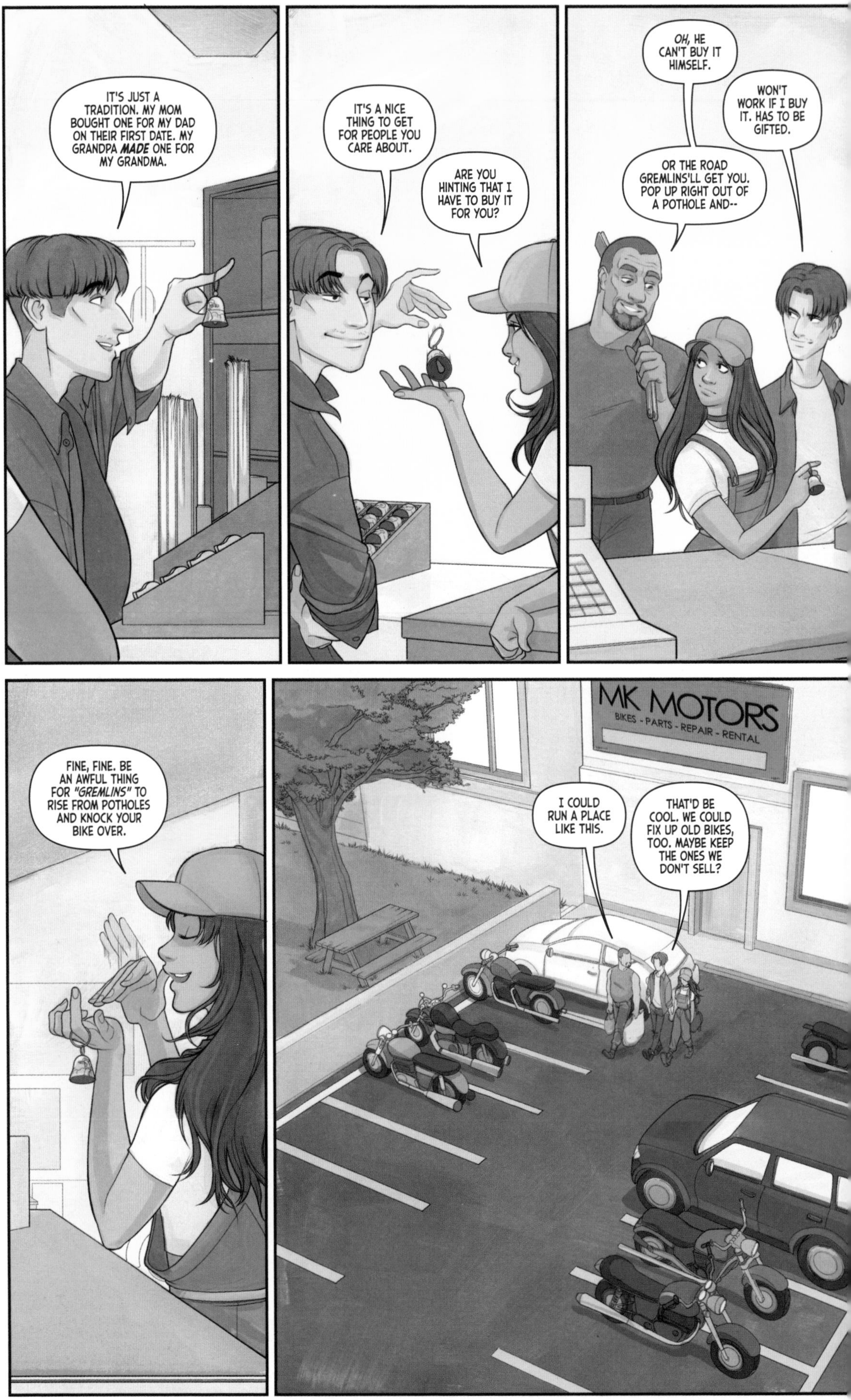
IT'S JUST A TRADITION. MY MOM BOUGHT ONE FOR MY DAD ON THEIR FIRST DATE. MY GRANDPA *MADE* ONE FOR MY GRANDMA.
IT'S A NICE THING TO GET FOR PEOPLE YOU CARE ABOUT.
ARE YOU HINTING THAT I HAVE TO BUY IT FOR YOU?
OH, HE CAN'T BUY IT HIMSELF.
WON'T WORK IF I BUY IT. HAS TO BE GIFTED.
OR THE ROAD GREMLINS'LL GET YOU. POP UP RIGHT OUT OF A POTHOLE AND--
FINE, FINE. BE AN AWFUL THING FOR *"GREMLINS"* TO RISE FROM POTHOLES AND KNOCK YOUR BIKE OVER.
MK MOTORS
BIKES - PARTS - REPAIR - RENTAL
I COULD RUN A PLACE LIKE THIS.
THAT'D BE COOL. WE COULD FIX UP OLD BIKES, TOO. MAYBE KEEP THE ONES WE DON'T SELL?

SOUNDS GOOD TO ME. YOU TWO HEADED HOME?

THINK WE MIGHT RIDE DOWN TO THE RIVER FOR A BIT.

ALRIGHT, BE SAFE.

FUNNY HOW WE MADE IT HERE WITHOUT ANY PROBLEMS, SANS BELL.

I THINK YOU MAY BE GOOD LUCK, TOO.

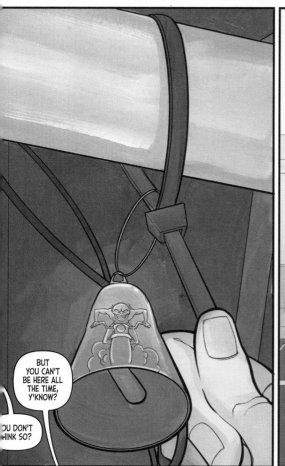

BUT YOU CAN'T BE HERE ALL THE TIME, Y'KNOW?

OU DON'T HINK SO?

MOST FOLK CAN'T.

MOST FOLK DON'T BELIEVE IN GREMLINS...

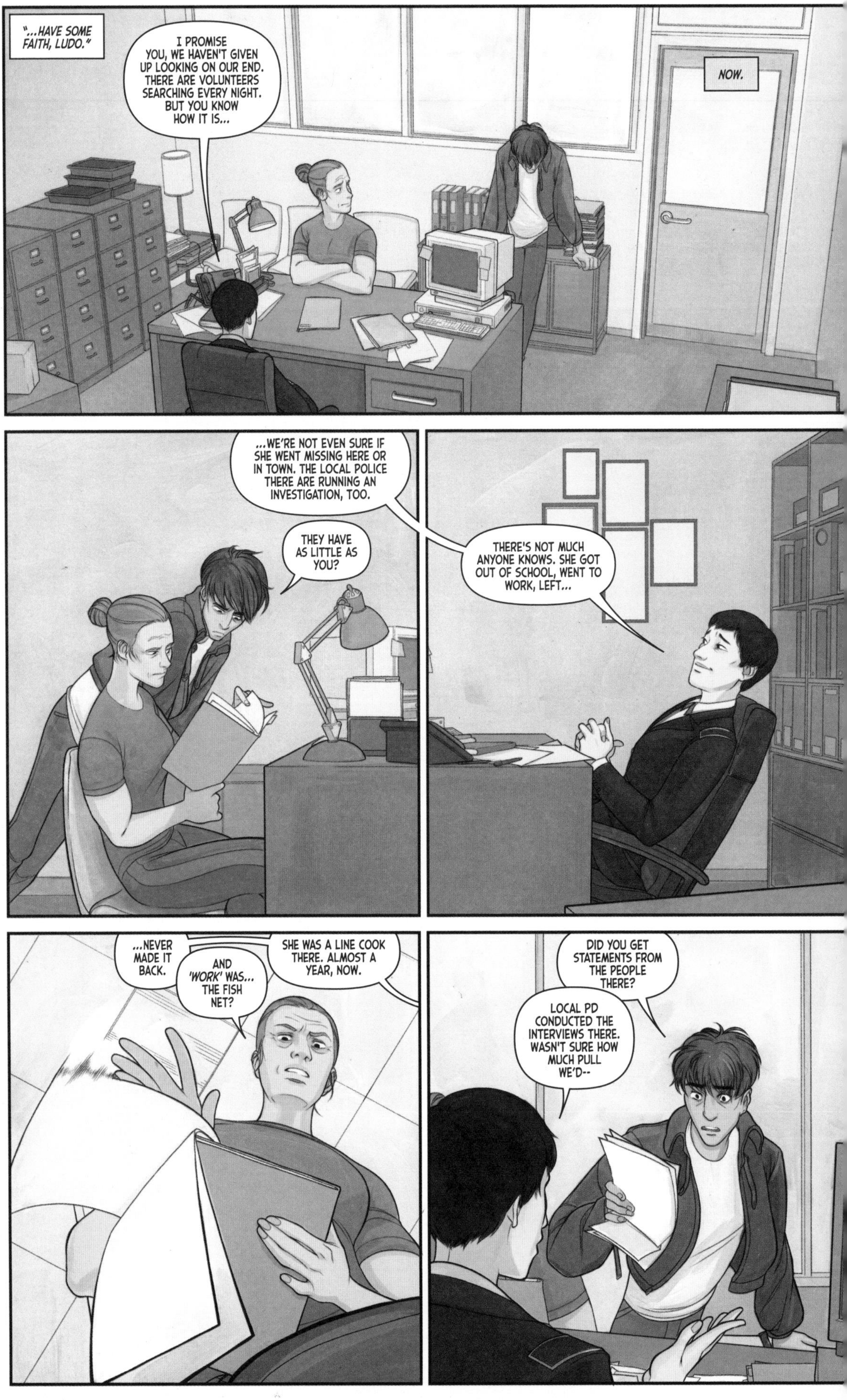
"...HAVE SOME FAITH, LUDO."
I PROMISE YOU, WE HAVEN'T GIVEN UP LOOKING ON OUR END. THERE ARE VOLUNTEERS SEARCHING EVERY NIGHT. BUT YOU KNOW HOW IT IS...
NOW.
...WE'RE NOT EVEN SURE IF SHE WENT MISSING HERE OR IN TOWN. THE LOCAL POLICE THERE ARE RUNNING AN INVESTIGATION, TOO.
THEY HAVE AS LITTLE AS YOU?
THERE'S NOT MUCH ANYONE KNOWS. SHE GOT OUT OF SCHOOL, WENT TO WORK, LEFT...
...NEVER MADE IT BACK.
AND 'WORK' WAS... THE FISH NET?
SHE WAS A LINE COOK THERE. ALMOST A YEAR, NOW.
DID YOU GET STATEMENTS FROM THE PEOPLE THERE?
LOCAL PD CONDUCTED THE INTERVIEWS THERE. WASN'T SURE HOW MUCH PULL WE'D--

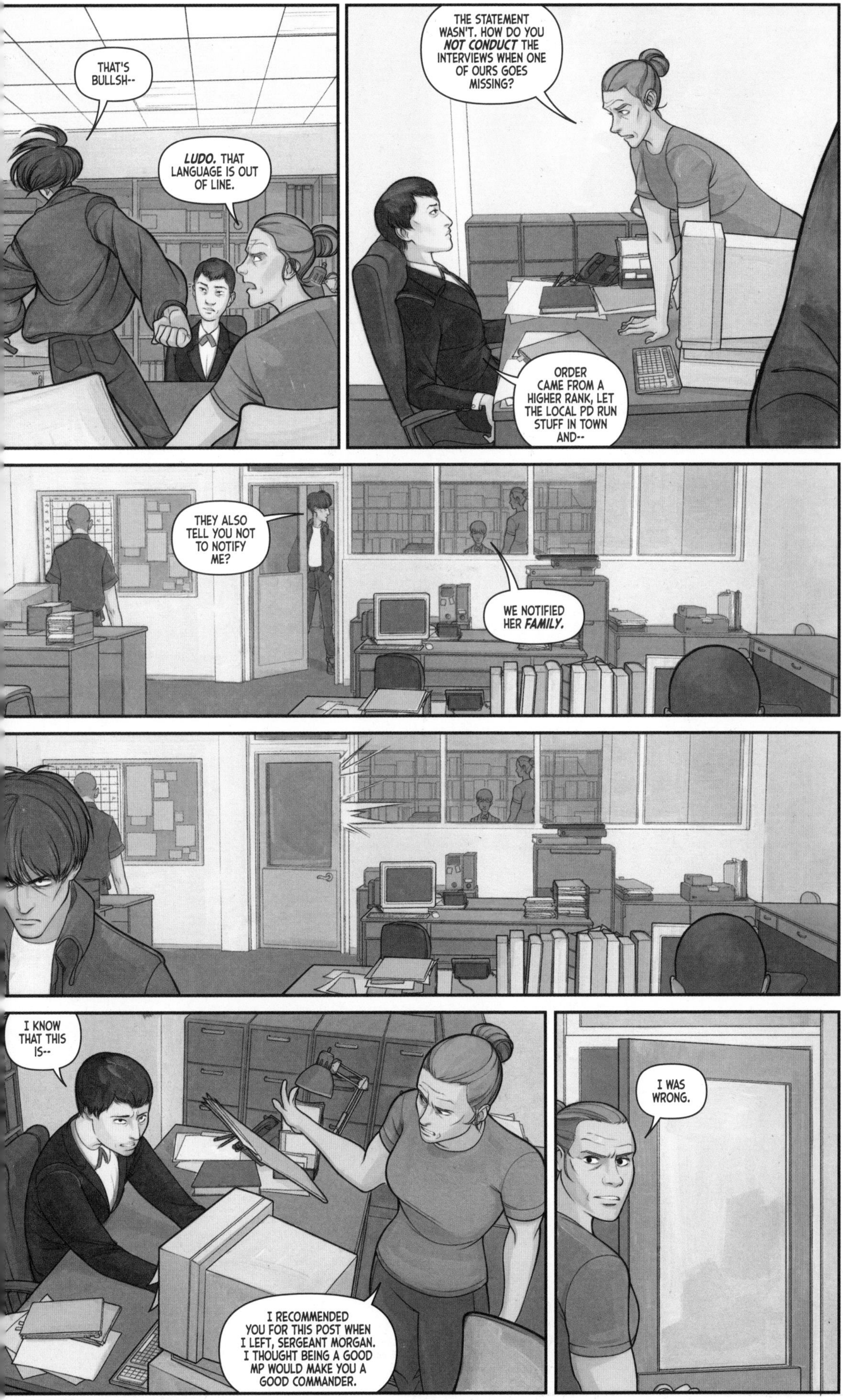
THAT'S BULLSH--
LUDO. THAT LANGUAGE IS OUT OF LINE.
THE STATEMENT WASN'T. HOW DO YOU NOT CONDUCT THE INTERVIEWS WHEN ONE OF OURS GOES MISSING?
ORDER CAME FROM A HIGHER RANK, LET THE LOCAL PD RUN STUFF IN TOWN AND--
THEY ALSO TELL YOU NOT TO NOTIFY ME?
WE NOTIFIED HER FAMILY.
I KNOW THAT THIS IS--
I RECOMMENDED YOU FOR THIS POST WHEN I LEFT, SERGEANT MORGAN. I THOUGHT BEING A GOOD MP WOULD MAKE YOU A GOOD COMMANDER.
I WAS WRONG.

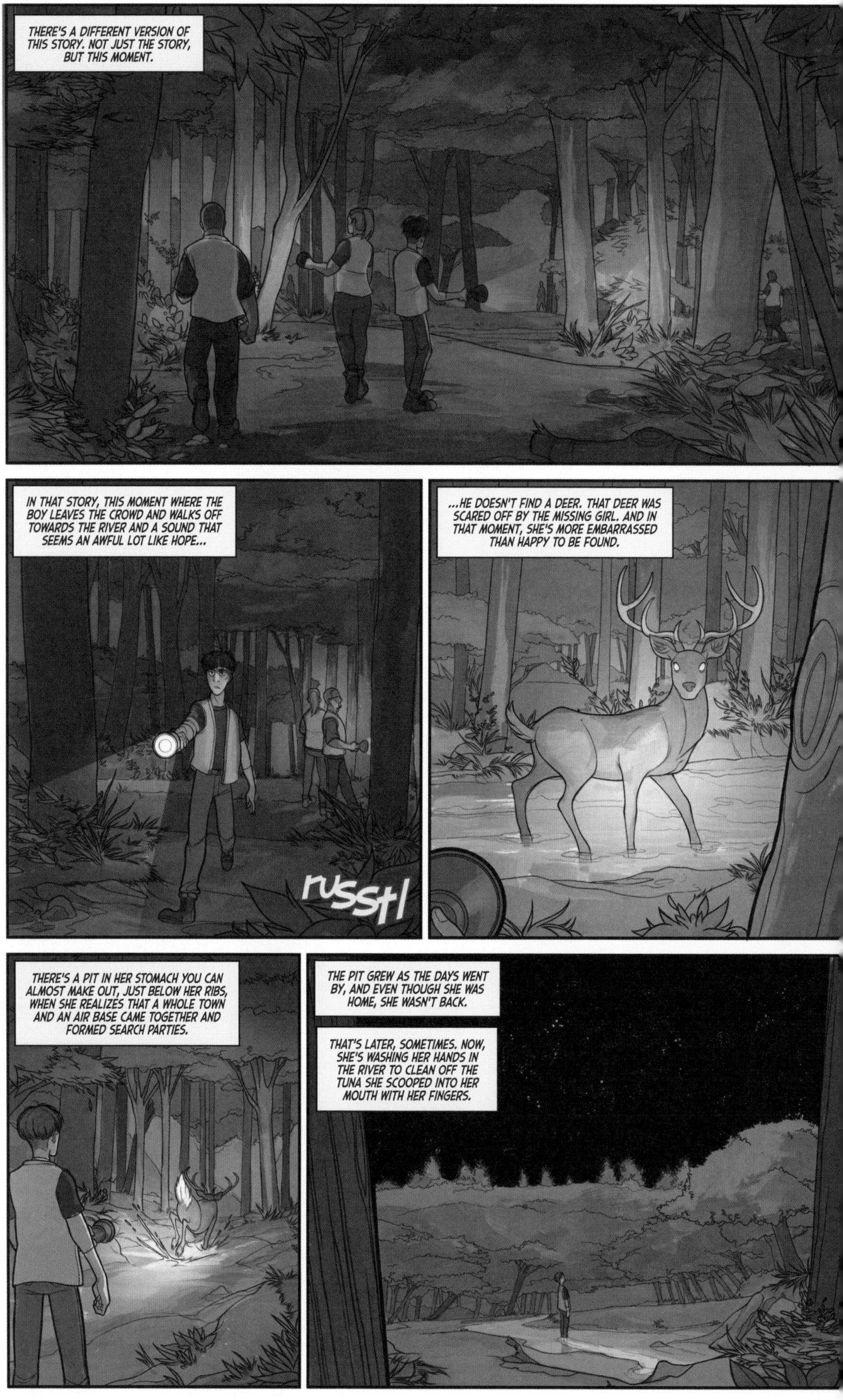
THERE'S A DIFFERENT VERSION OF THIS STORY. NOT JUST THE STORY, BUT THIS MOMENT.
IN THAT STORY, THIS MOMENT WHERE THE BOY LEAVES THE CROWD AND WALKS OFF TOWARDS THE RIVER AND A SOUND THAT SEEMS AN AWFUL LOT LIKE HOPE...
russtl
...HE DOESN'T FIND A DEER. THAT DEER WAS SCARED OFF BY THE MISSING GIRL. AND IN THAT MOMENT, SHE'S MORE EMBARRASSED THAN HAPPY TO BE FOUND.
THERE'S A PIT IN HER STOMACH YOU CAN ALMOST MAKE OUT, JUST BELOW HER RIBS, WHEN SHE REALIZES THAT A WHOLE TOWN AND AN AIR BASE CAME TOGETHER AND FORMED SEARCH PARTIES.
THE PIT GREW AS THE DAYS WENT BY, AND EVEN THOUGH SHE WAS HOME, SHE WASN'T BACK.
THAT'S LATER, SOMETIMES. NOW, SHE'S WASHING HER HANDS IN THE RIVER TO CLEAN OFF THE TUNA SHE SCOOPED INTO HER MOUTH WITH HER FINGERS.

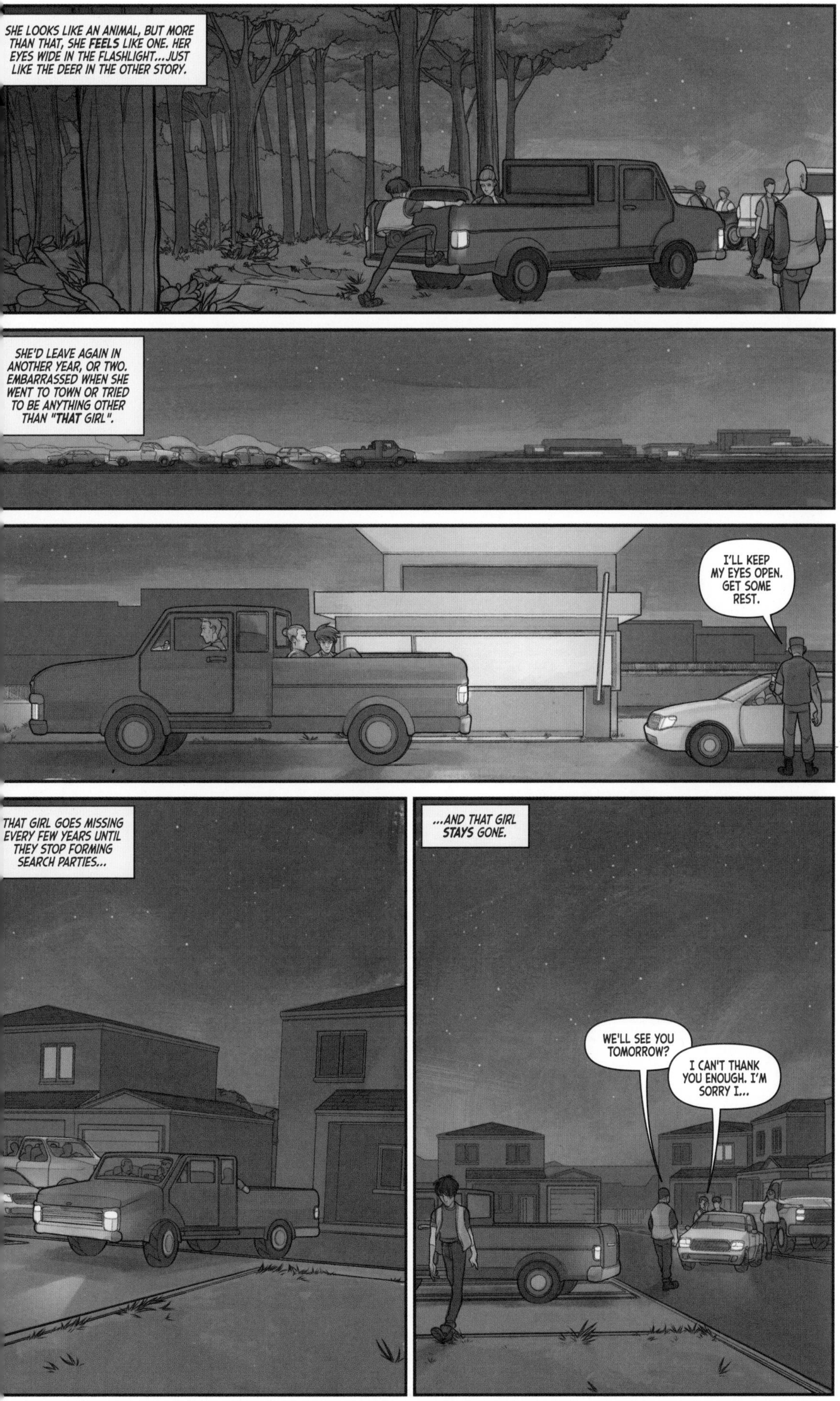
SHE LOOKS LIKE AN ANIMAL, BUT MORE THAN THAT, SHE **FEELS** LIKE ONE. HER EYES WIDE IN THE FLASHLIGHT...JUST LIKE THE DEER IN THE OTHER STORY.
SHE'D LEAVE AGAIN IN ANOTHER YEAR, OR TWO. EMBARRASSED WHEN SHE WENT TO TOWN OR TRIED TO BE ANYTHING OTHER THAN "**THAT** GIRL".
I'LL KEEP MY EYES OPEN. GET SOME REST.
THAT GIRL GOES MISSING EVERY FEW YEARS UNTIL THEY STOP FORMING SEARCH PARTIES...
...AND THAT GIRL **STAYS** GONE.
WE'LL SEE YOU TOMORROW?
I CAN'T THANK YOU ENOUGH. I'M SORRY I...

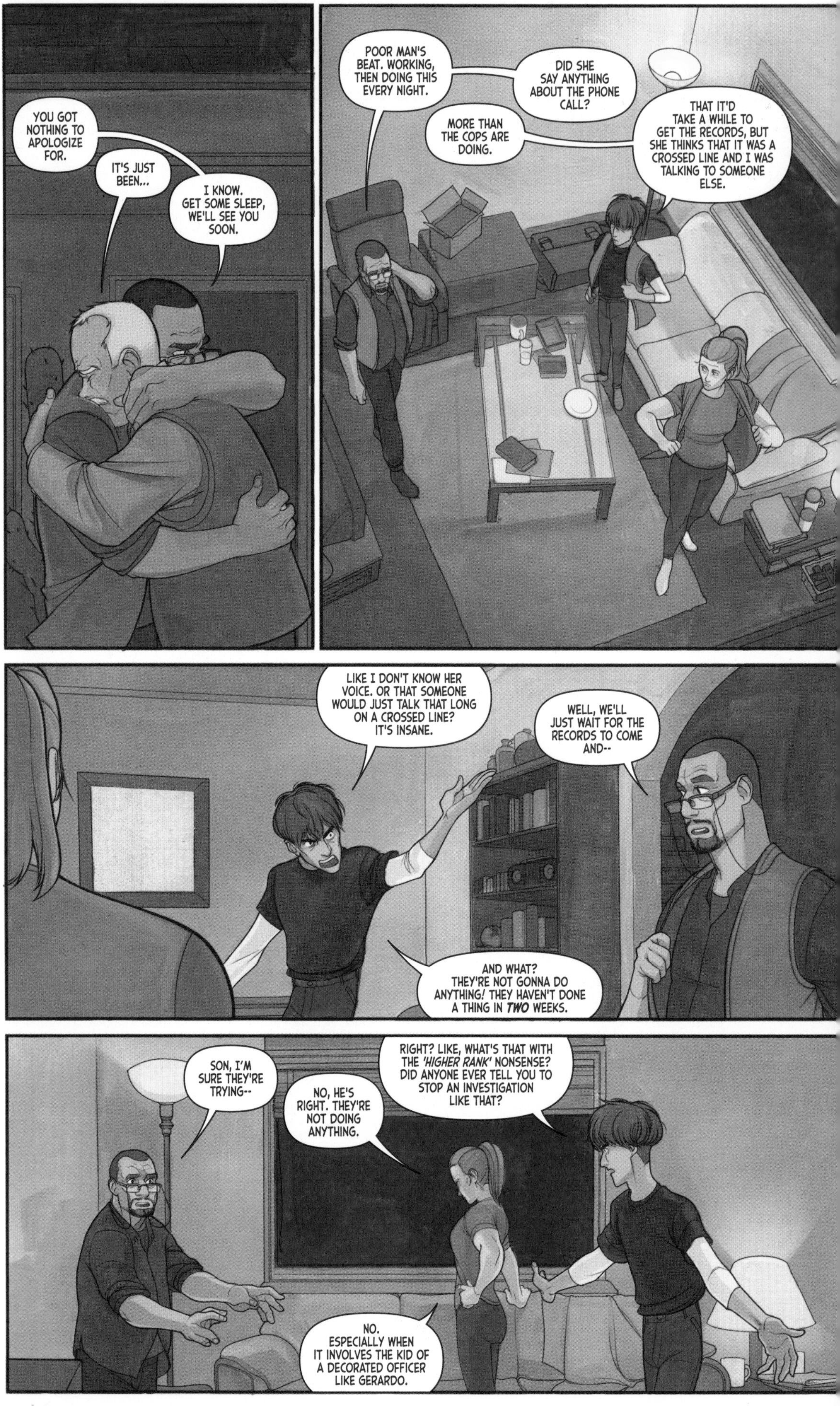
YOU GOT NOTHING TO APOLOGIZE FOR.
IT'S JUST BEEN...
I KNOW. GET SOME SLEEP, WE'LL SEE YOU SOON.
POOR MAN'S BEAT. WORKING, THEN DOING THIS EVERY NIGHT.
MORE THAN THE COPS ARE DOING.
DID SHE SAY ANYTHING ABOUT THE PHONE CALL?
THAT IT'D TAKE A WHILE TO GET THE RECORDS, BUT SHE THINKS THAT IT WAS A CROSSED LINE AND I WAS TALKING TO SOMEONE ELSE.
LIKE I DON'T KNOW HER VOICE. OR THAT SOMEONE WOULD JUST TALK THAT LONG ON A CROSSED LINE? IT'S INSANE.
WELL, WE'LL JUST WAIT FOR THE RECORDS TO COME AND--
AND WHAT? THEY'RE NOT GONNA DO ANYTHING! THEY HAVEN'T DONE A THING IN ***TWO*** WEEKS.
SON, I'M SURE THEY'RE TRYING--
NO, HE'S RIGHT. THEY'RE NOT DOING ANYTHING.
RIGHT? LIKE, WHAT'S THAT WITH THE *'HIGHER RANK'* NONSENSE? DID ANYONE EVER TELL YOU TO STOP AN INVESTIGATION LIKE THAT?
NO. ESPECIALLY WHEN IT INVOLVES THE KID OF A DECORATED OFFICER LIKE GERARDO.

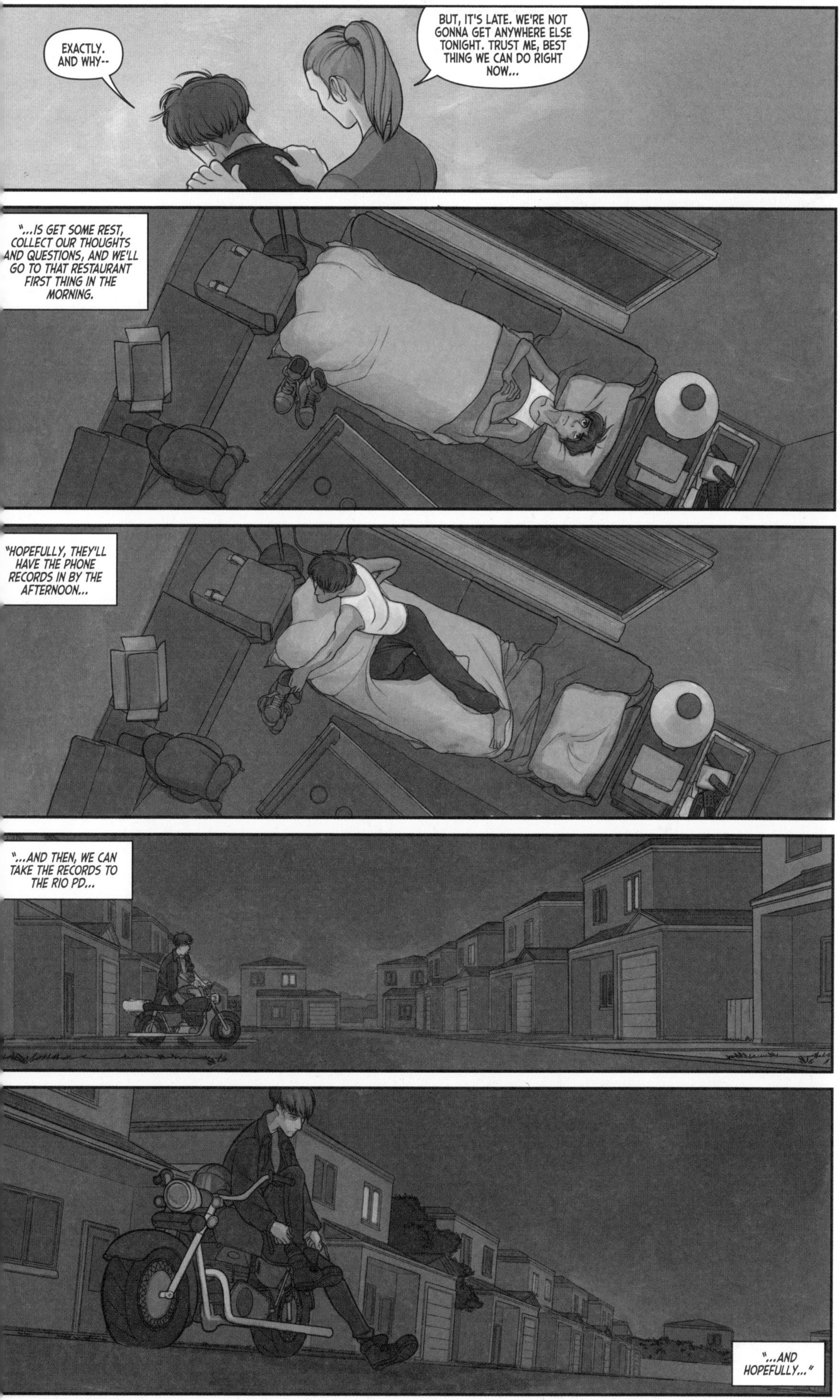
EXACTLY. AND WHY--
BUT, IT'S LATE. WE'RE NOT GONNA GET ANYWHERE ELSE TONIGHT. TRUST ME, BEST THING WE CAN DO RIGHT NOW...
"...IS GET SOME REST, COLLECT OUR THOUGHTS AND QUESTIONS, AND WE'LL GO TO THAT RESTAURANT FIRST THING IN THE MORNING.
"HOPEFULLY, THEY'LL HAVE THE PHONE RECORDS IN BY THE AFTERNOON...
"...AND THEN, WE CAN TAKE THE RECORDS TO THE RIO PD...
"...AND HOPEFULLY..."

Part II: A Ribbon of Road

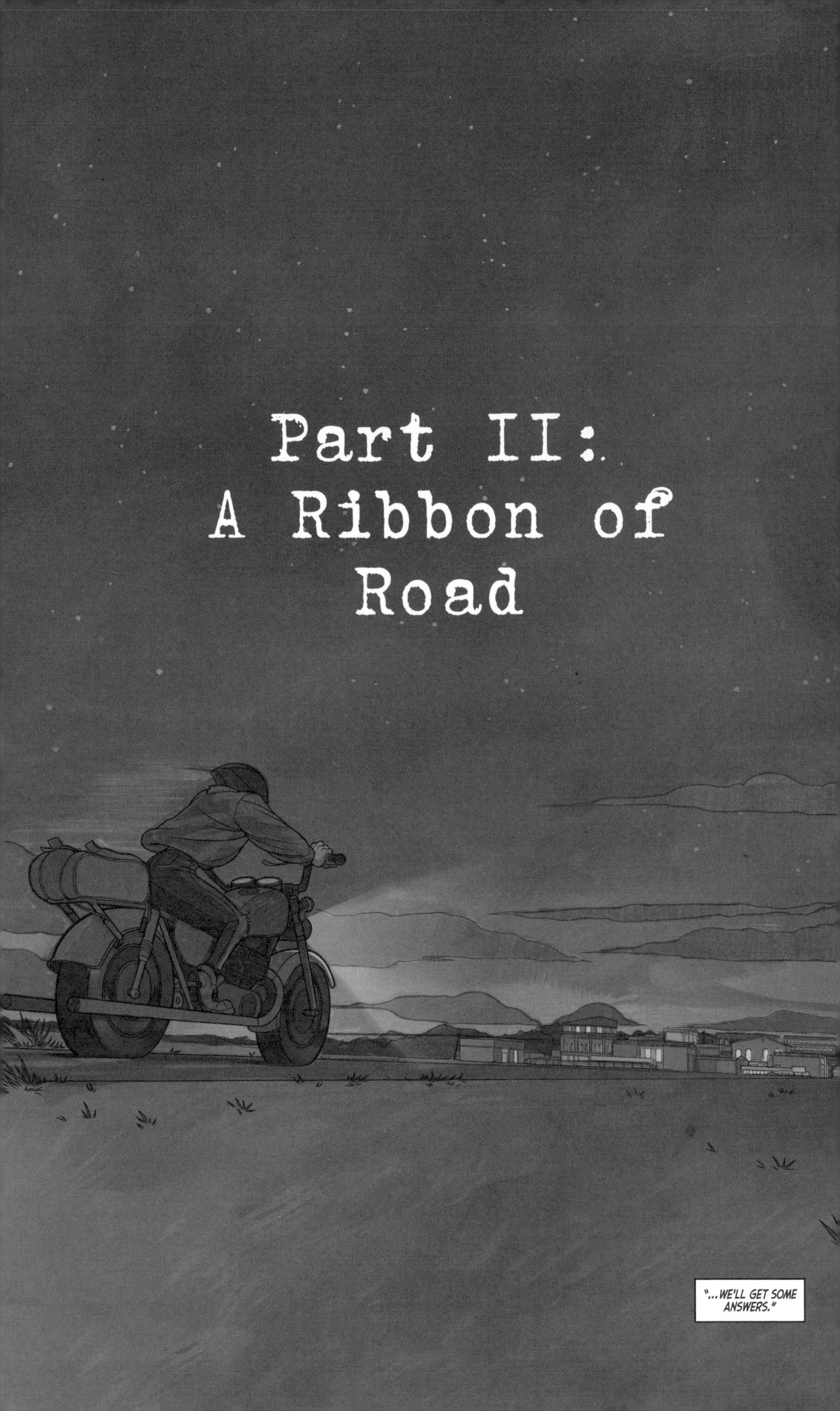
"...WE'LL GET SOME ANSWERS."

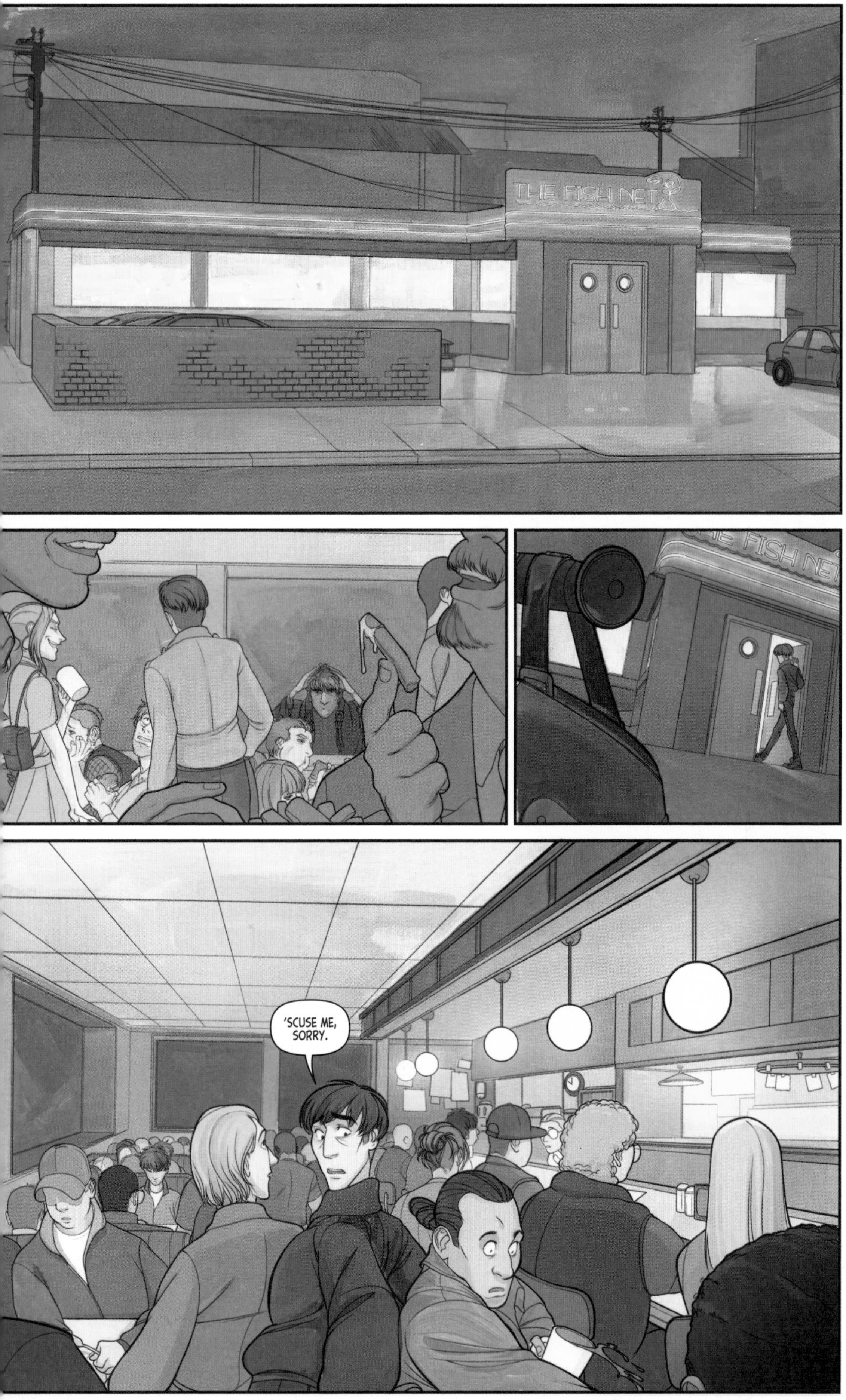
THE FISH NET
'SCUSE ME, SORRY.

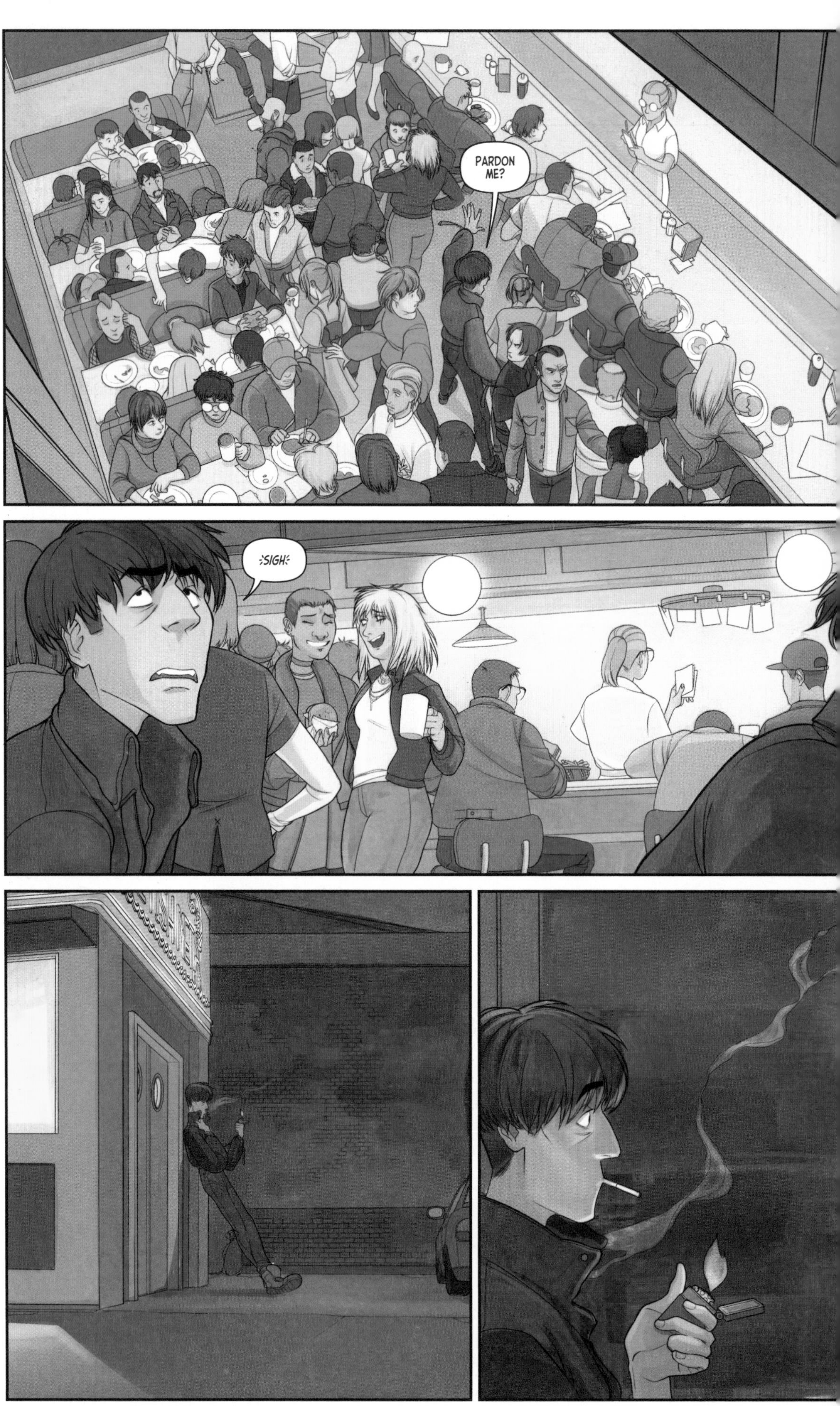
PARDON ME?
SIGH

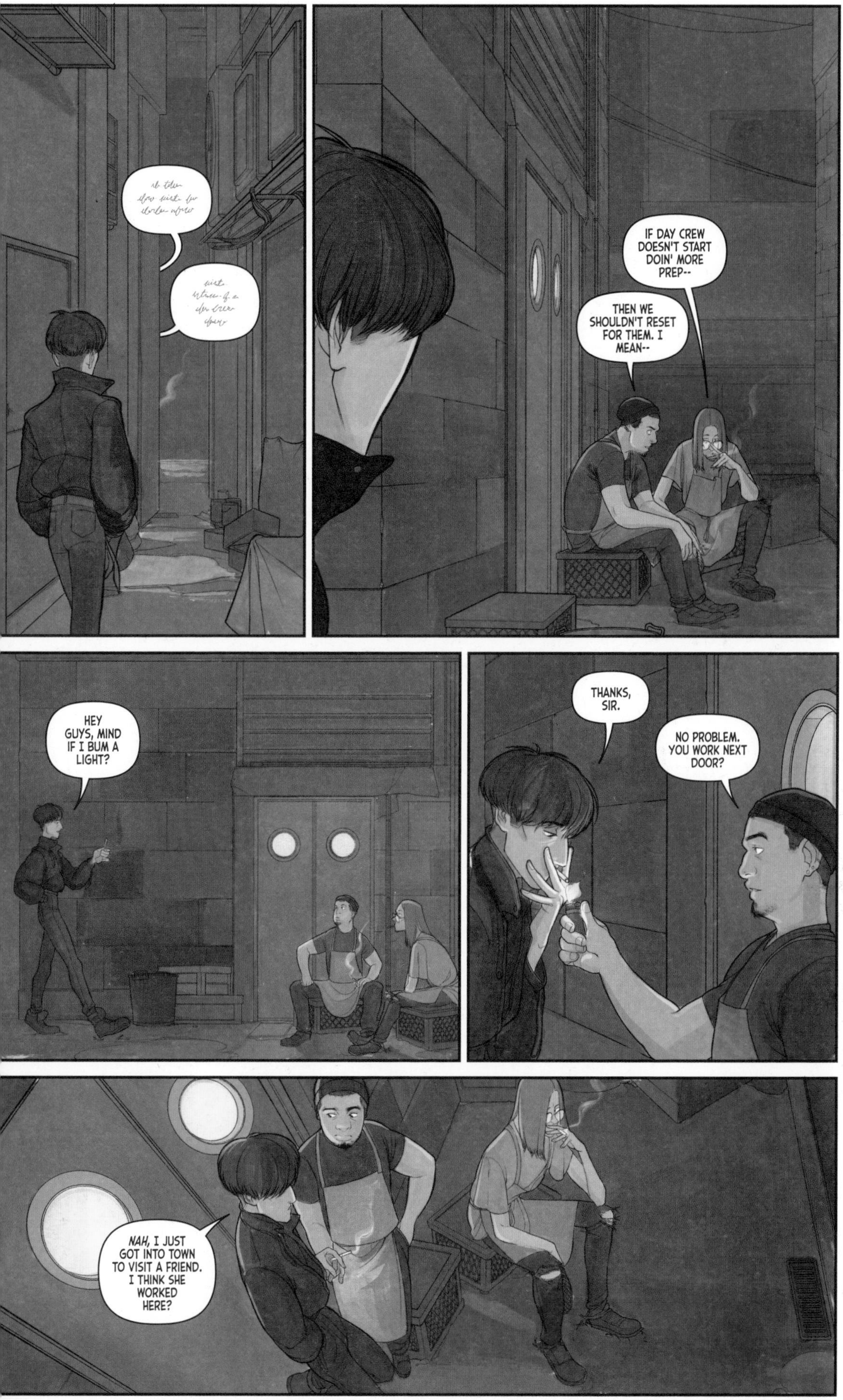
IF DAY CREW DOESN'T START DOIN' MORE PREP--
THEN WE SHOULDN'T RESET FOR THEM. I MEAN--
HEY GUYS, MIND IF I BUM A LIGHT?
THANKS, SIR.
NO PROBLEM. YOU WORK NEXT DOOR?
NAH, I JUST GOT INTO TOWN TO VISIT A FRIEND. I THINK SHE WORKED HERE?

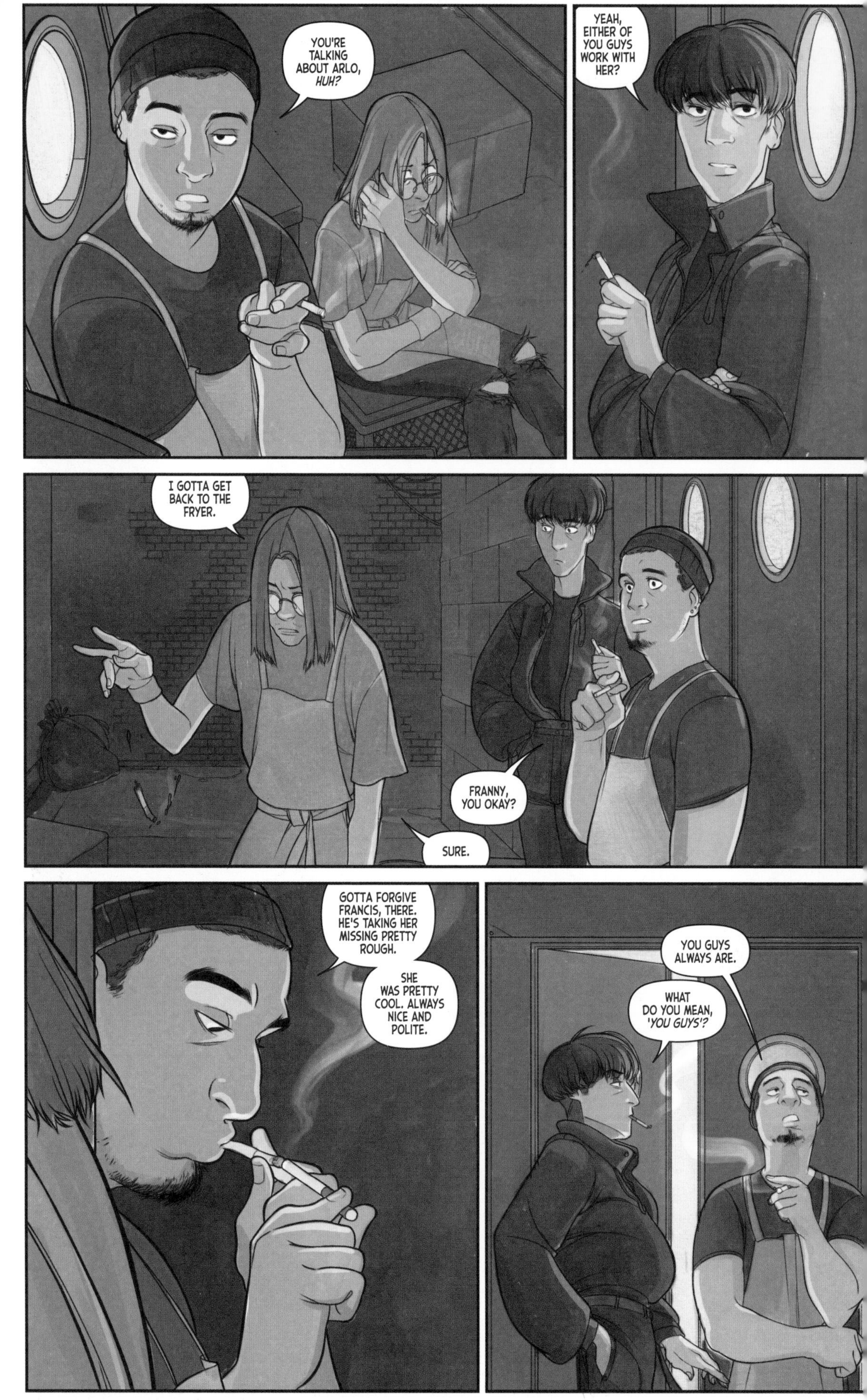

YOU'RE TALKING ABOUT ARLO, *HUH?*
YEAH, EITHER OF YOU GUYS WORK WITH HER?
I GOTTA GET BACK TO THE FRYER.
FRANNY, YOU OKAY?
SURE.
GOTTA FORGIVE FRANCIS, THERE. HE'S TAKING HER MISSING PRETTY ROUGH.
SHE WAS PRETTY COOL. ALWAYS NICE AND POLITE.
YOU GUYS ALWAYS ARE.
WHAT DO YOU MEAN, *'YOU GUYS'?*

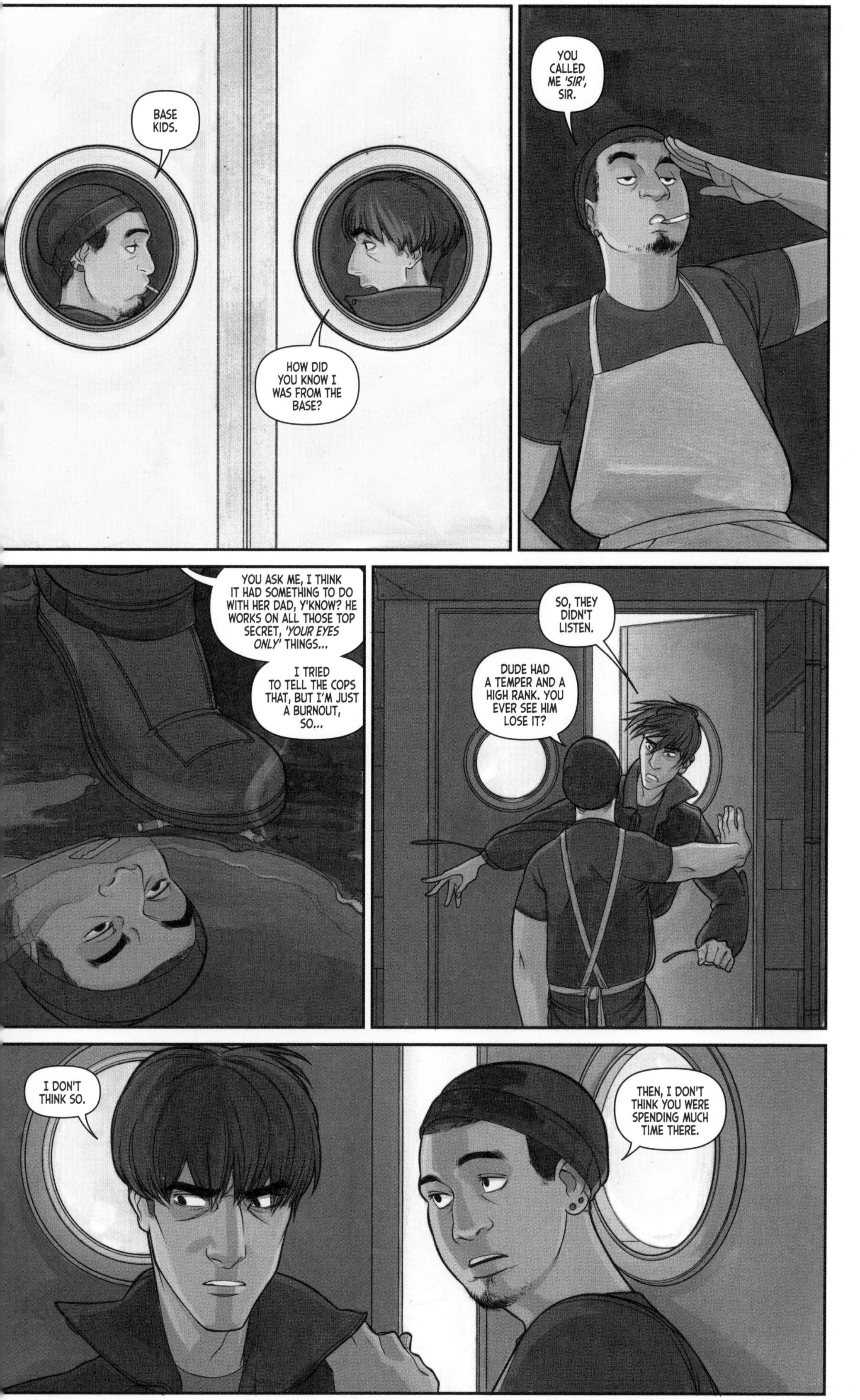
BASE KIDS.
HOW DID YOU KNOW I WAS FROM THE BASE?
YOU CALLED ME *'SIR'*, SIR.
YOU ASK ME, I THINK IT HAD SOMETHING TO DO WITH HER DAD, Y'KNOW? HE WORKS ON ALL THOSE TOP SECRET, *'YOUR EYES ONLY'* THINGS...
I TRIED TO TELL THE COPS THAT, BUT I'M JUST A BURNOUT, SO...
SO, THEY DIDN'T LISTEN.
DUDE HAD A TEMPER AND A HIGH RANK. YOU EVER SEE HIM LOSE IT?
I DON'T THINK SO.
THEN, I DON'T THINK YOU WERE SPENDING MUCH TIME THERE.

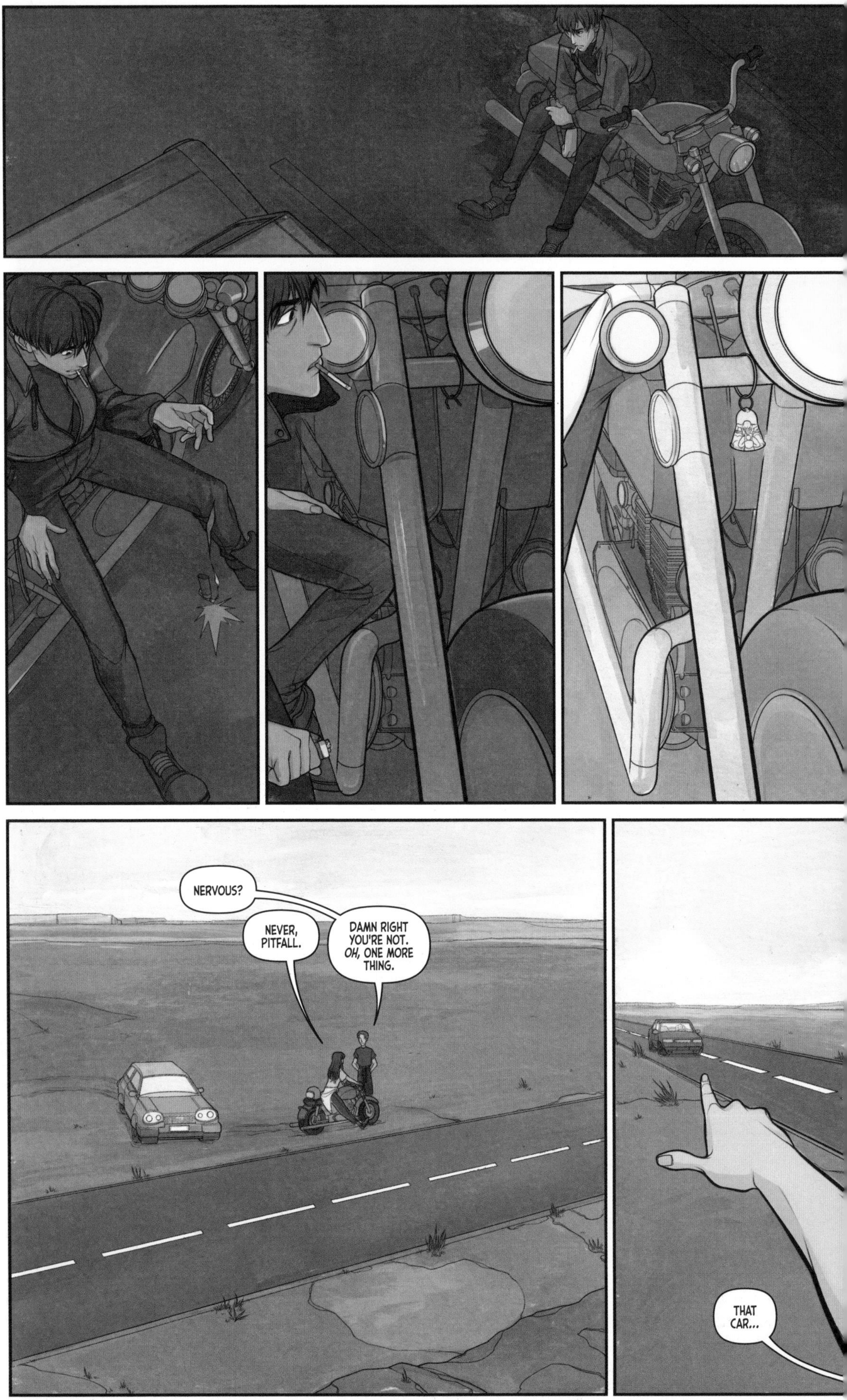
NERVOUS?
NEVER, PITFALL.
DAMN RIGHT YOU'RE NOT. *OH,* ONE MORE THING.
THAT CAR...

"...WANTS YOU DEAD."

THAT ONE TOO. YOU GOTTA RIDE LIKE ALL THESE DRIVERS ARE HITMEN--

AND I'M JOHNNY MNEMONIC?

IF THAT'S WHAT WORKS FOR YOU.

RIDE LIKE JOHNNY MNEMONIC--

"--DODGING HITMEN AND ASSASSINS..."

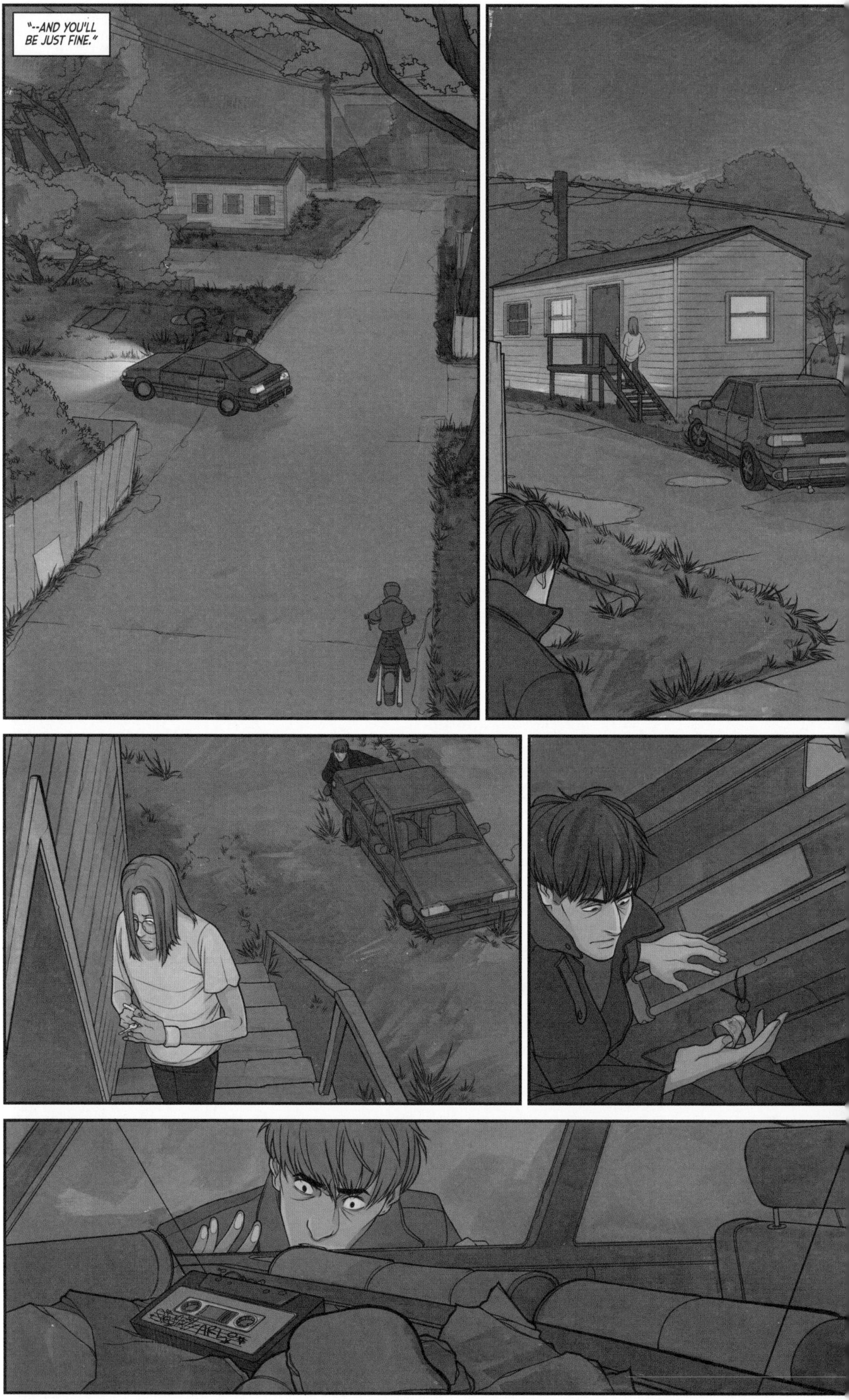
"--AND YOU'LL BE JUST FINE."

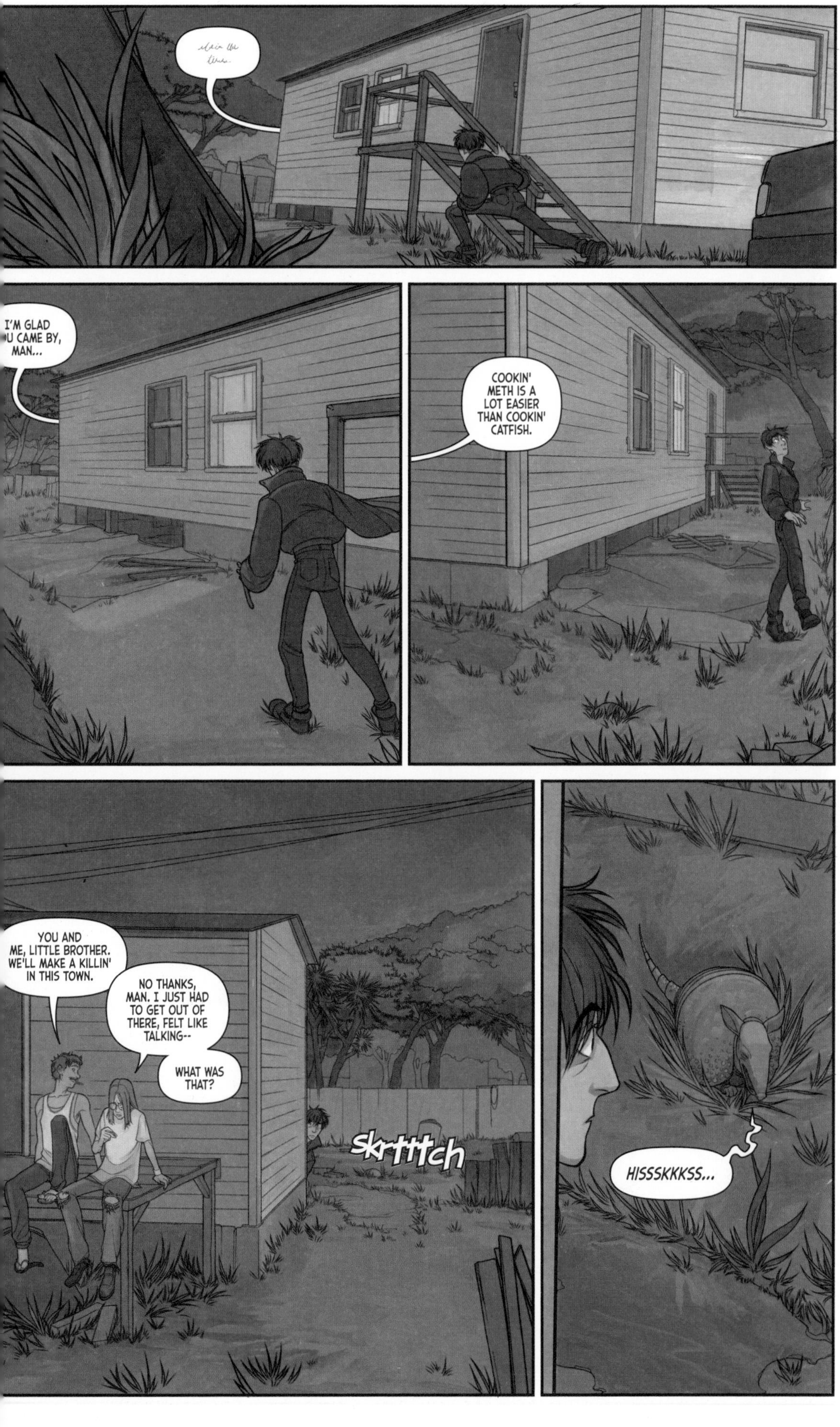
I'M GLAD U CAME BY, MAN...
COOKIN' METH IS A LOT EASIER THAN COOKIN' CATFISH.
YOU AND ME, LITTLE BROTHER. WE'LL MAKE A KILLIN' IN THIS TOWN.
NO THANKS, MAN. I JUST HAD TO GET OUT OF THERE, FELT LIKE TALKING--
WHAT WAS THAT?
SKRTTTCH
HISSSKKKSS...

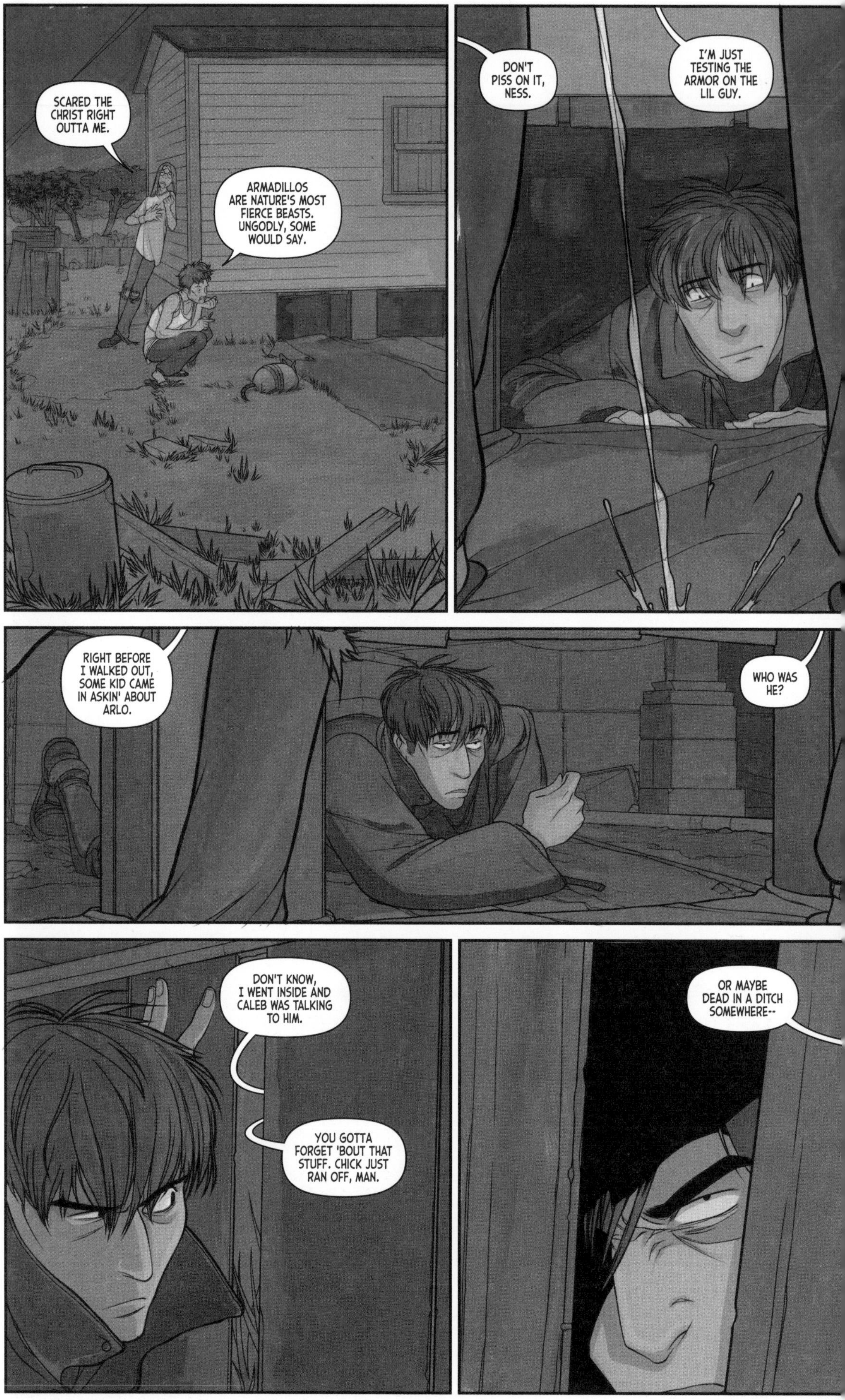
SCARED THE CHRIST RIGHT OUTTA ME.
ARMADILLOS ARE NATURE'S MOST FIERCE BEASTS. UNGODLY, SOME WOULD SAY.
DON'T PISS ON IT, NESS.
I'M JUST TESTING THE ARMOR ON THE LIL GUY.
RIGHT BEFORE I WALKED OUT, SOME KID CAME IN ASKIN' ABOUT ARLO.
WHO WAS HE?
DON'T KNOW, I WENT INSIDE AND CALEB WAS TALKING TO HIM.
YOU GOTTA FORGET 'BOUT THAT STUFF. CHICK JUST RAN OFF, MAN.
OR MAYBE DEAD IN A DITCH SOMEWHERE--

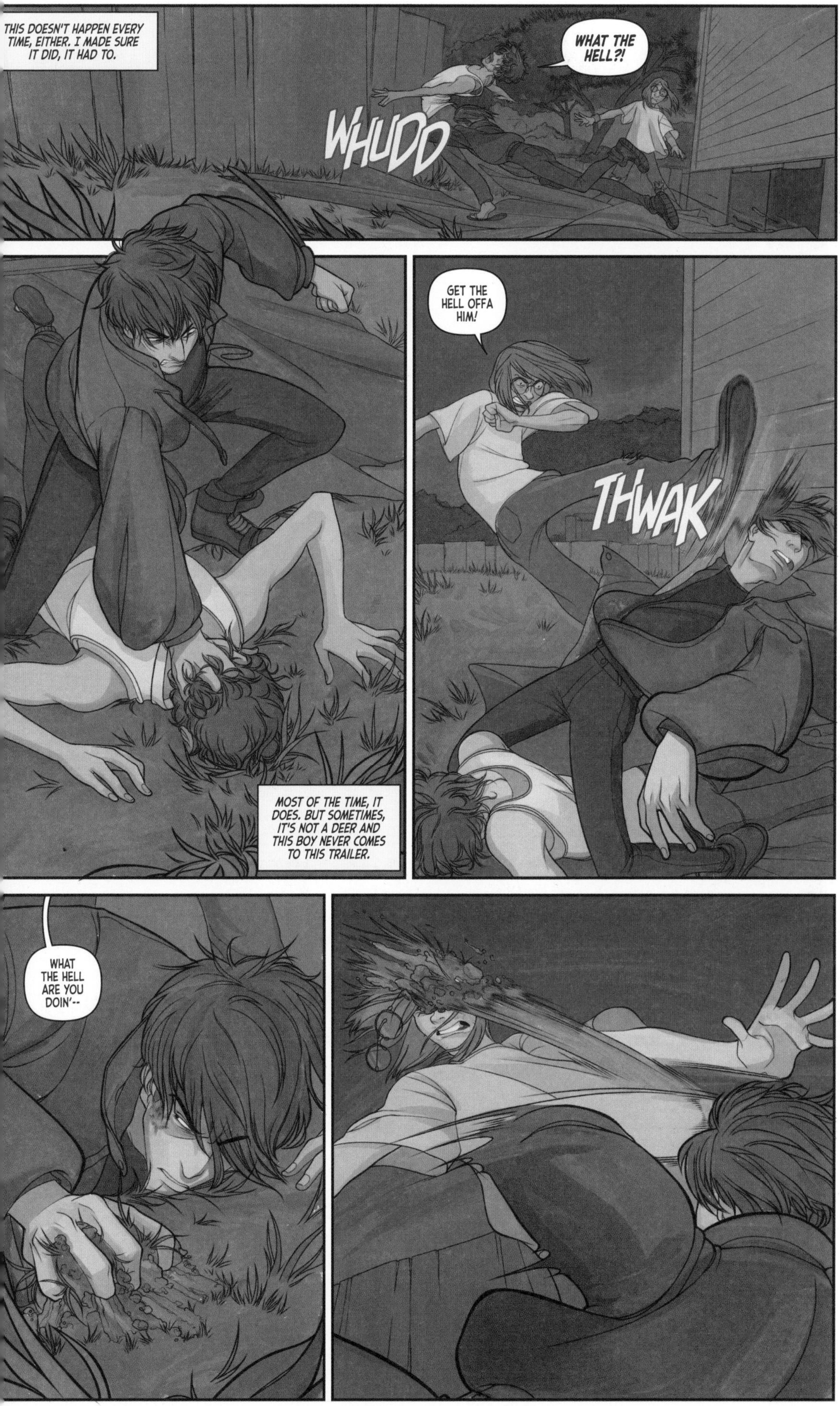
THIS DOESN'T HAPPEN EVERY TIME, EITHER. I MADE SURE IT DID, IT HAD TO.
WHAT THE HELL?!
WHUDD
MOST OF THE TIME, IT DOES. BUT SOMETIMES, IT'S NOT A DEER AND THIS BOY NEVER COMES TO THIS TRAILER.
GET THE HELL OFFA HIM!
THWAK
WHAT THE HELL ARE YOU DOIN'--

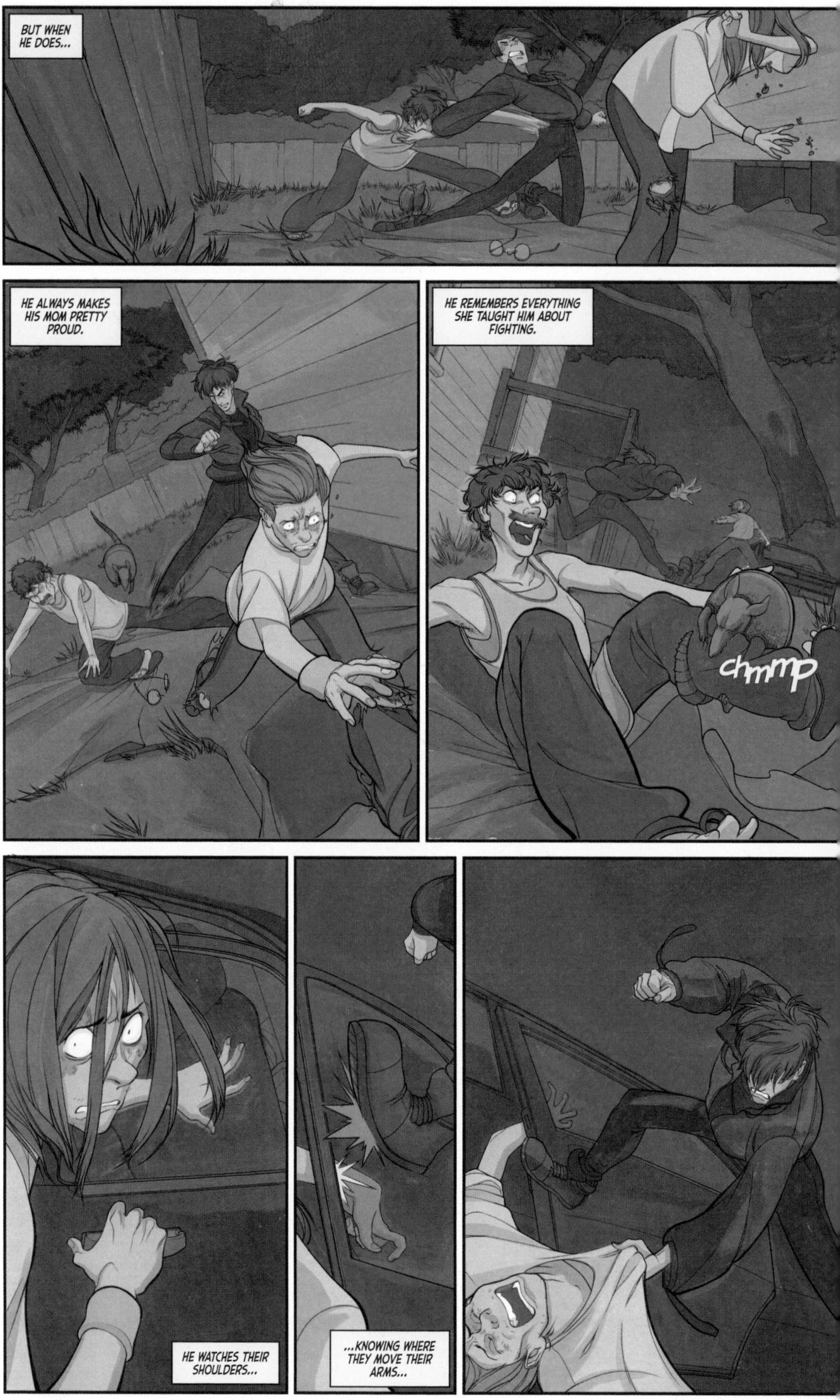
BUT WHEN HE DOES...
HE ALWAYS MAKES HIS MOM PRETTY PROUD.
HE REMEMBERS EVERYTHING SHE TAUGHT HIM ABOUT FIGHTING.
chmmp
HE WATCHES THEIR SHOULDERS...
...KNOWING WHERE THEY MOVE THEIR ARMS...

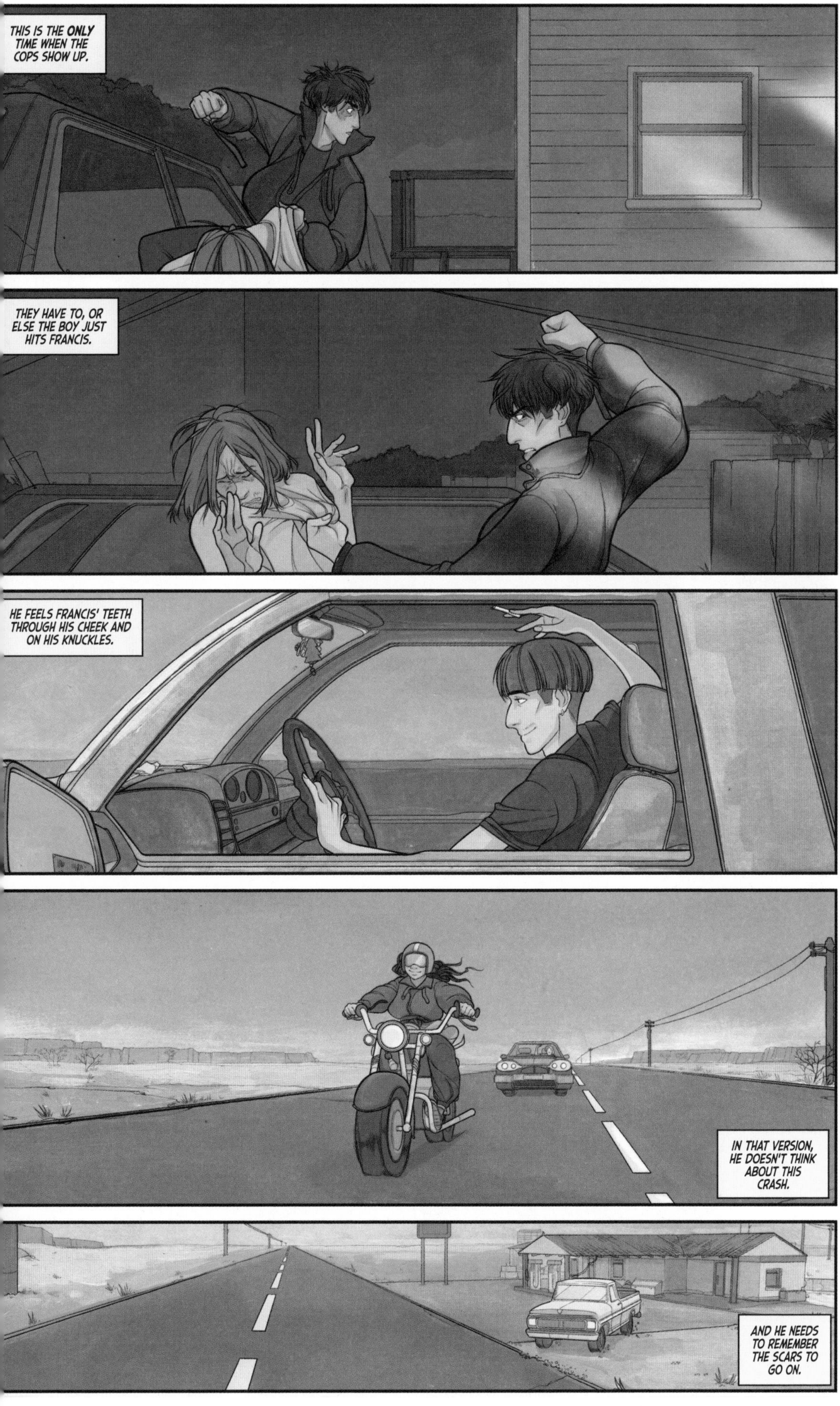
THIS IS THE ONLY TIME WHEN THE COPS SHOW UP.
THEY HAVE TO, OR ELSE THE BOY JUST HITS FRANCIS.
HE FEELS FRANCIS' TEETH THROUGH HIS CHEEK AND ON HIS KNUCKLES.
IN THAT VERSION, HE DOESN'T THINK ABOUT THIS CRASH.
AND HE NEEDS TO REMEMBER THE SCARS TO GO ON.

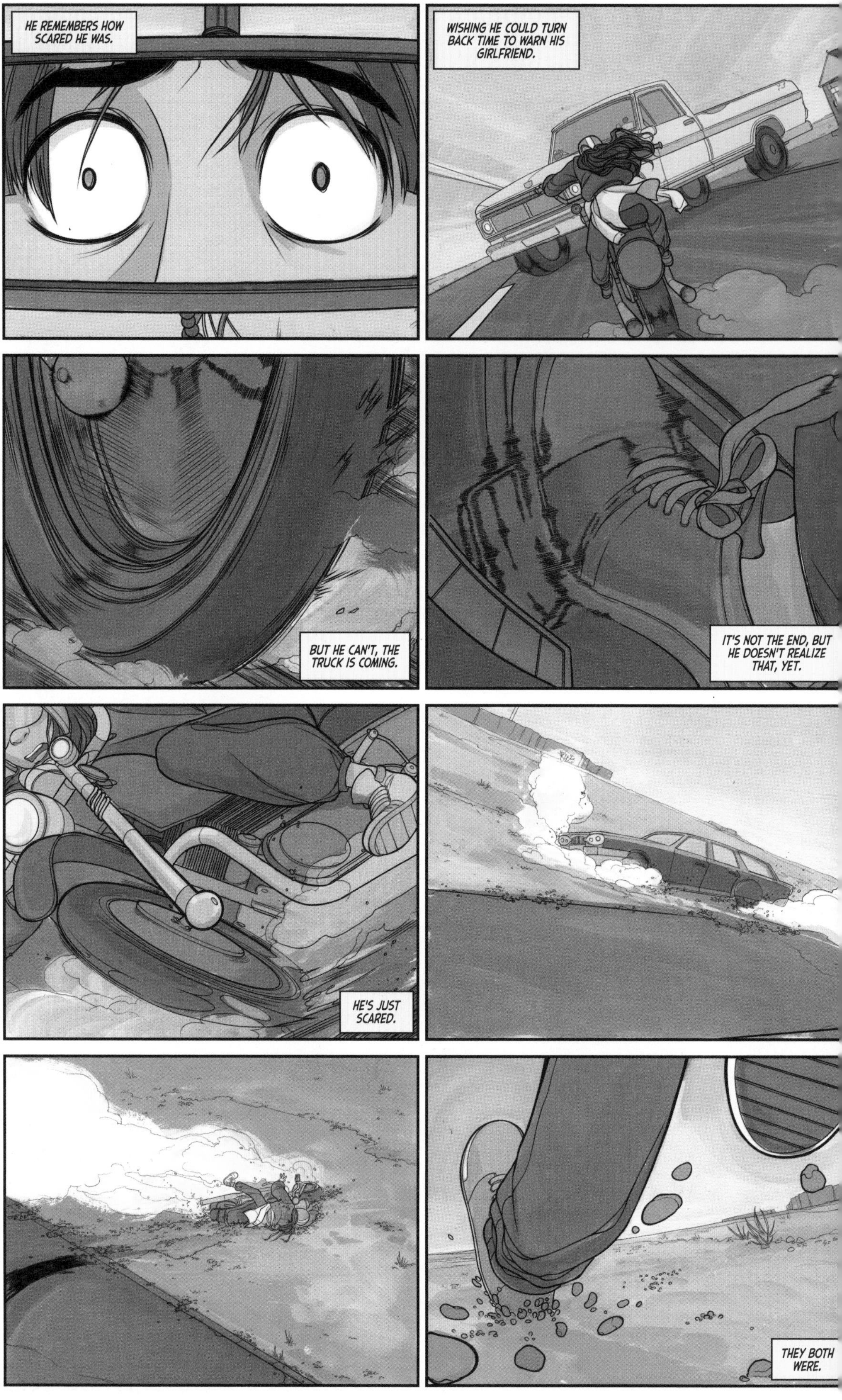
HE REMEMBERS HOW SCARED HE WAS.
WISHING HE COULD TURN BACK TIME TO WARN HIS GIRLFRIEND.
BUT HE CAN'T, THE TRUCK IS COMING.
IT'S NOT THE END, BUT HE DOESN'T REALIZE THAT, YET.
HE'S JUST SCARED.
THEY BOTH WERE.

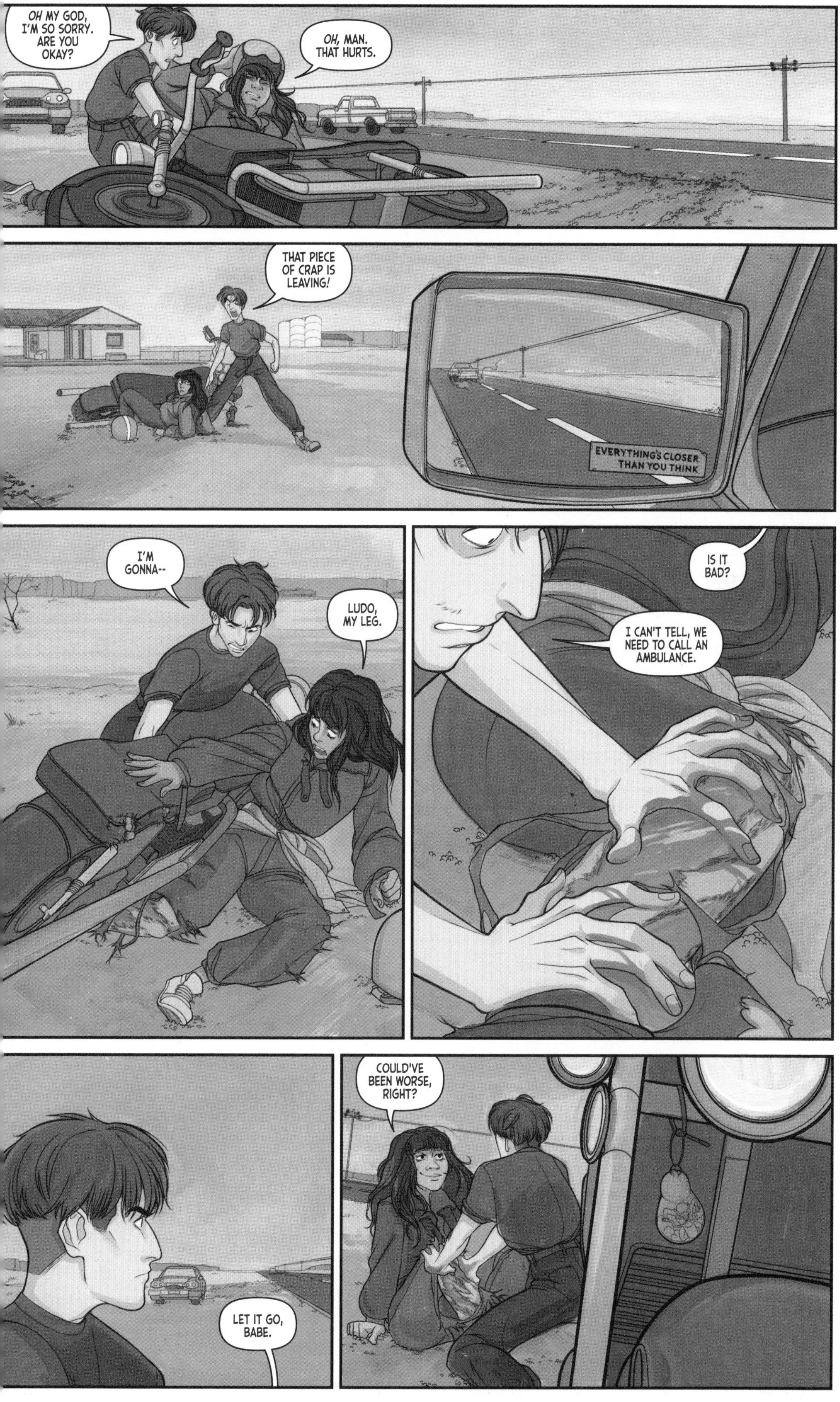
OH MY GOD, I'M SO SORRY. ARE YOU OKAY?
OH, MAN. THAT HURTS.
THAT PIECE OF CRAP IS LEAVING!
EVERYTHING'S CLOSER THAN YOU THINK
I'M GONNA--
LUDO, MY LEG.
IS IT BAD?
I CAN'T TELL, WE NEED TO CALL AN AMBULANCE.
LET IT GO, BABE.
COULD'VE BEEN WORSE, RIGHT?

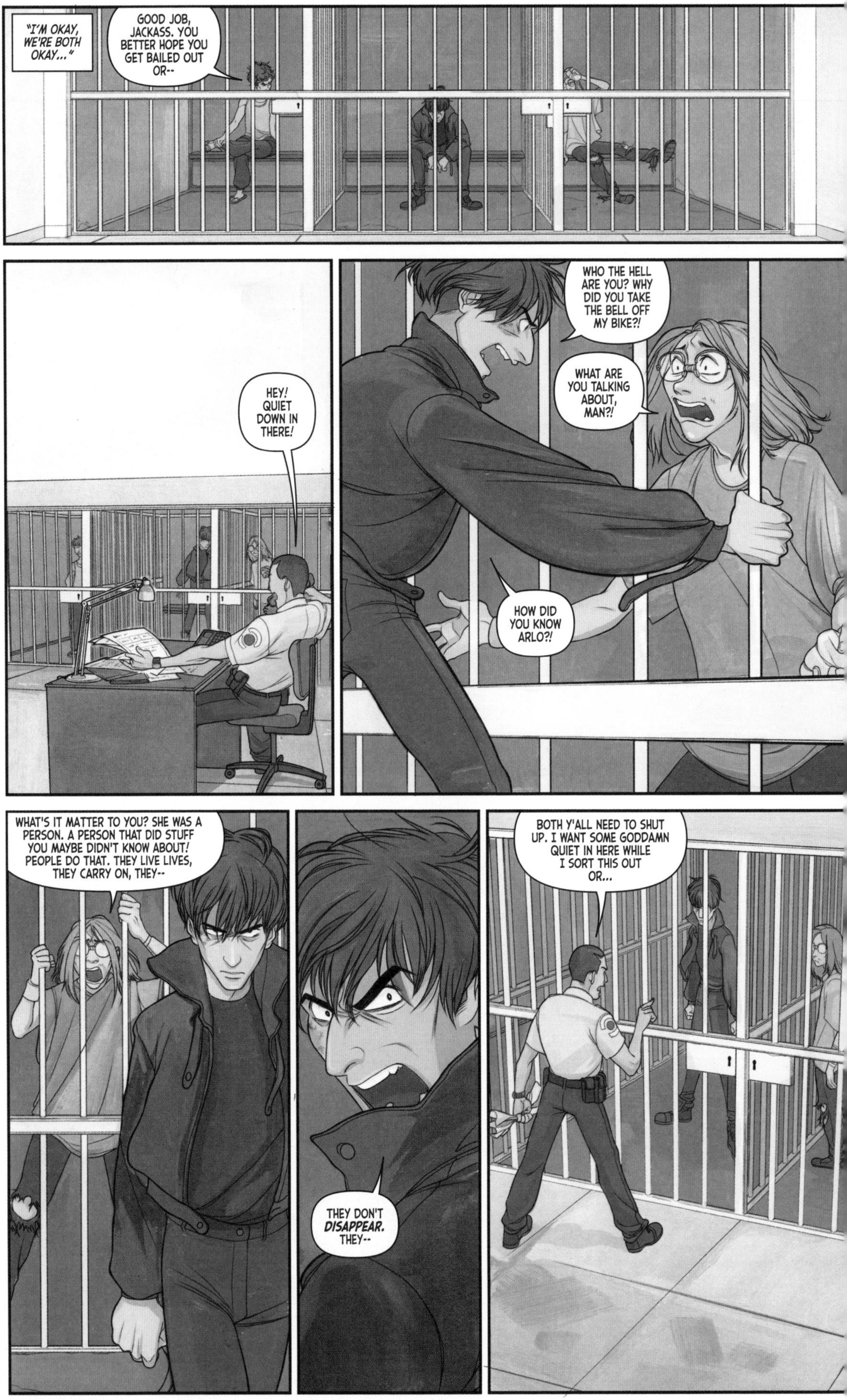
"I'M OKAY, WE'RE BOTH OKAY..."
GOOD JOB, JACKASS. YOU BETTER HOPE YOU GET BAILED OUT OR--
HEY! QUIET DOWN IN THERE!
WHO THE HELL ARE YOU? WHY DID YOU TAKE THE BELL OFF MY BIKE?!
WHAT ARE YOU TALKING ABOUT, MAN?!
HOW DID YOU KNOW ARLO?!
WHAT'S IT MATTER TO YOU? SHE WAS A PERSON. A PERSON THAT DID STUFF YOU MAYBE DIDN'T KNOW ABOUT! PEOPLE DO THAT. THEY LIVE LIVES, THEY CARRY ON, THEY--
THEY DON'T *DISAPPEAR.* THEY--
BOTH Y'ALL NEED TO SHUT UP. I WANT SOME GODDAMN QUIET IN HERE WHILE I SORT THIS OUT OR...

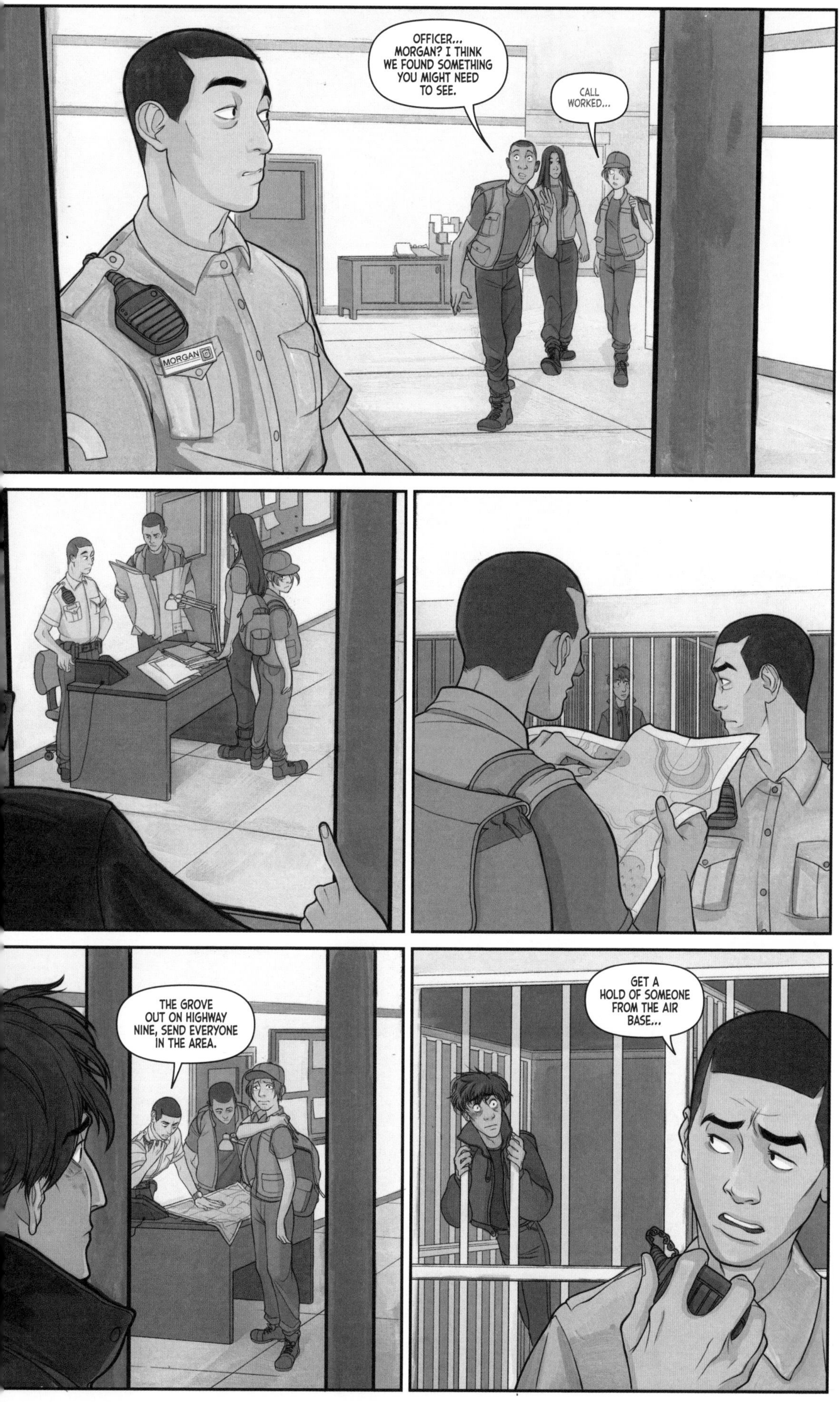
OFFICER... MORGAN? I THINK WE FOUND SOMETHING YOU MIGHT NEED TO SEE.
CALL WORKED...
MORGAN
THE GROVE OUT ON HIGHWAY NINE, SEND EVERYONE IN THE AREA.
GET A HOLD OF SOMEONE FROM THE AIR BASE...

"...THEY'RE GONNA NEED TO BE THERE, TOO."

RIO AZUL POLICE DEPARTMENT

POLICE LINE DO NOT CROSS   POLICE LINE DO NO

DO NOT CROSS   POLICE L

AUL COUNTY HOSPITAL 4

24 NEWS — BREAKING NEWS
LIVE UPDATE: BODY OF MISSING GIRL FOUN

LEGISLATOR STATES 'NO COMMENT' REGARDING LAX STAFFING FOR NATIONAL PARKS · | · CASES OF

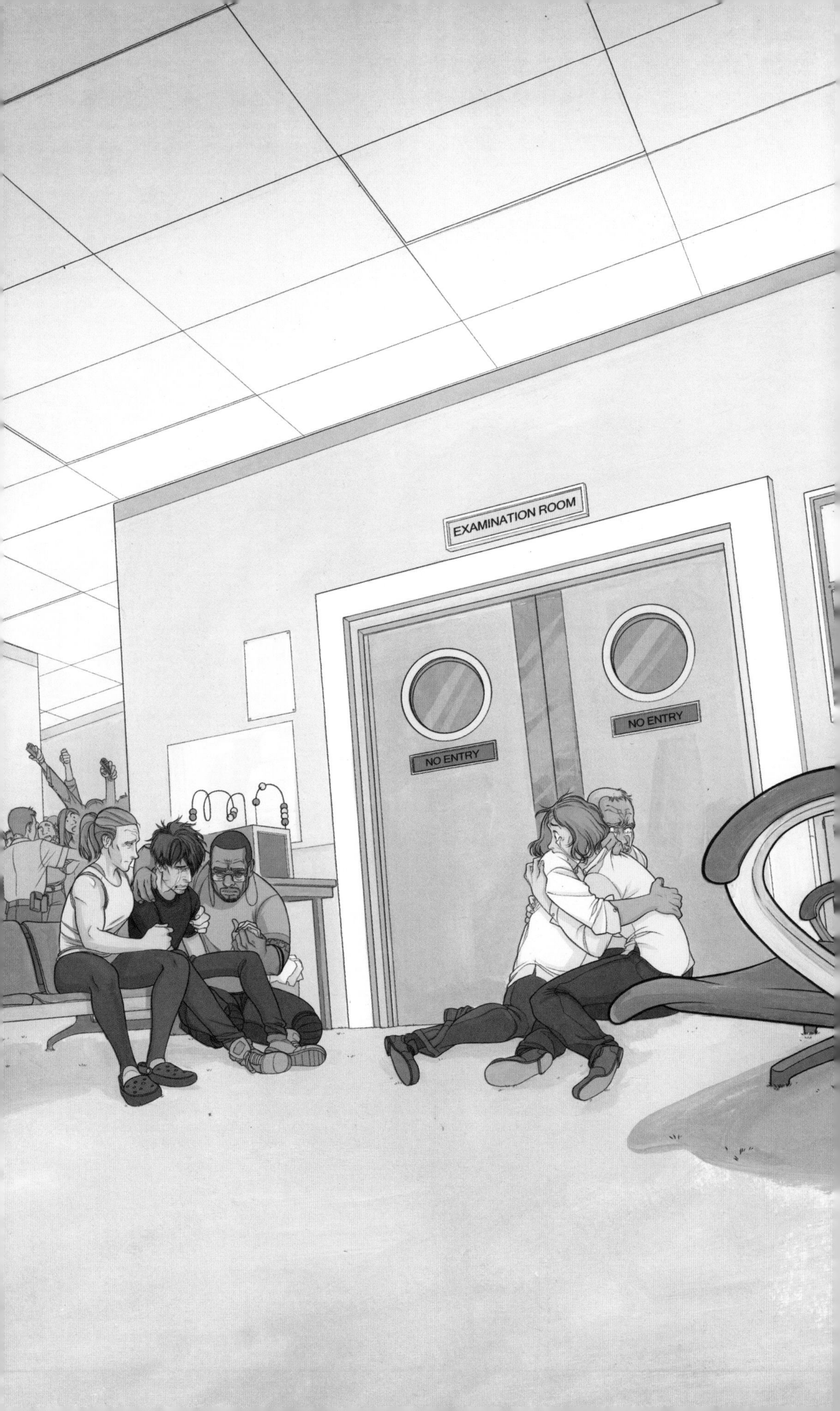
EXAMINATION ROOM
NO ENTRY
NO ENTRY

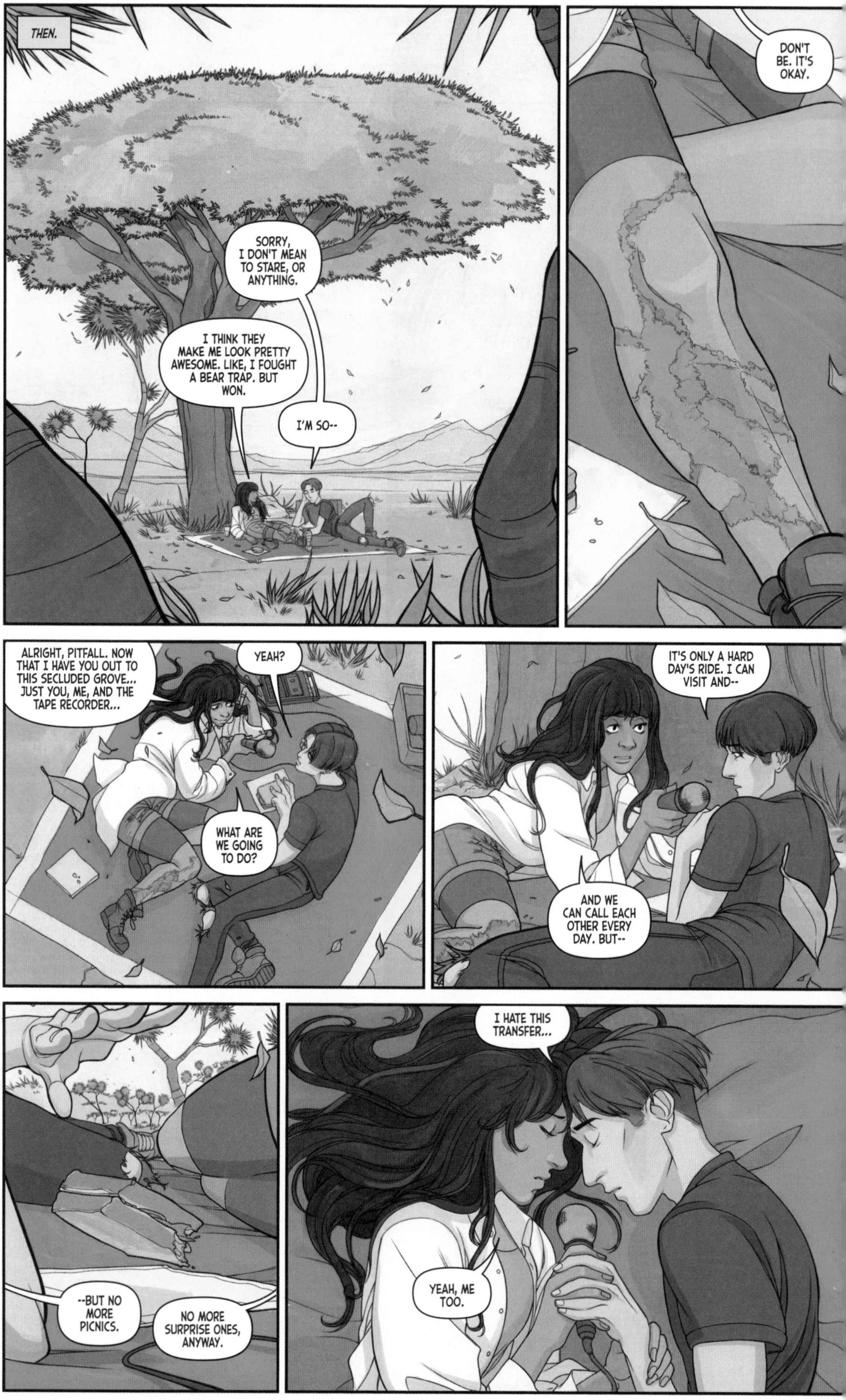
THEN.
SORRY, I DON'T MEAN TO STARE, OR ANYTHING.
I THINK THEY MAKE ME LOOK PRETTY AWESOME. LIKE, I FOUGHT A BEAR TRAP. BUT WON.
I'M SO--
DON'T BE. IT'S OKAY.
ALRIGHT, PITFALL. NOW THAT I HAVE YOU OUT TO THIS SECLUDED GROVE... JUST YOU, ME, AND THE TAPE RECORDER...
YEAH?
WHAT ARE WE GOING TO DO?
IT'S ONLY A HARD DAY'S RIDE. I CAN VISIT AND--
AND WE CAN CALL EACH OTHER EVERY DAY. BUT--
--BUT NO MORE PICNICS.
NO MORE SURPRISE ONES, ANYWAY.
I HATE THIS TRANSFER...
YEAH, ME TOO.

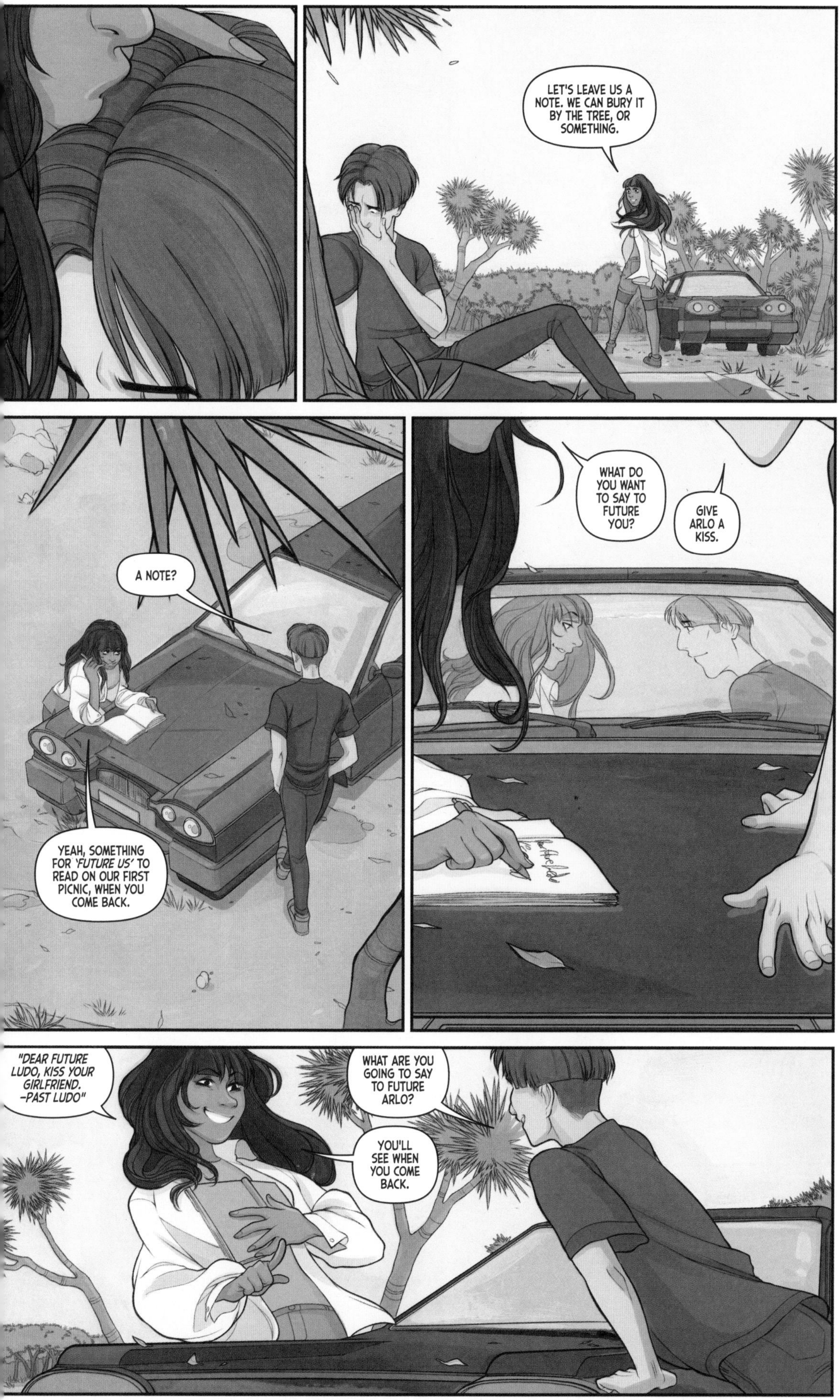
LET'S LEAVE US A NOTE. WE CAN BURY IT BY THE TREE, OR SOMETHING.
A NOTE?
YEAH, SOMETHING FOR *'FUTURE US'* TO READ ON OUR FIRST PICNIC, WHEN YOU COME BACK.
WHAT DO YOU WANT TO SAY TO FUTURE YOU?
GIVE ARLO A KISS.
"DEAR FUTURE LUDO, KISS YOUR GIRLFRIEND. -PAST LUDO"
WHAT ARE YOU GOING TO SAY TO FUTURE ARLO?
YOU'LL SEE WHEN YOU COME BACK.

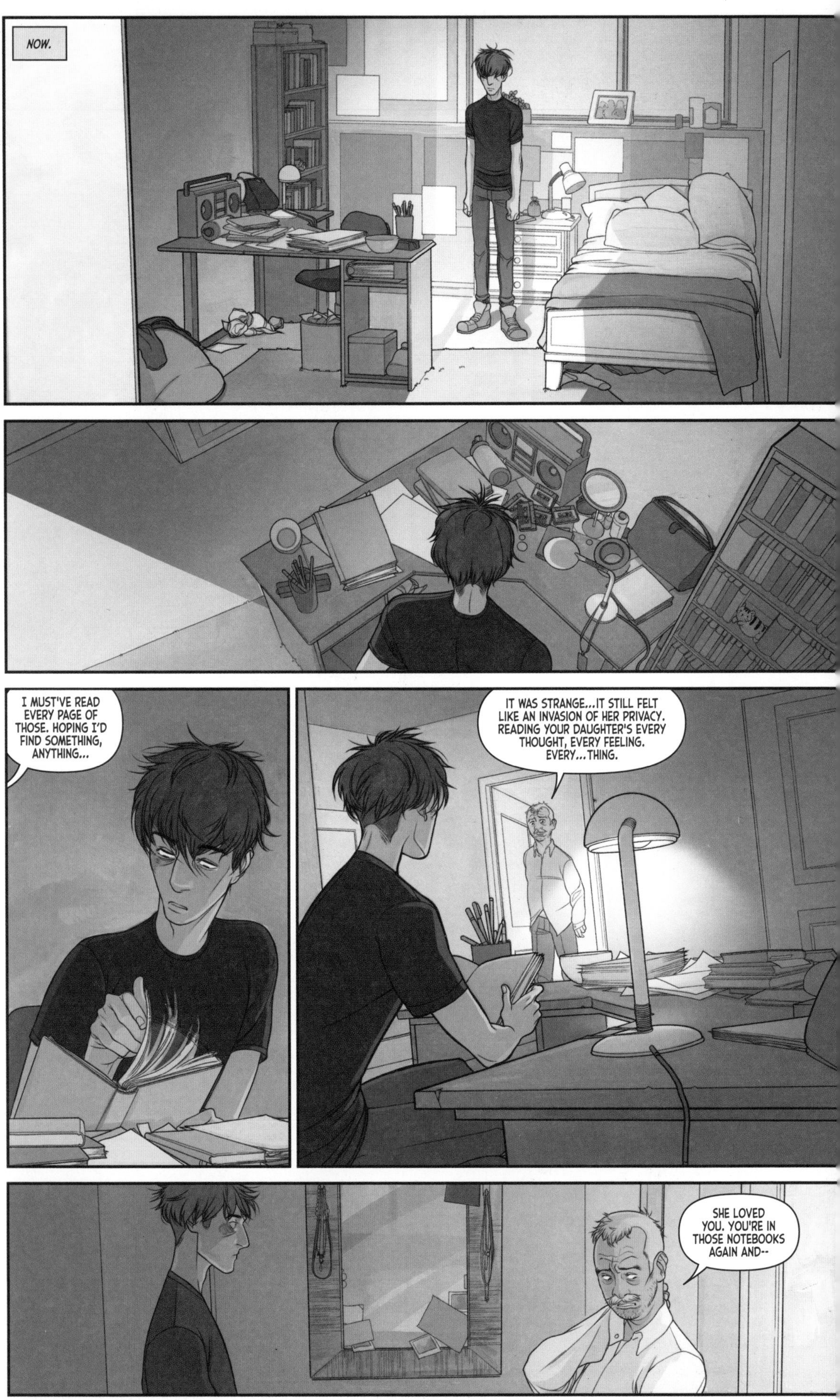
NOW.
I MUST'VE READ EVERY PAGE OF THOSE. HOPING I'D FIND SOMETHING, ANYTHING...
IT WAS STRANGE...IT STILL FELT LIKE AN INVASION OF HER PRIVACY. READING YOUR DAUGHTER'S EVERY THOUGHT, EVERY FEELING. EVERY...THING.
SHE LOVED YOU. YOU'RE IN THOSE NOTEBOOKS AGAIN AND--

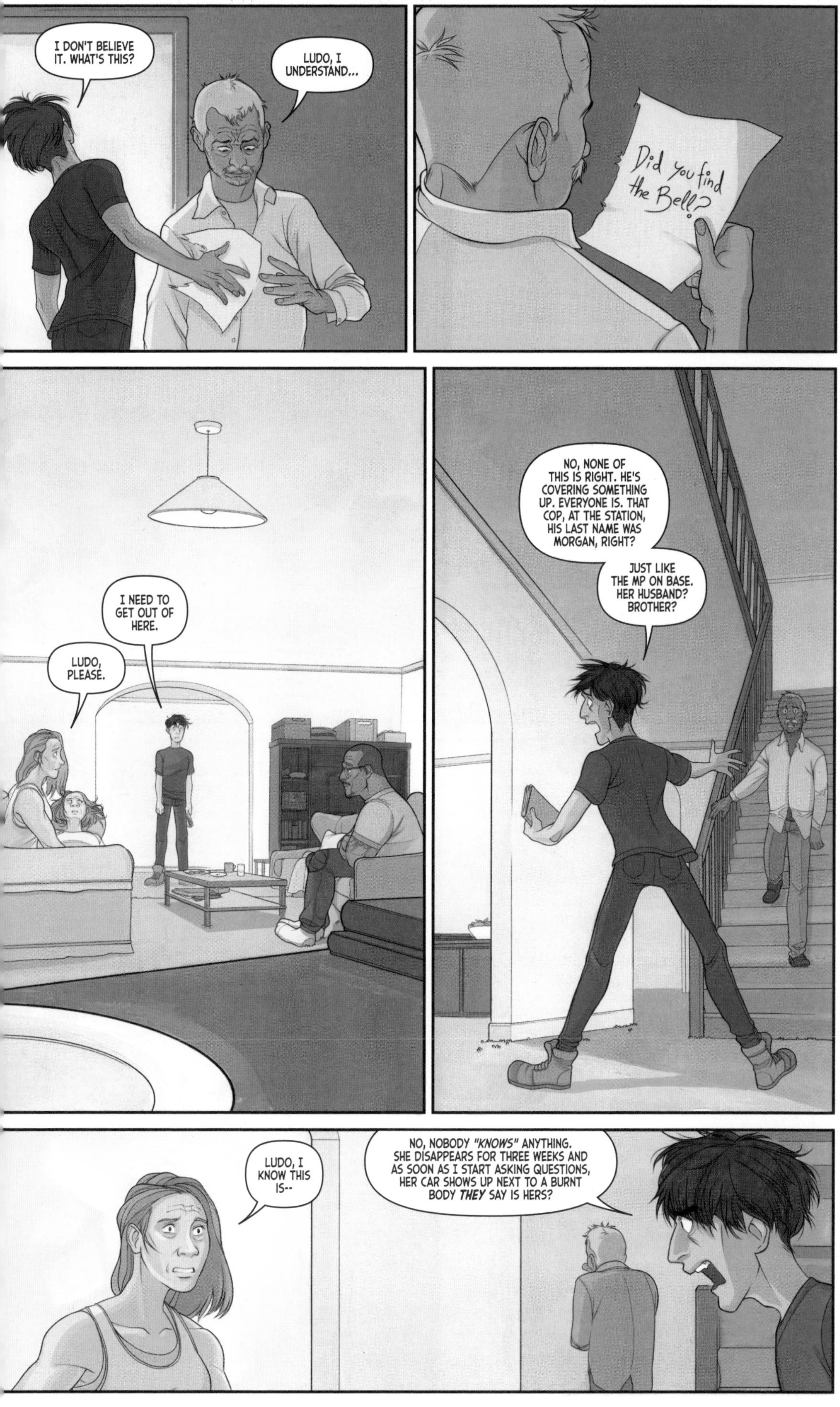
I DON'T BELIEVE IT. WHAT'S THIS?
LUDO, I UNDERSTAND...
Did you find the Bell?
I NEED TO GET OUT OF HERE.
LUDO, PLEASE.
NO, NONE OF THIS IS RIGHT. HE'S COVERING SOMETHING UP. EVERYONE IS. THAT COP, AT THE STATION, HIS LAST NAME WAS MORGAN, RIGHT?
JUST LIKE THE MP ON BASE. HER HUSBAND? BROTHER?
LUDO, I KNOW THIS IS--
NO, NOBODY "KNOWS" ANYTHING. SHE DISAPPEARS FOR THREE WEEKS AND AS SOON AS I START ASKING QUESTIONS, HER CAR SHOWS UP NEXT TO A BURNT BODY THEY SAY IS HERS?

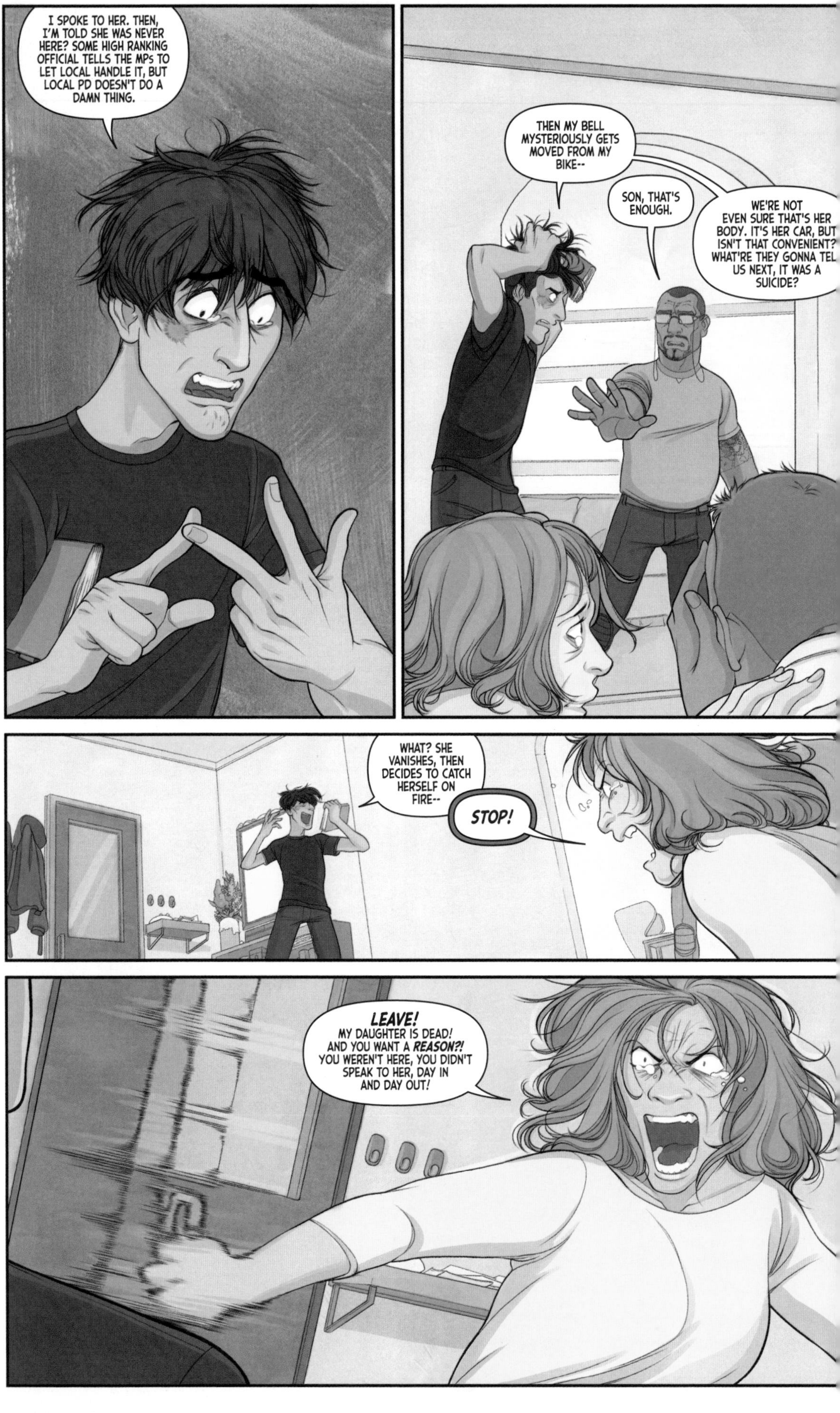
I SPOKE TO HER. THEN, I'M TOLD SHE WAS NEVER HERE? SOME HIGH RANKING OFFICIAL TELLS THE MPs TO LET LOCAL HANDLE IT, BUT LOCAL PD DOESN'T DO A DAMN THING.
THEN MY BELL MYSTERIOUSLY GETS MOVED FROM MY BIKE--
SON, THAT'S ENOUGH.
WE'RE NOT EVEN SURE THAT'S HER BODY. IT'S HER CAR, BUT ISN'T THAT CONVENIENT? WHAT'RE THEY GONNA TEL US NEXT, IT WAS A SUICIDE?
WHAT? SHE VANISHES, THEN DECIDES TO CATCH HERSELF ON FIRE--
STOP!
LEAVE! MY DAUGHTER IS DEAD! AND YOU WANT A REASON?! YOU WEREN'T HERE, YOU DIDN'T SPEAK TO HER, DAY IN AND DAY OUT!

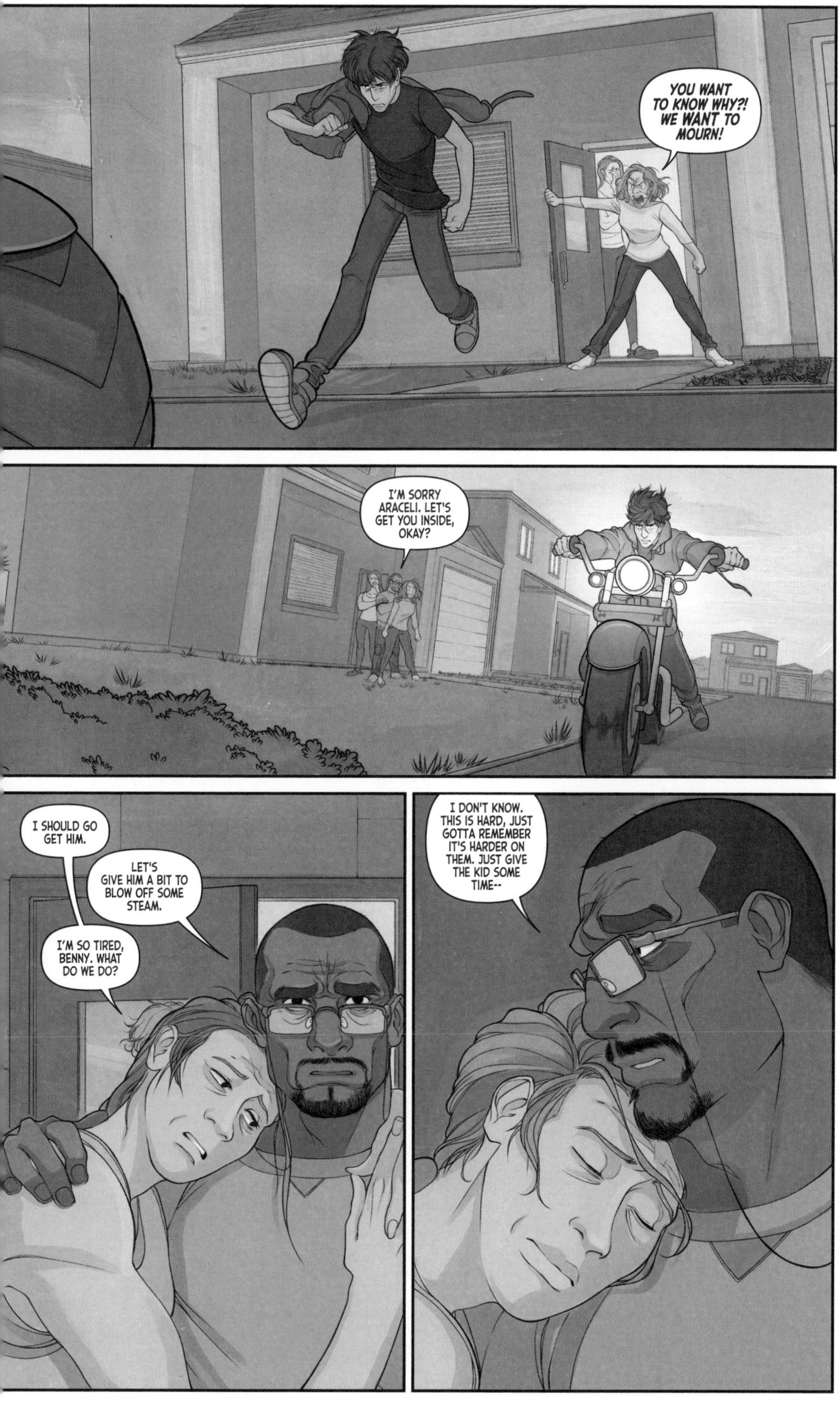
YOU WANT TO KNOW WHY?! WE WANT TO MOURN!
I'M SORRY ARACELI. LET'S GET YOU INSIDE, OKAY?
I SHOULD GO GET HIM.
LET'S GIVE HIM A BIT TO BLOW OFF SOME STEAM.
I'M SO TIRED, BENNY. WHAT DO WE DO?
I DON'T KNOW. THIS IS HARD, JUST GOTTA REMEMBER IT'S HARDER ON THEM. JUST GIVE THE KID SOME TIME--

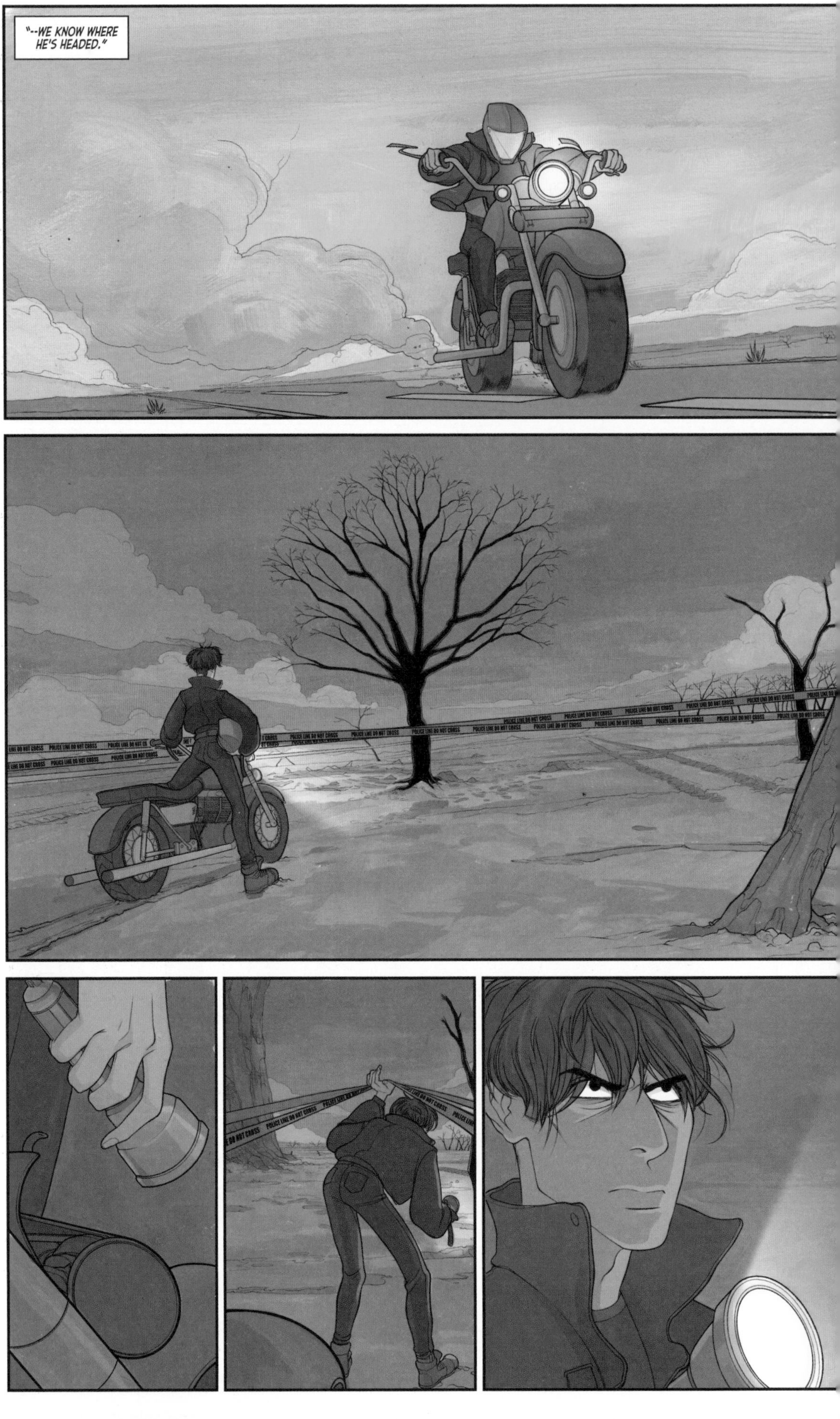
"--WE KNOW WHERE HE'S HEADED."
POLICE LINE DO NOT CROSS

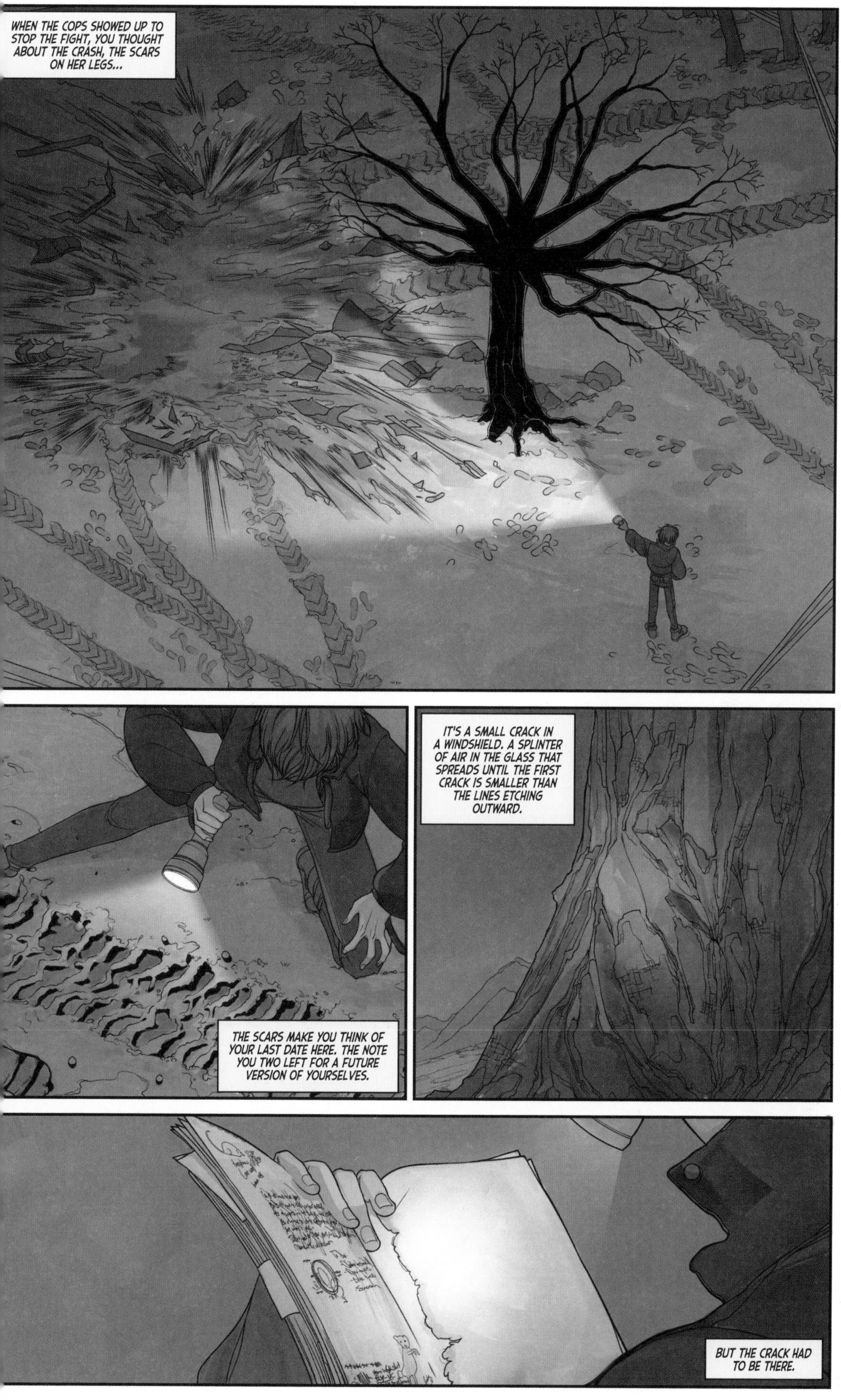
WHEN THE COPS SHOWED UP TO STOP THE FIGHT, YOU THOUGHT ABOUT THE CRASH, THE SCARS ON HER LEGS...
THE SCARS MAKE YOU THINK OF YOUR LAST DATE HERE. THE NOTE YOU TWO LEFT FOR A FUTURE VERSION OF YOURSELVES.
IT'S A SMALL CRACK IN A WINDSHIELD. A SPLINTER OF AIR IN THE GLASS THAT SPREADS UNTIL THE FIRST CRACK IS SMALLER THAN THE LINES ETCHING OUTWARD.
BUT THE CRACK HAD TO BE THERE.

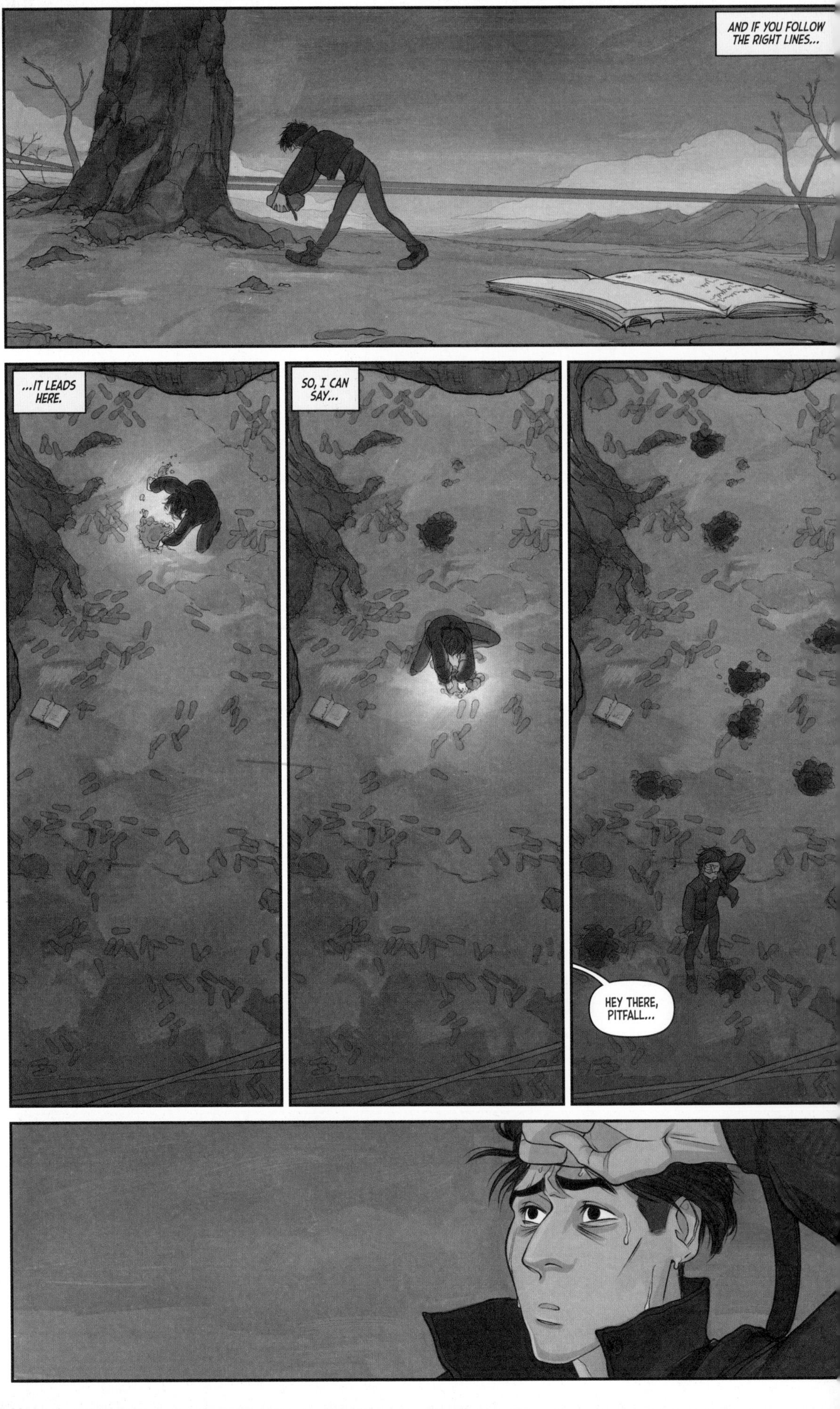
AND IF YOU FOLLOW THE RIGHT LINES...
...IT LEADS HERE.
SO, I CAN SAY...
HEY THERE, PITFALL...

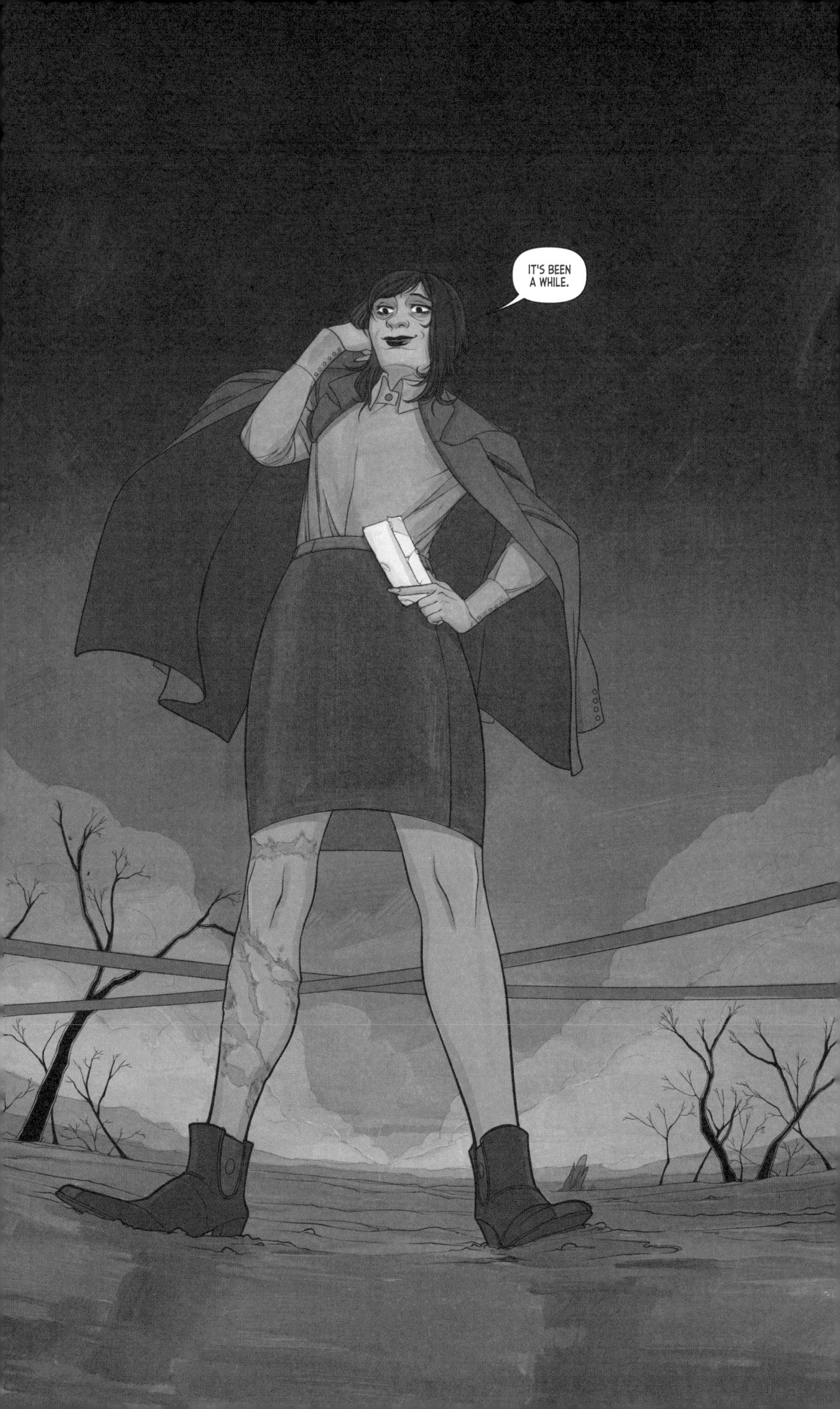
IT'S BEEN A WHILE.

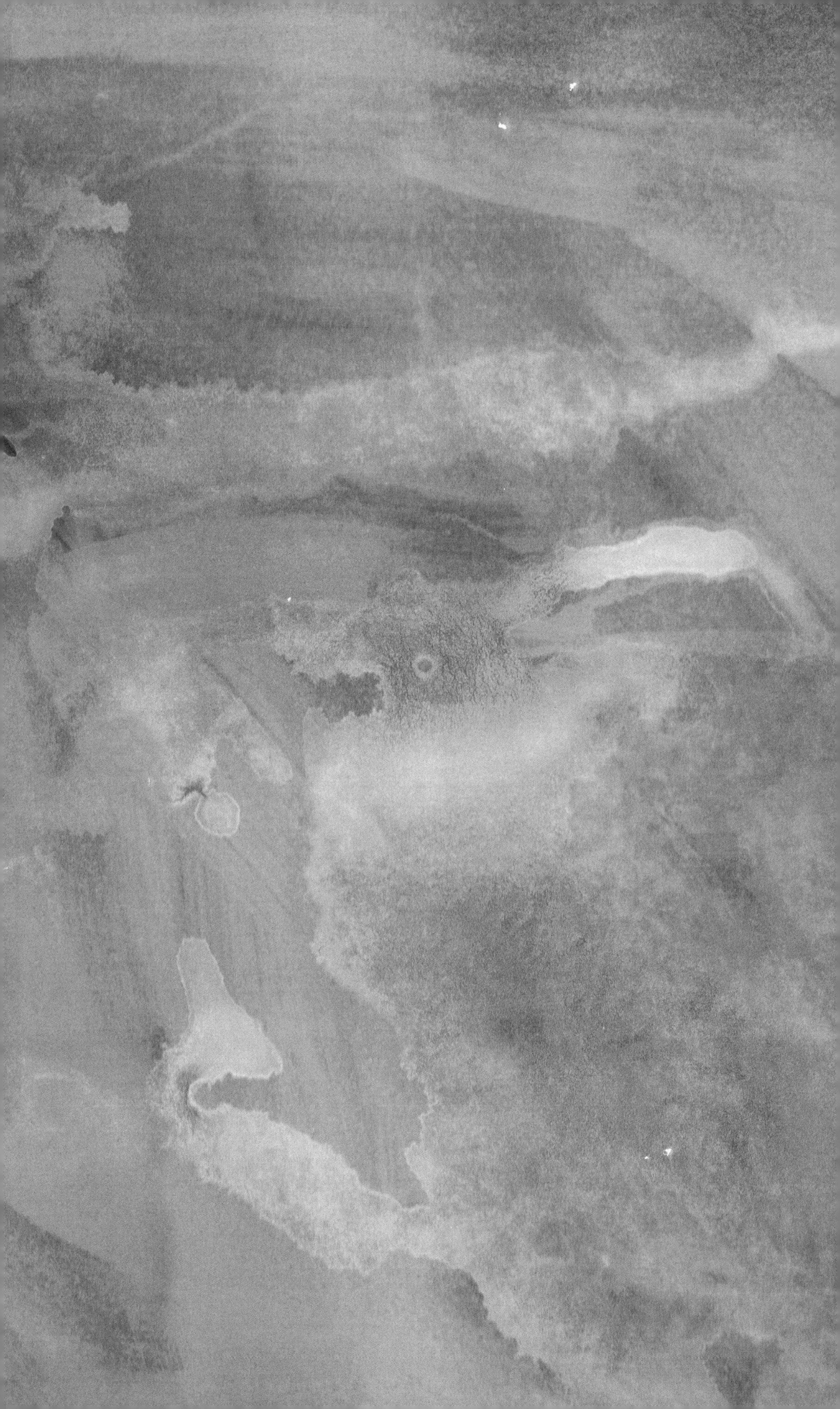

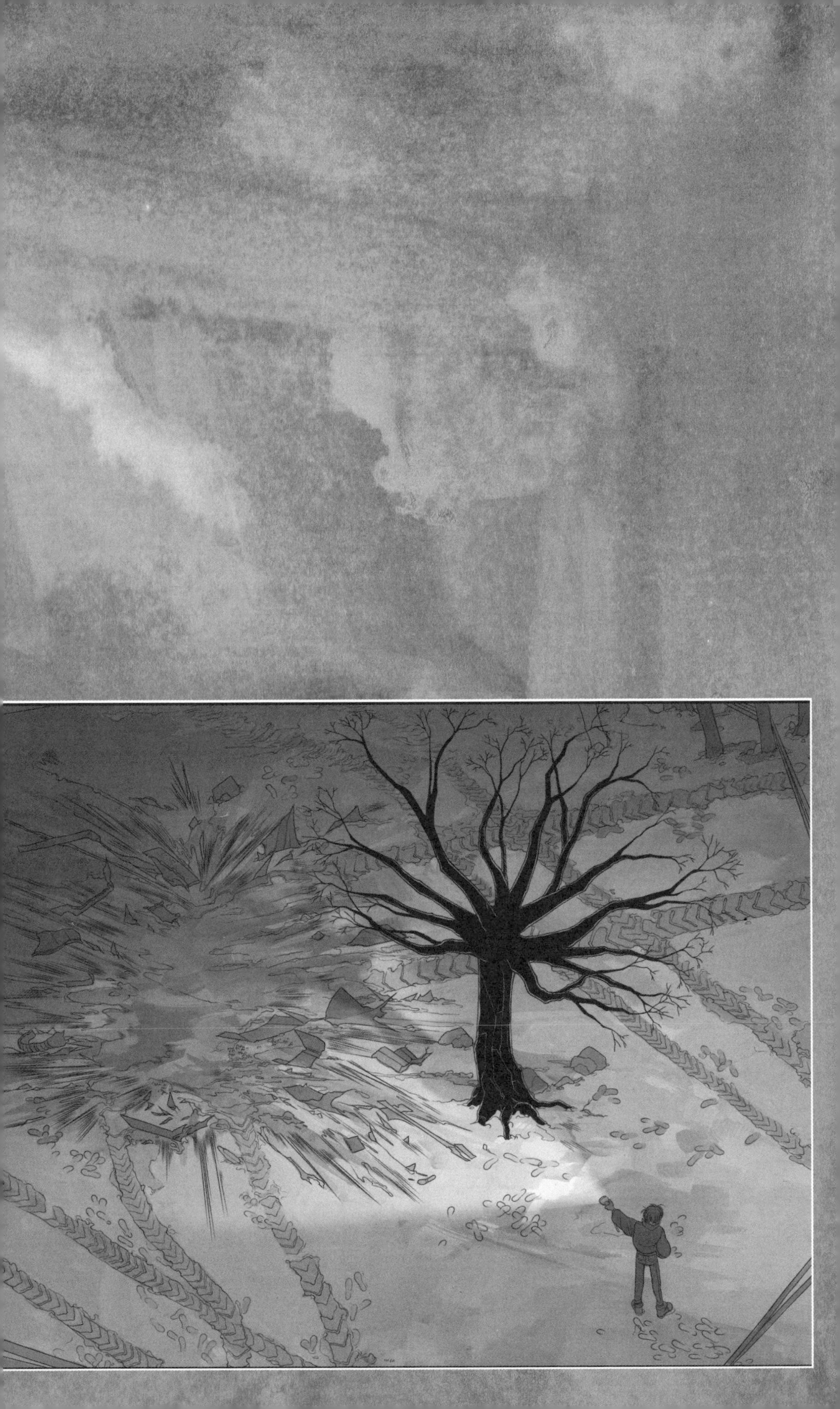

CHAPTER THREE

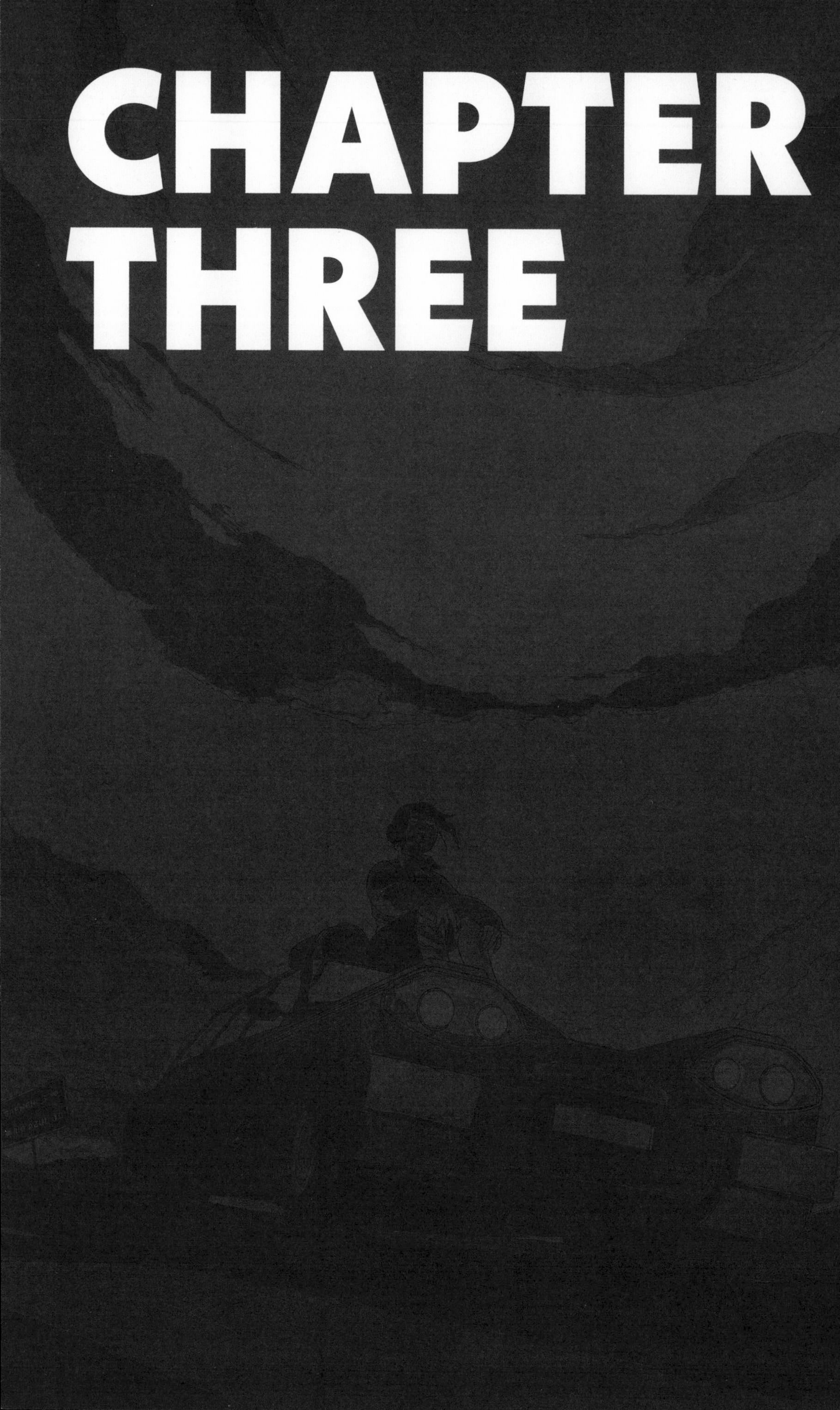

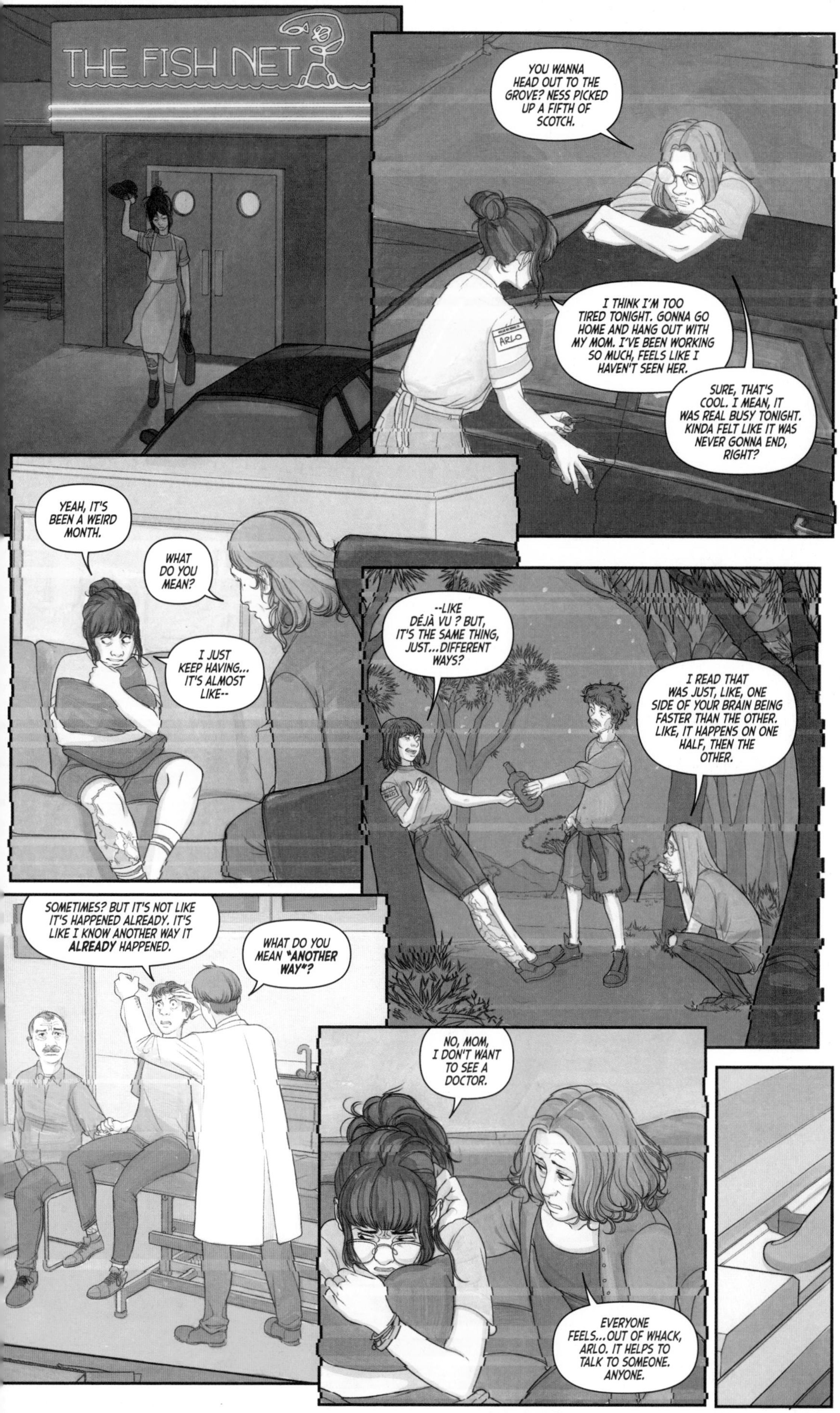

THE FISH NET
YOU WANNA HEAD OUT TO THE GROVE? NESS PICKED UP A FIFTH OF SCOTCH.
ARLO
I THINK I'M TOO TIRED TONIGHT. GONNA GO HOME AND HANG OUT WITH MY MOM. I'VE BEEN WORKING SO MUCH, FEELS LIKE I HAVEN'T SEEN HER.
SURE, THAT'S COOL. I MEAN, IT WAS REAL BUSY TONIGHT. KINDA FELT LIKE IT WAS NEVER GONNA END, RIGHT?
YEAH, IT'S BEEN A WEIRD MONTH.
WHAT DO YOU MEAN?
I JUST KEEP HAVING... IT'S ALMOST LIKE--
--LIKE DÉJÀ VU ? BUT, IT'S THE SAME THING, JUST...DIFFERENT WAYS?
I READ THAT WAS JUST, LIKE, ONE SIDE OF YOUR BRAIN BEING FASTER THAN THE OTHER. LIKE, IT HAPPENS ON ONE HALF, THEN THE OTHER.
SOMETIMES? BUT IT'S NOT LIKE IT'S HAPPENED ALREADY. IT'S LIKE I KNOW ANOTHER WAY IT **ALREADY** HAPPENED.
WHAT DO YOU MEAN **"ANOTHER WAY"**?
NO, MOM, I DON'T WANT TO SEE A DOCTOR.
EVERYONE FEELS...OUT OF WHACK, ARLO. IT HELPS TO TALK TO SOMEONE. ANYONE.

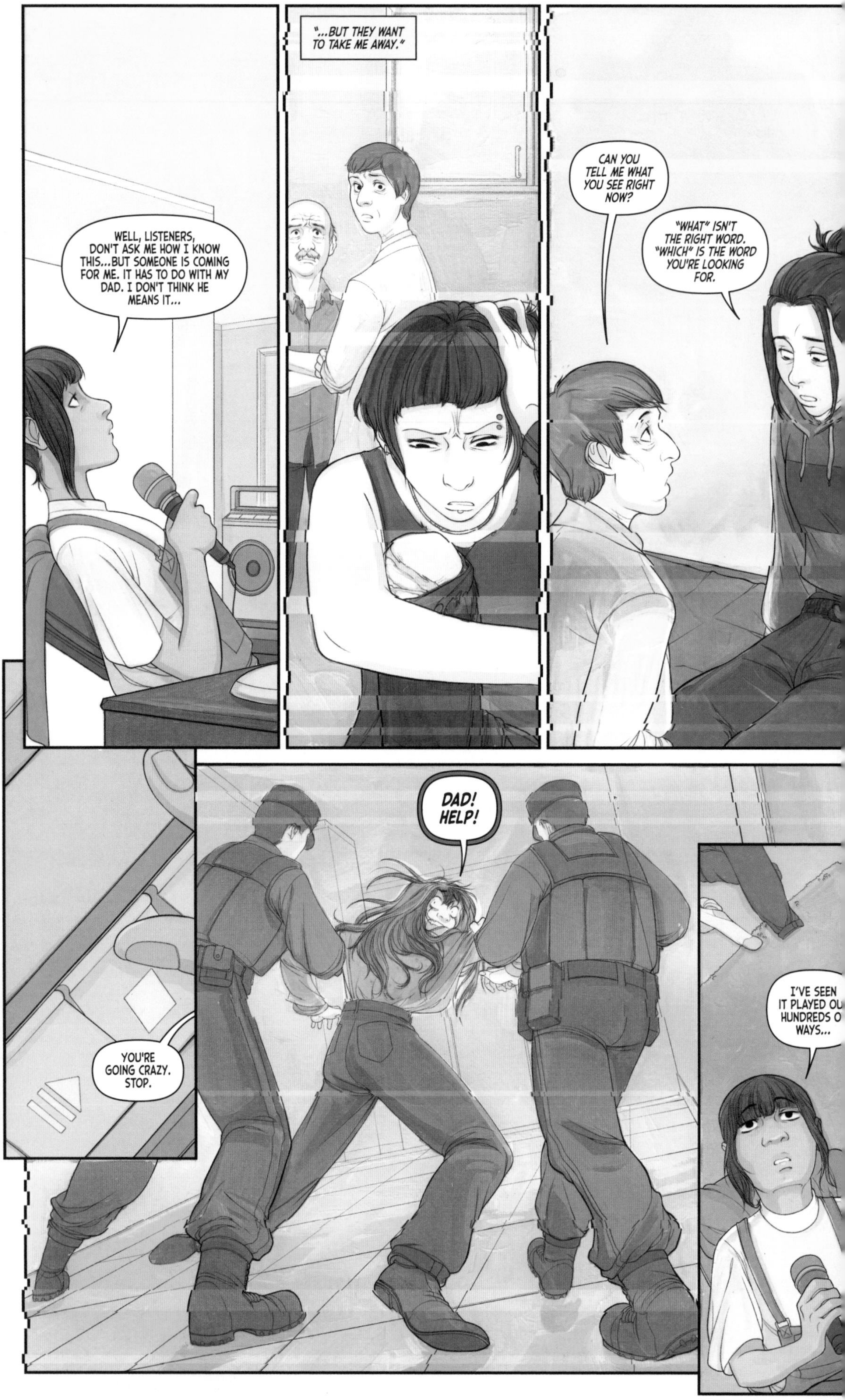
WELL, LISTENERS, DON'T ASK ME HOW I KNOW THIS...BUT SOMEONE IS COMING FOR ME. IT HAS TO DO WITH MY DAD. I DON'T THINK HE MEANS IT...
"...BUT THEY WANT TO TAKE ME AWAY."
CAN YOU TELL ME WHAT YOU SEE RIGHT NOW?
"WHAT" ISN'T THE RIGHT WORD. "WHICH" IS THE WORD YOU'RE LOOKING FOR.
YOU'RE GOING CRAZY. STOP.
DAD! HELP!
I'VE SEEN IT PLAYED OU HUNDREDS O WAYS...

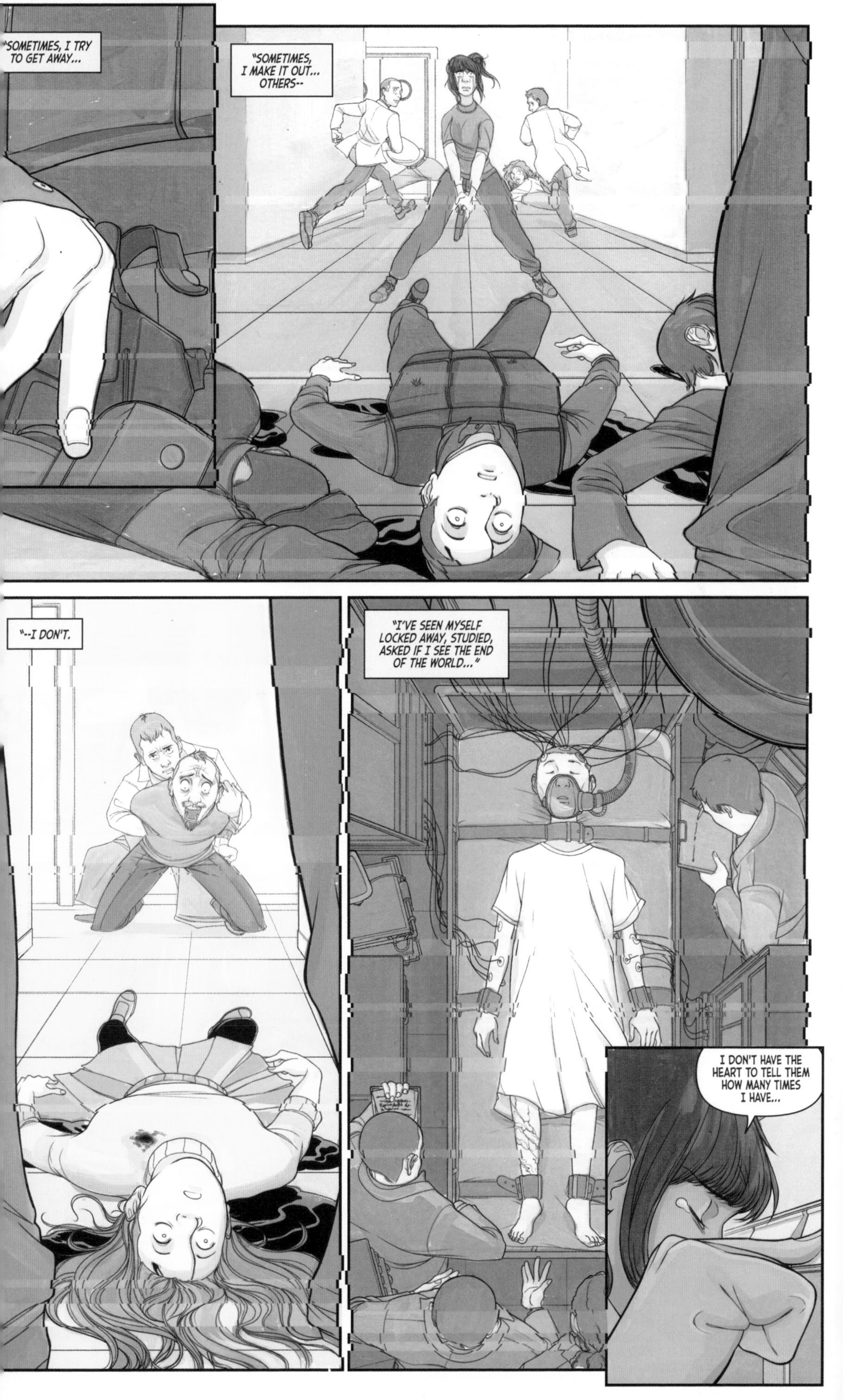
"SOMETIMES, I TRY TO GET AWAY...
"SOMETIMES, I MAKE IT OUT... OTHERS--
"--I DON'T.
"I'VE SEEN MYSELF LOCKED AWAY, STUDIED, ASKED IF I SEE THE END OF THE WORLD..."
I DON'T HAVE THE HEART TO TELL THEM HOW MANY TIMES I HAVE...

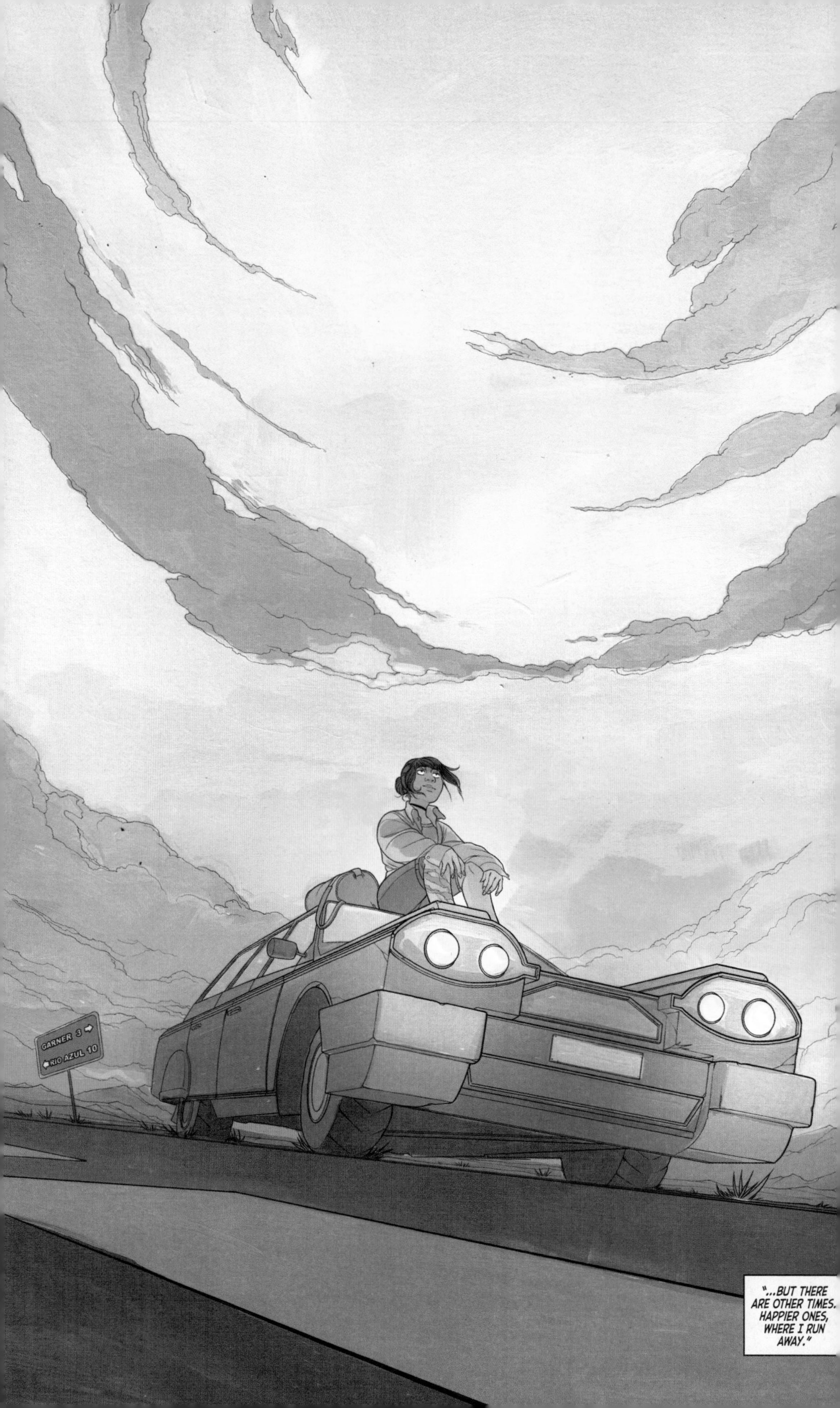
GARNER 3
RIO AZUL 10
"...BUT THERE ARE OTHER TIMES. HAPPIER ONES, WHERE I RUN AWAY."

Part III: A Skipping Tape

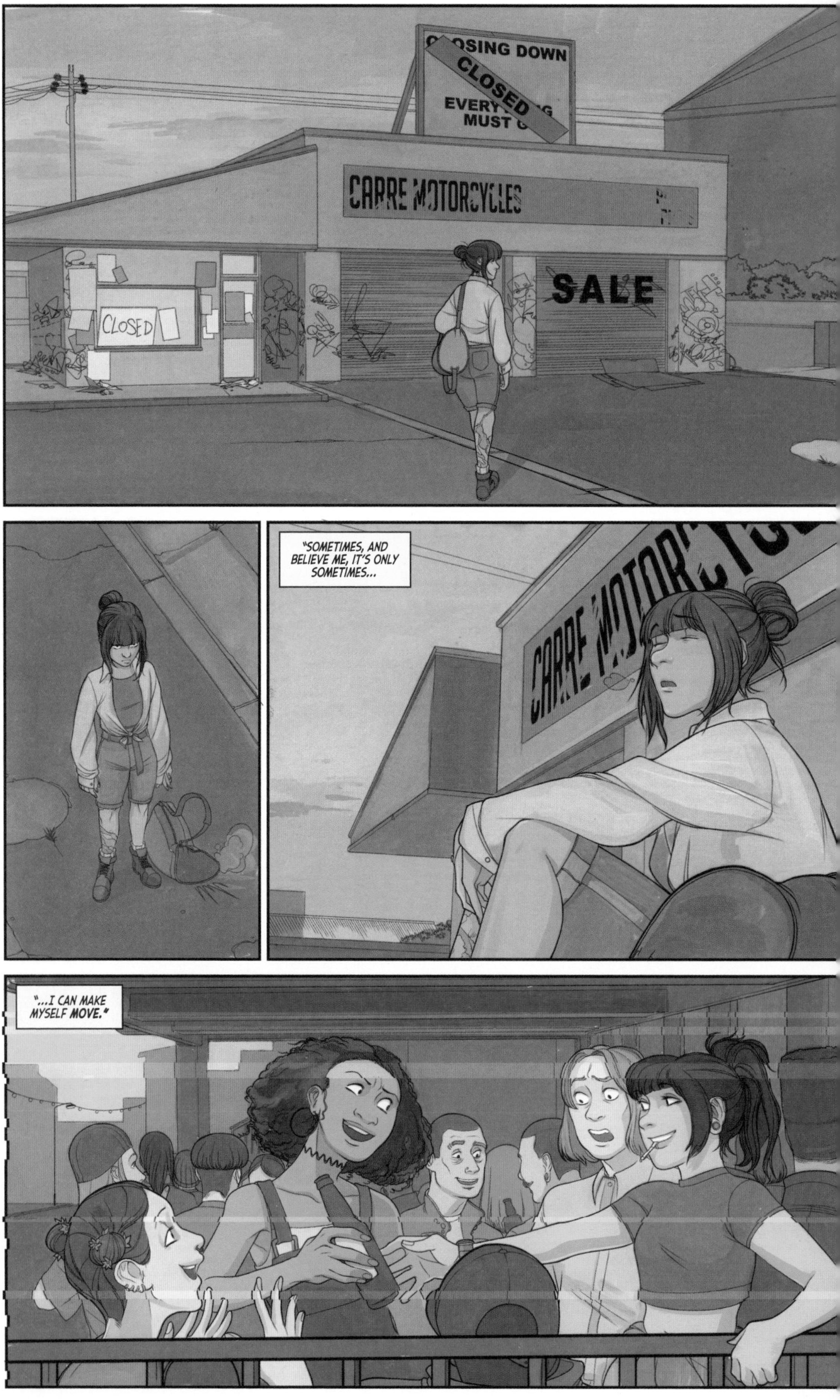
CLOSED
CARRE MOTORCYCLES
CLOSED
SALE
"SOMETIMES, AND BELIEVE ME, IT'S ONLY SOMETIMES...
"...I CAN MAKE MYSELF MOVE."

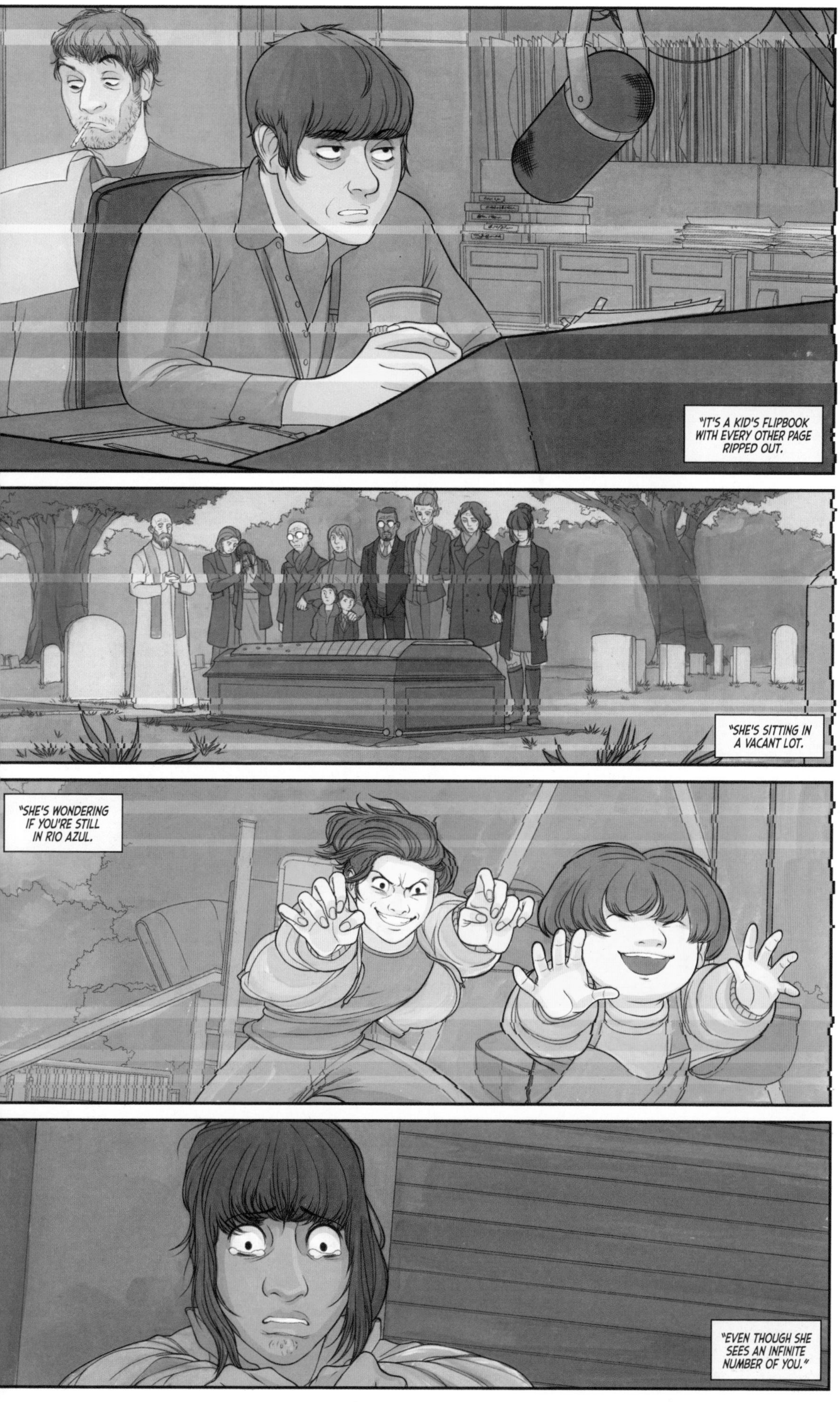
"IT'S A KID'S FLIPBOOK WITH EVERY OTHER PAGE RIPPED OUT.
"SHE'S SITTING IN A VACANT LOT.
"SHE'S WONDERING IF YOU'RE STILL IN RIO AZUL.
"EVEN THOUGH SHE SEES AN INFINITE NUMBER OF YOU."

"BUT THERE'S ONE FUTURE, IN PARTICULAR, WHERE IF SHE SQUINTS **JUST RIGHT** AND THE SHADOWS WORK WITH HER...

"...SHE CAN MAKE HIM OUT. SMILING BIG AND BROAD WITH THE SAME LAUGH HER DAUGHTER WILL EVENTUALLY HAVE.

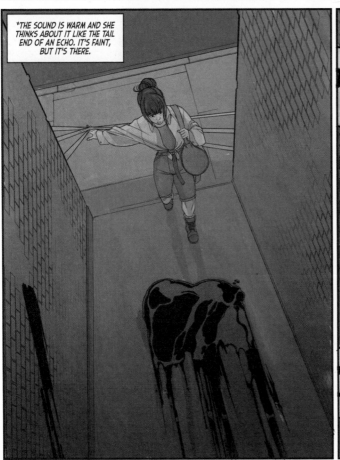

"THE SOUND IS WARM AND SHE THINKS ABOUT IT LIKE THE TAIL END OF AN ECHO. IT'S FAINT, BUT IT'S THERE.

POLICE LINE DO NOT

CE LINE DO NOT CRO

"YOU'RE GOING TO HAVE TO UNDERSTAND THAT, LUDO. IT'S **THERE**, NOT HERE..."

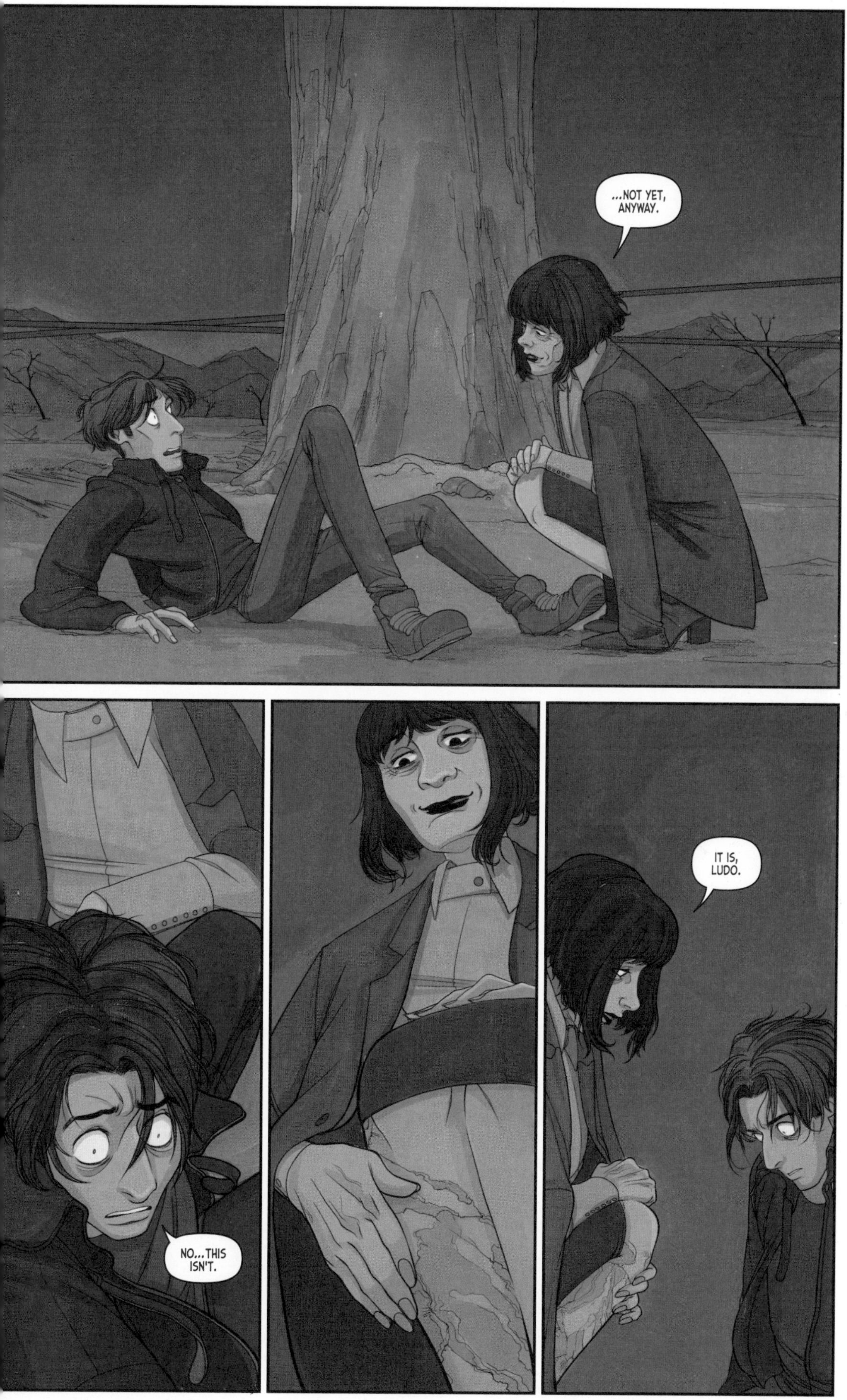
...NOT YET, ANYWAY.
NO...THIS ISN'T.
IT IS, LUDO.

LOOK, I DON'T KNOW WHO YOU ARE, BUT--

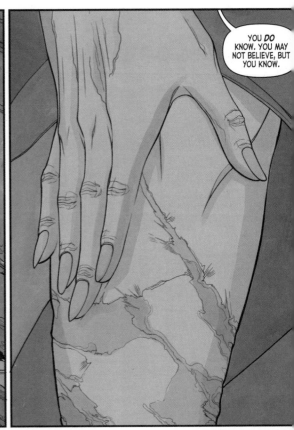

YOU *DO* KNOW. YOU MAY NOT BELIEVE, BUT YOU KNOW.

IF YOU KNOW WHERE ARLO IS, YOU NEED--

LUDO, YOU CAN'T KEEP TRYING TO BEND EVERYONE TO YOUR WHIMS. SOMETIMES THE WORLD IS LIKE THE OLD MAN YOU FOUND IN THE ALLEY.

IT HAPPENS AROUND US, *DESPITE US.*

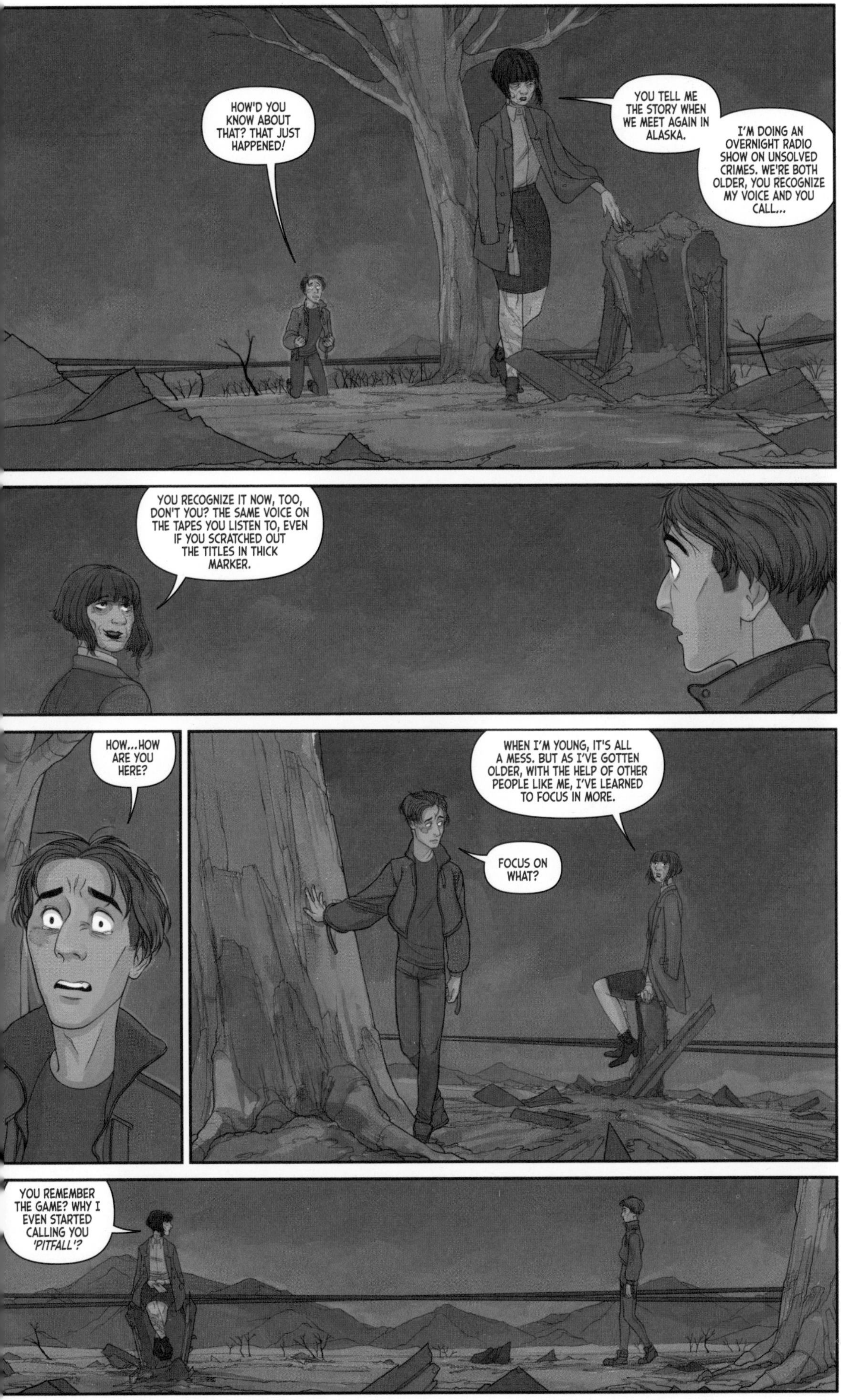
HOW'D YOU KNOW ABOUT THAT? THAT JUST HAPPENED!
YOU TELL ME THE STORY WHEN WE MEET AGAIN IN ALASKA.
I'M DOING AN OVERNIGHT RADIO SHOW ON UNSOLVED CRIMES. WE'RE BOTH OLDER, YOU RECOGNIZE MY VOICE AND YOU CALL...
YOU RECOGNIZE IT NOW, TOO, DON'T YOU? THE SAME VOICE ON THE TAPES YOU LISTEN TO, EVEN IF YOU SCRATCHED OUT THE TITLES IN THICK MARKER.
HOW...HOW ARE YOU HERE?
WHEN I'M YOUNG, IT'S ALL A MESS. BUT AS I'VE GOTTEN OLDER, WITH THE HELP OF OTHER PEOPLE LIKE ME, I'VE LEARNED TO FOCUS IN MORE.
FOCUS ON WHAT?
YOU REMEMBER THE GAME? WHY I EVEN STARTED CALLING YOU 'PITFALL'?

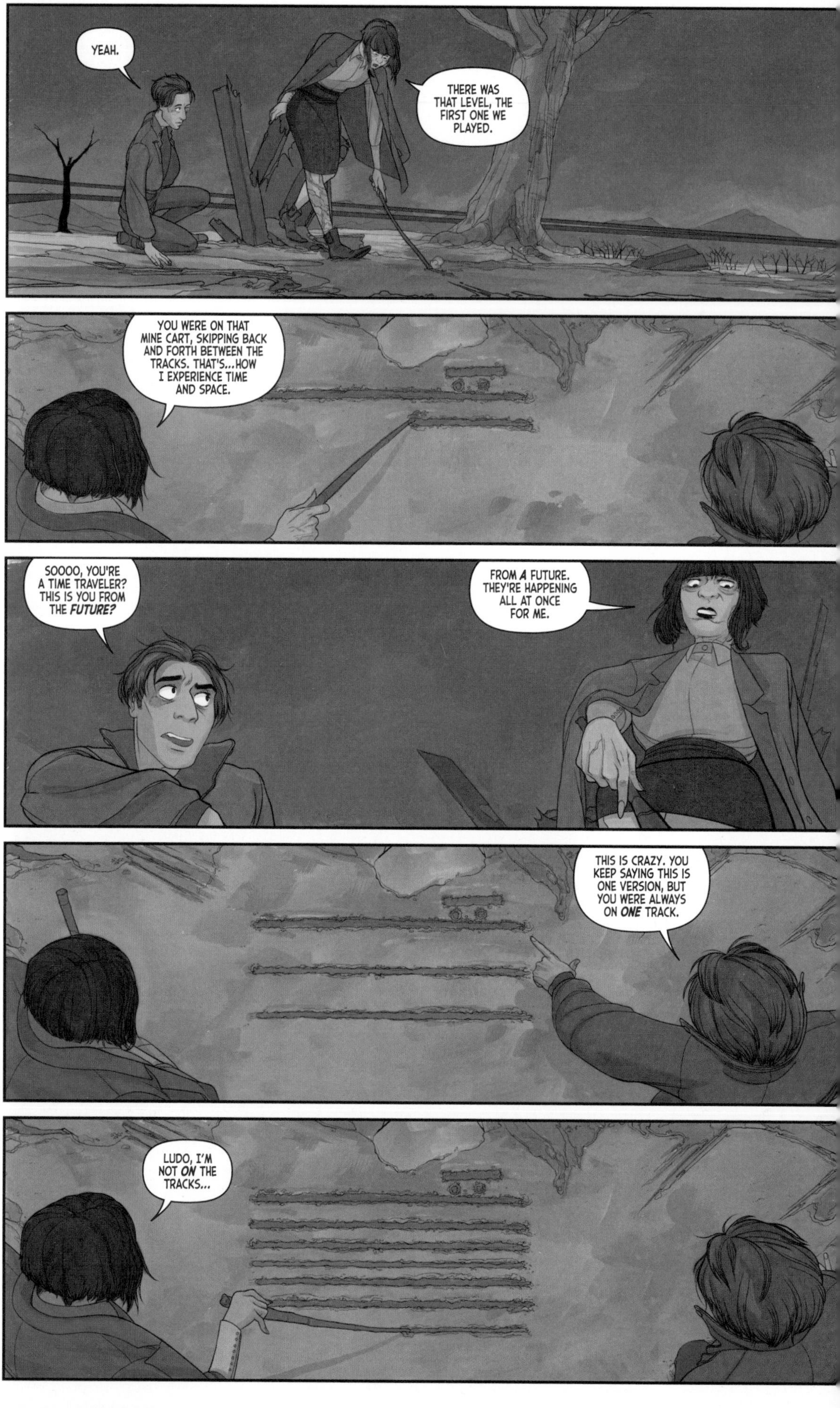
YEAH.
THERE WAS THAT LEVEL, THE FIRST ONE WE PLAYED.
YOU WERE ON THAT MINE CART, SKIPPING BACK AND FORTH BETWEEN THE TRACKS. THAT'S...HOW I EXPERIENCE TIME AND SPACE.
SOOOO, YOU'RE A TIME TRAVELER? THIS IS YOU FROM THE ***FUTURE?***
FROM ***A*** FUTURE. THEY'RE HAPPENING ALL AT ONCE FOR ME.
THIS IS CRAZY. YOU KEEP SAYING THIS IS ONE VERSION, BUT YOU WERE ALWAYS ON ***ONE*** TRACK.
LUDO, I'M NOT ***ON*** THE TRACKS...

"*...I AM THE TRACKS.*"

BEFORE.

WHEN DO WE CALL THE COPS?

AFTER YOU MOVE THE GREMLIN BELL.

WE KEEP DOING THIS, AND I KEEP FORGETTING.

YOU'RE THE ONLY ONE WHO CAN BRING US ALL HERE, GUS. I CAN HANDLE REMEMBERING THE ORDER OF IT ALL.

THAT'S WHY WE'RE ALL HERE. WE'RE A FAMILY.

CAN WE SAY SOMETHING TO DAD IF WE SEE HIM?

YOU TELL ME, PENNY. I CAN'T SEE WHEN I'M NOT WITH YOU. WHAT DO YOU SEE?

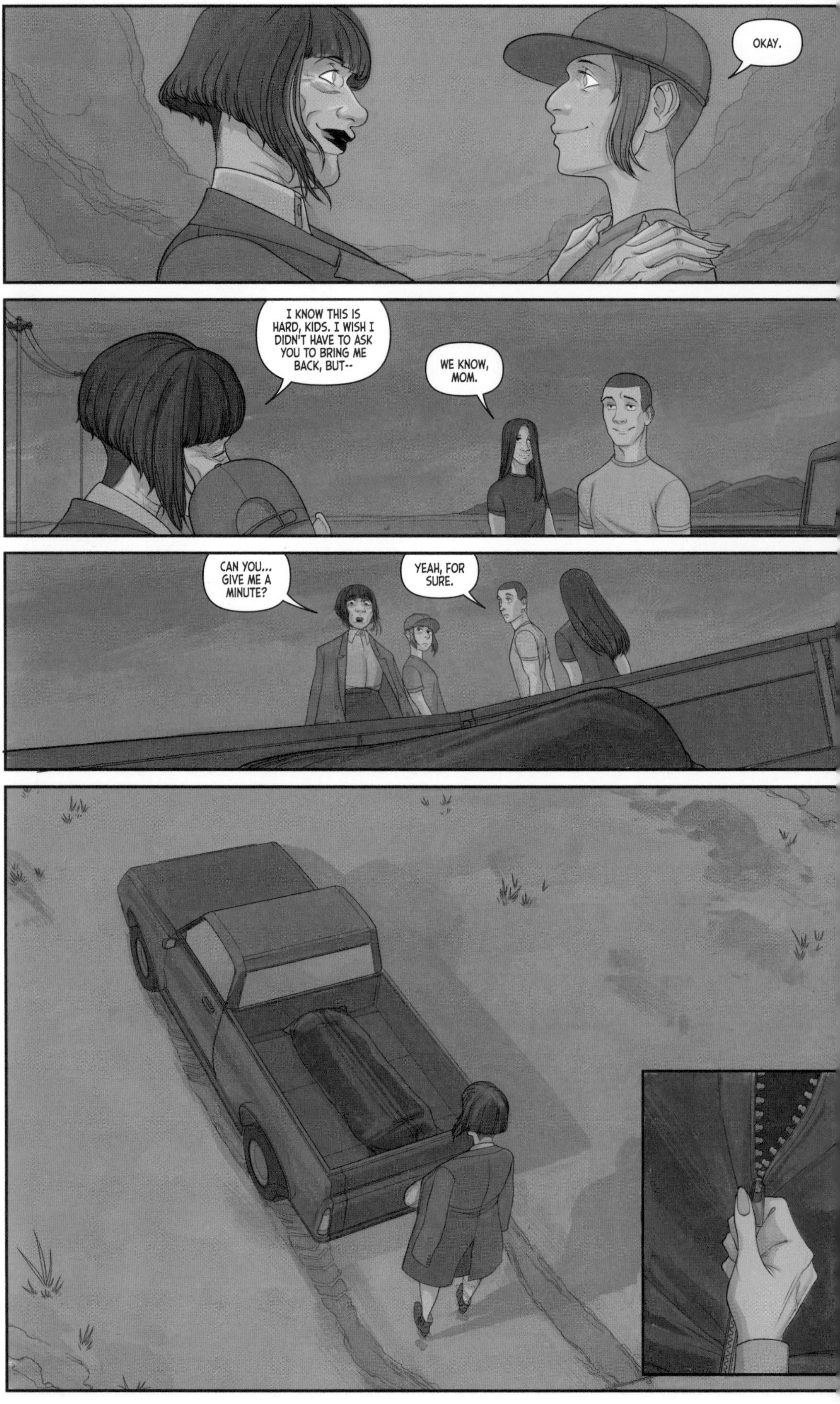
OKAY.
I KNOW THIS IS HARD, KIDS. I WISH I DIDN'T HAVE TO ASK YOU TO BRING ME BACK, BUT--
WE KNOW, MOM.
CAN YOU... GIVE ME A MINUTE?
YEAH, FOR SURE.

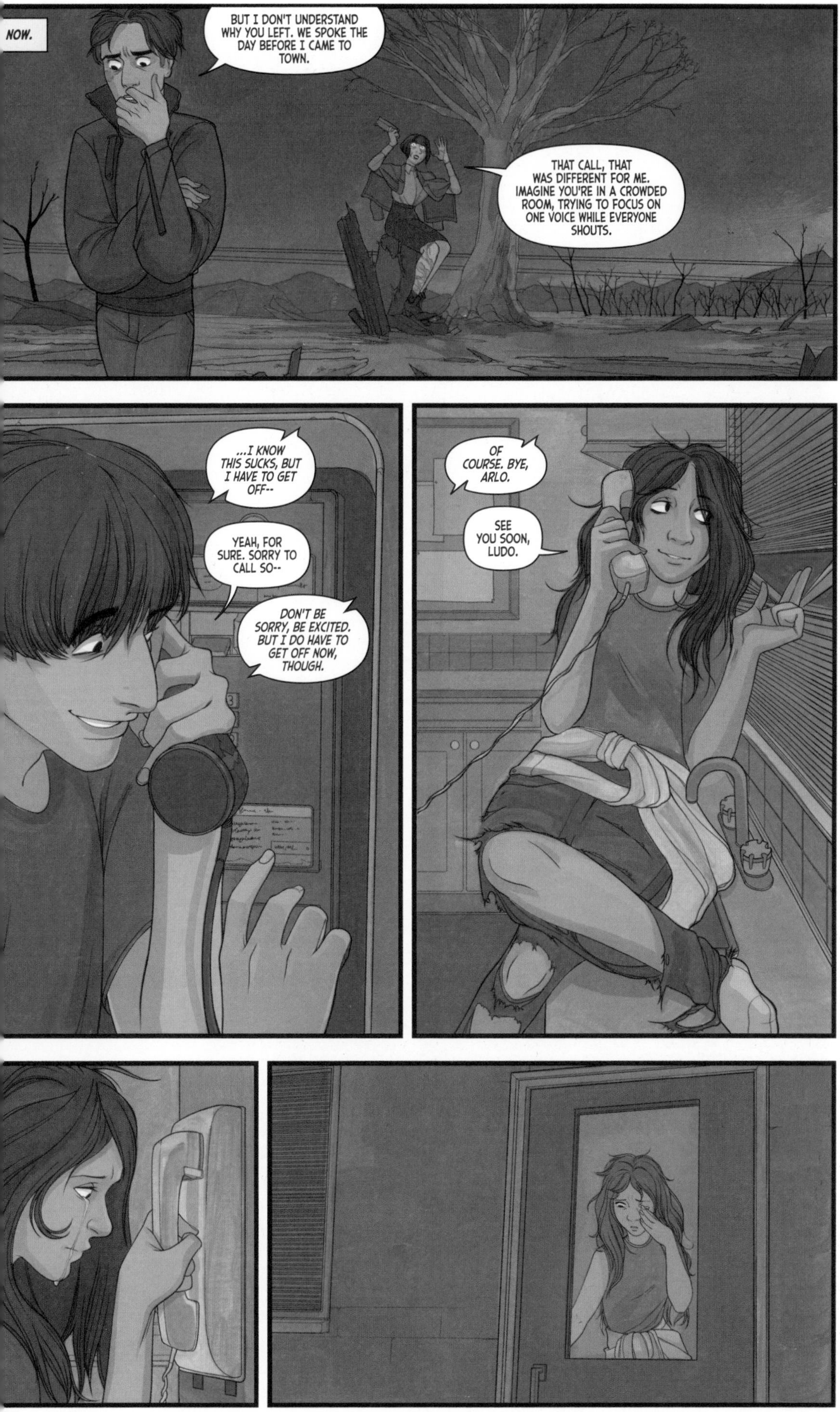
NOW.
BUT I DON'T UNDERSTAND WHY YOU LEFT. WE SPOKE THE DAY BEFORE I CAME TO TOWN.
THAT CALL, THAT WAS DIFFERENT FOR ME. IMAGINE YOU'RE IN A CROWDED ROOM, TRYING TO FOCUS ON ONE VOICE WHILE EVERYONE SHOUTS.
...I KNOW THIS SUCKS, BUT I HAVE TO GET OFF--
YEAH, FOR SURE. SORRY TO CALL SO--
DON'T BE SORRY, BE EXCITED. BUT I DO HAVE TO GET OFF NOW, THOUGH.
OF COURSE. BYE, ARLO.
SEE YOU SOON, LUDO.

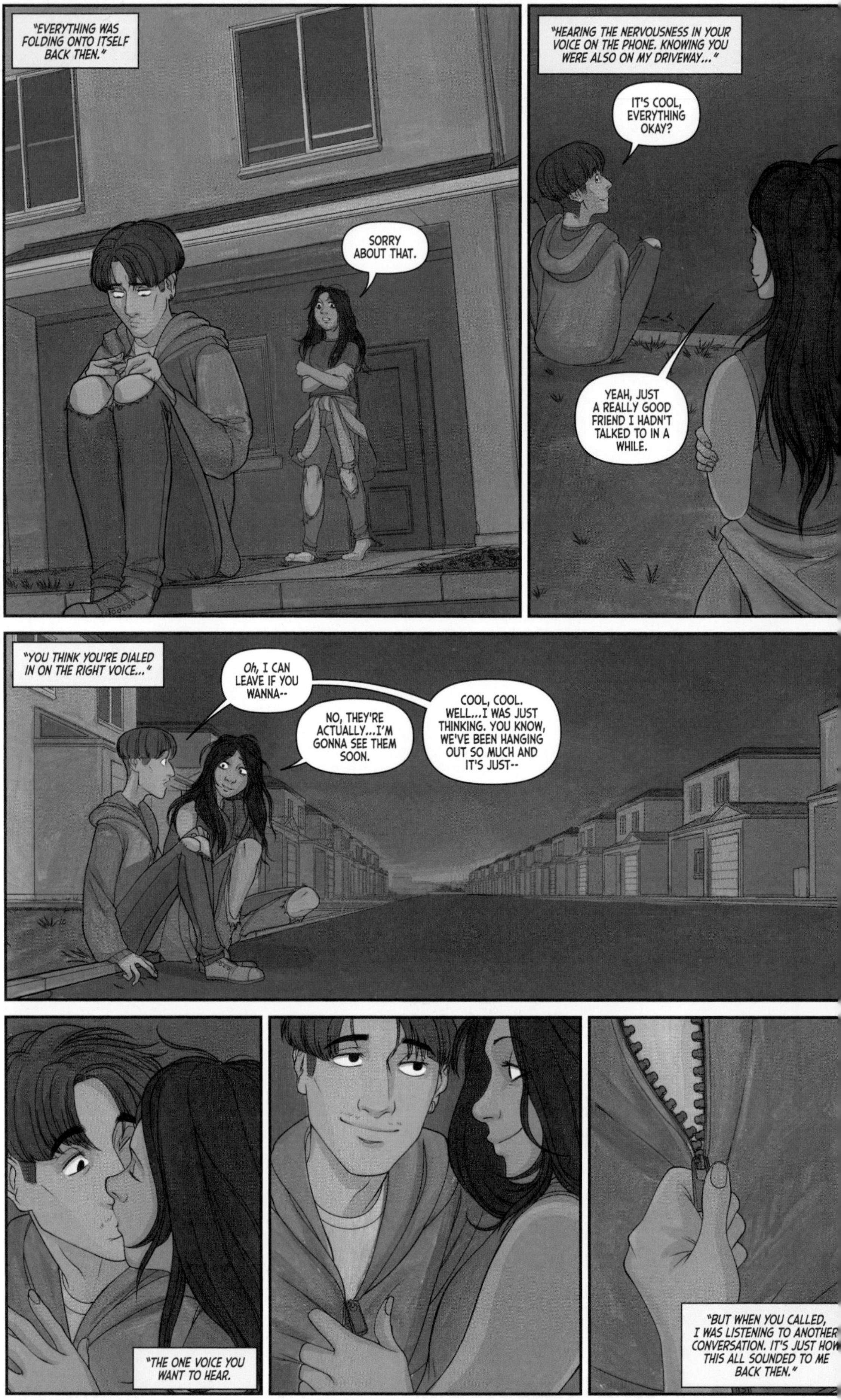
"EVERYTHING WAS FOLDING ONTO ITSELF BACK THEN."
SORRY ABOUT THAT.
"HEARING THE NERVOUSNESS IN YOUR VOICE ON THE PHONE. KNOWING YOU WERE ALSO ON MY DRIVEWAY..."
IT'S COOL, EVERYTHING OKAY?
YEAH, JUST A REALLY GOOD FRIEND I HADN'T TALKED TO IN A WHILE.
"YOU THINK YOU'RE DIALED IN ON THE RIGHT VOICE..."
Oh, I CAN LEAVE IF YOU WANNA--
NO, THEY'RE ACTUALLY...I'M GONNA SEE THEM SOON.
COOL, COOL. WELL...I WAS JUST THINKING. YOU KNOW, WE'VE BEEN HANGING OUT SO MUCH AND IT'S JUST--
"THE ONE VOICE YOU WANT TO HEAR.
"BUT WHEN YOU CALLED, I WAS LISTENING TO ANOTHER CONVERSATION. IT'S JUST HOW THIS ALL SOUNDED TO ME BACK THEN."

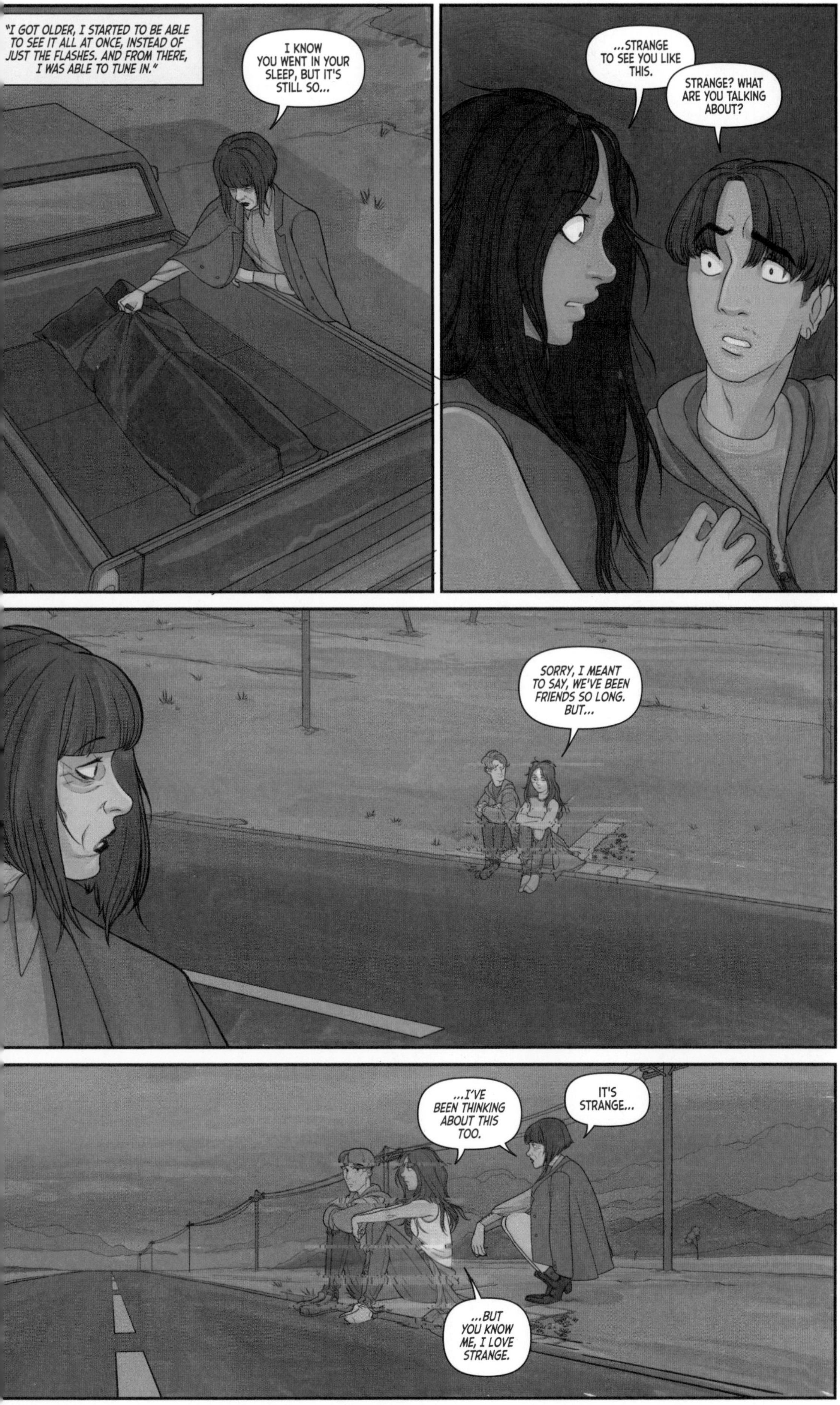
"I GOT OLDER, I STARTED TO BE ABLE TO SEE IT ALL AT ONCE, INSTEAD OF JUST THE FLASHES. AND FROM THERE, I WAS ABLE TO TUNE IN."
I KNOW YOU WENT IN YOUR SLEEP, BUT IT'S STILL SO...
...STRANGE TO SEE YOU LIKE THIS.
STRANGE? WHAT ARE YOU TALKING ABOUT?
SORRY, I MEANT TO SAY, WE'VE BEEN FRIENDS SO LONG. BUT...
...I'VE BEEN THINKING ABOUT THIS TOO.
IT'S STRANGE...
...BUT YOU KNOW ME, I LOVE STRANGE.

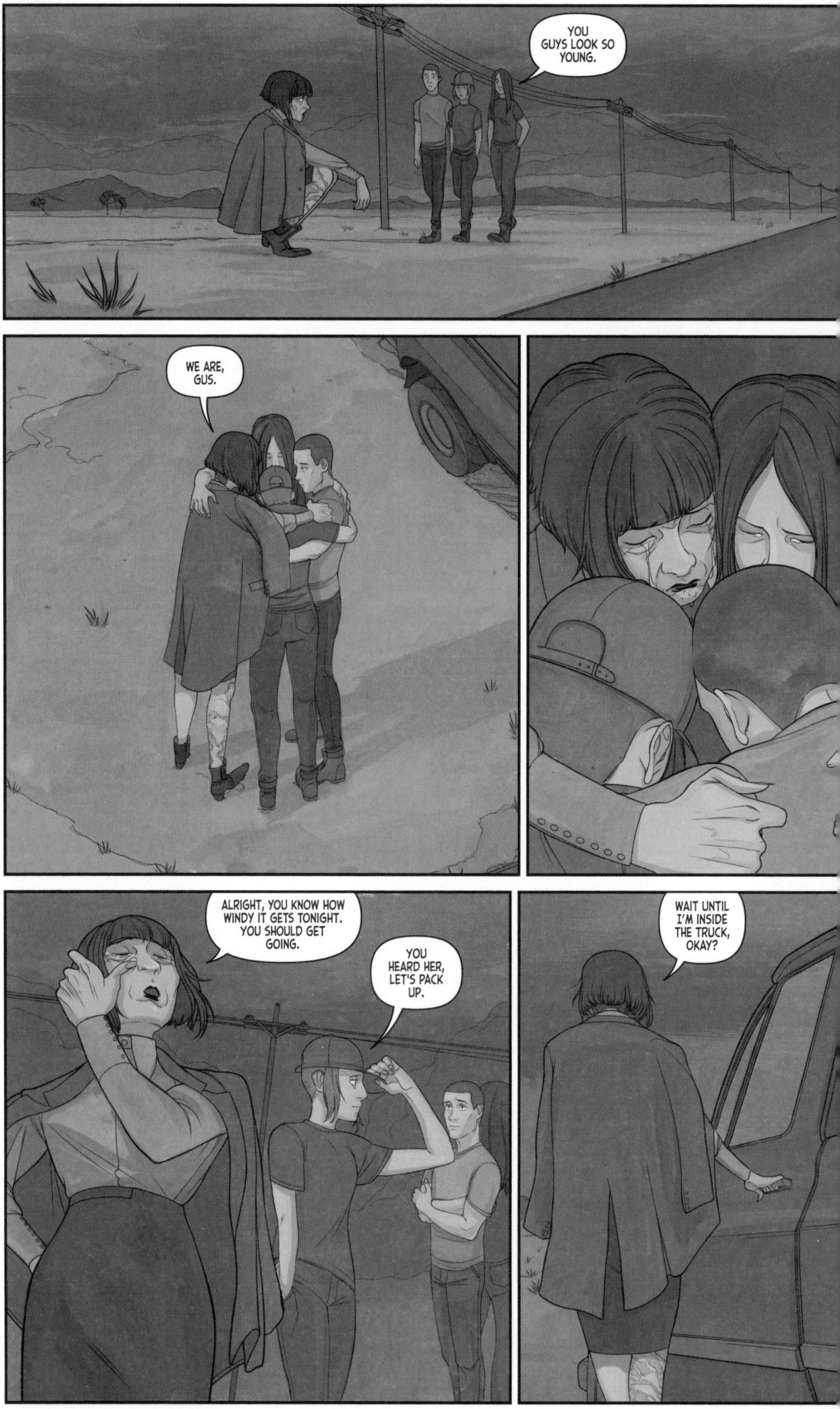
YOU GUYS LOOK SO YOUNG.
WE ARE, GUS.
ALRIGHT, YOU KNOW HOW WINDY IT GETS TONIGHT. YOU SHOULD GET GOING.
YOU HEARD HER, LET'S PACK UP.
WAIT UNTIL I'M INSIDE THE TRUCK, OKAY?

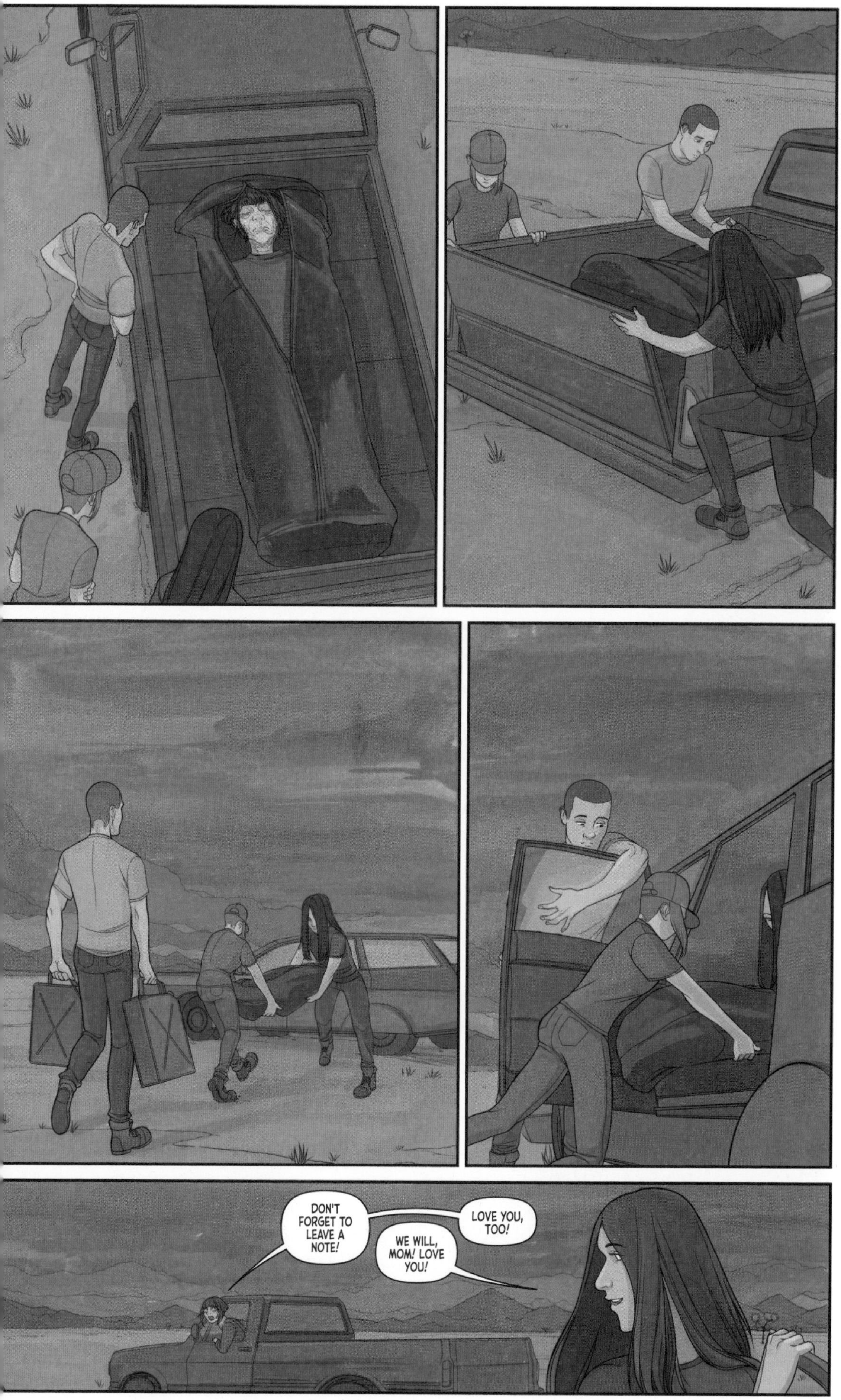

DON'T FORGET TO LEAVE A NOTE!
WE WILL, MOM! LOVE YOU!
LOVE YOU, TOO!

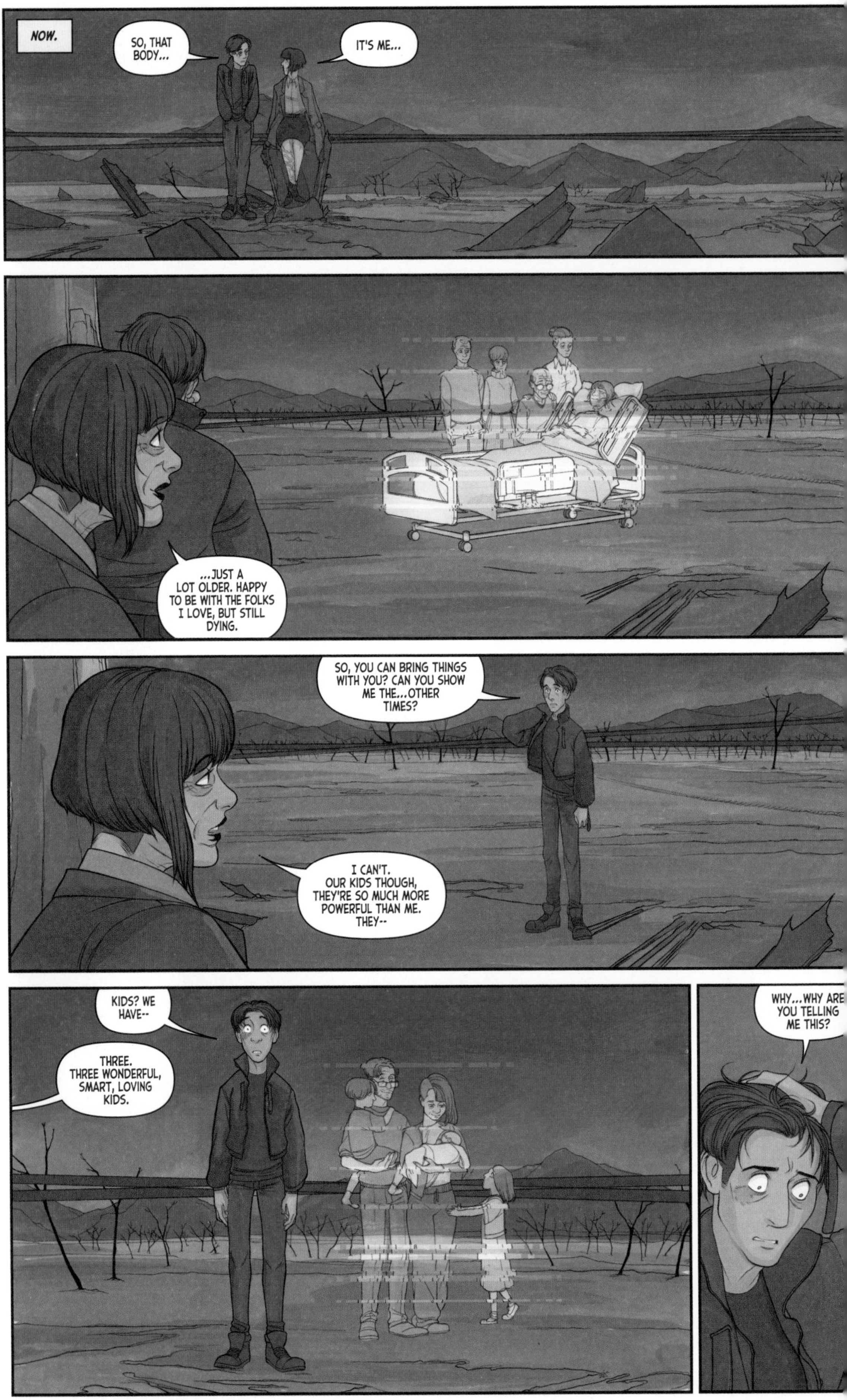
NOW.
SO, THAT BODY...
IT'S ME...
...JUST A LOT OLDER. HAPPY TO BE WITH THE FOLKS I LOVE, BUT STILL DYING.
SO, YOU CAN BRING THINGS WITH YOU? CAN YOU SHOW ME THE...OTHER TIMES?
I CAN'T. OUR KIDS THOUGH, THEY'RE SO MUCH MORE POWERFUL THAN ME. THEY--
KIDS? WE HAVE--
THREE. THREE WONDERFUL, SMART, LOVING KIDS.
WHY...WHY ARE YOU TELLING ME THIS?

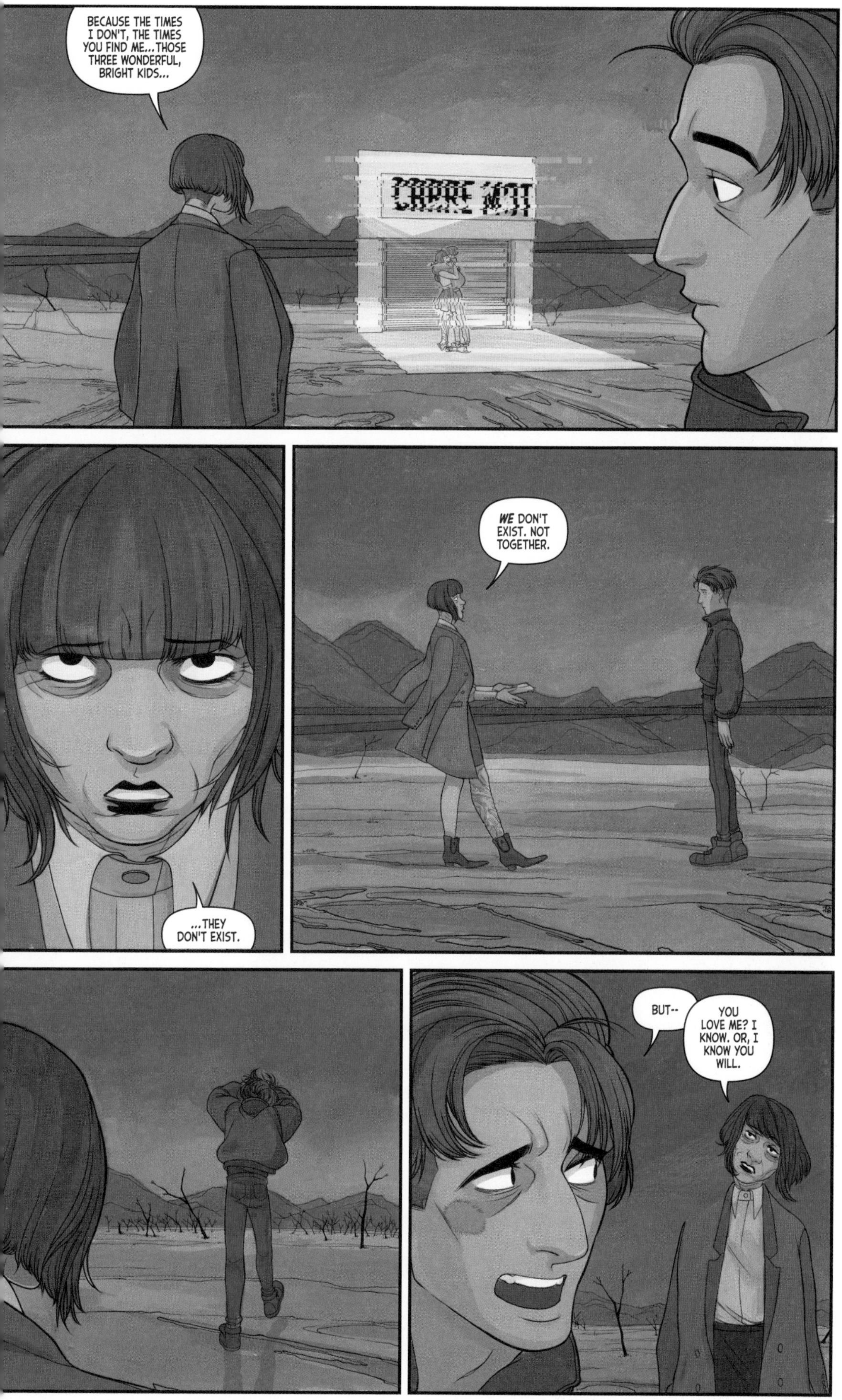
BECAUSE THE TIMES I DON'T, THE TIMES YOU FIND ME...THOSE THREE WONDERFUL, BRIGHT KIDS...
...THEY DON'T EXIST.
WE DON'T EXIST. NOT TOGETHER.
BUT--
YOU LOVE ME? I KNOW. OR, I KNOW YOU WILL.

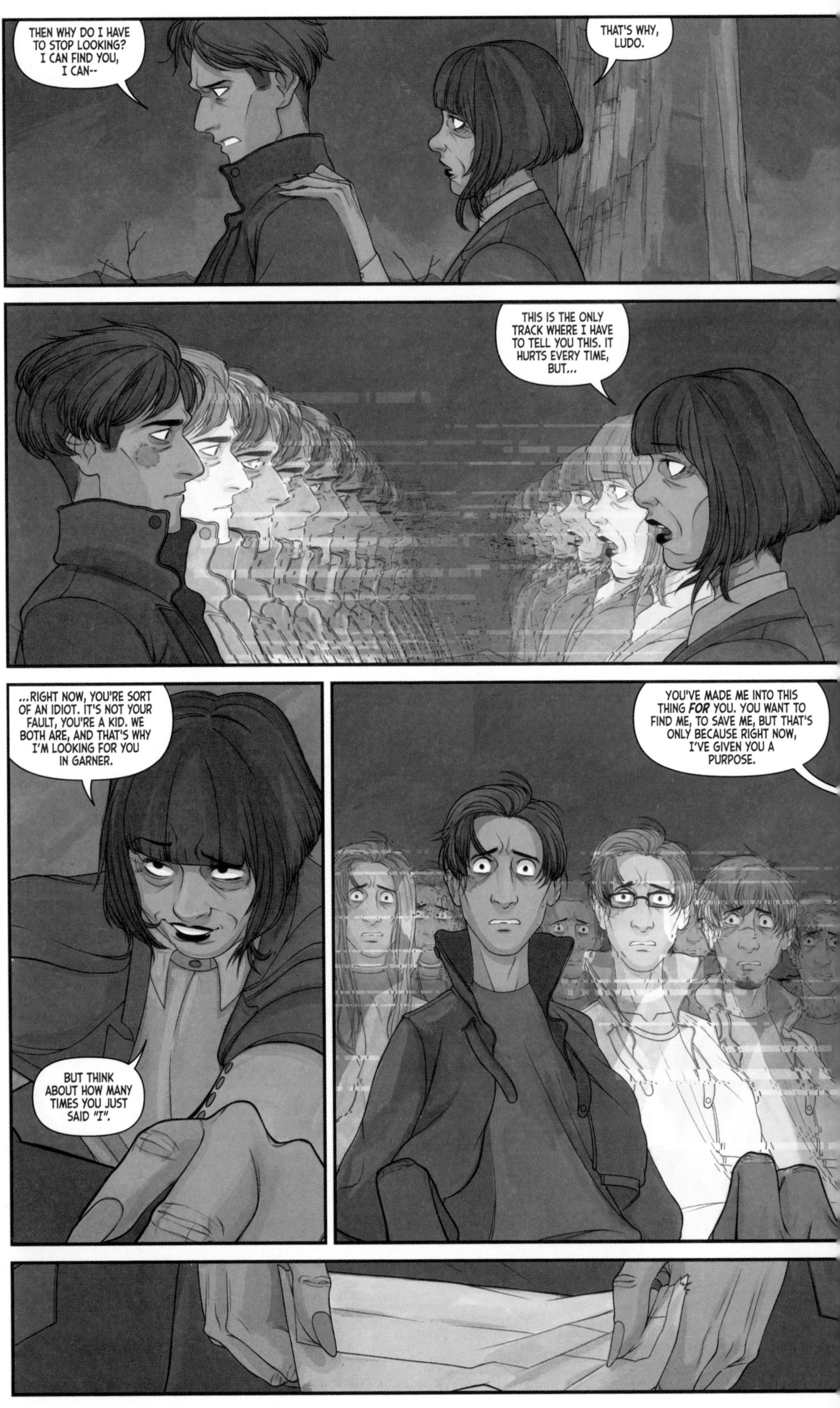
THEN WHY DO I HAVE TO STOP LOOKING? I CAN FIND YOU, I CAN--
THAT'S WHY, LUDO.
THIS IS THE ONLY TRACK WHERE I HAVE TO TELL YOU THIS. IT HURTS EVERY TIME, BUT...
...RIGHT NOW, YOU'RE SORT OF AN IDIOT. IT'S NOT YOUR FAULT, YOU'RE A KID. WE BOTH ARE, AND THAT'S WHY I'M LOOKING FOR YOU IN GARNER.
BUT THINK ABOUT HOW MANY TIMES YOU JUST SAID "*I*".
YOU'VE MADE ME INTO THIS THING ***FOR*** YOU. YOU WANT TO FIND ME, TO SAVE ME, BUT THAT'S ONLY BECAUSE RIGHT NOW, I'VE GIVEN YOU A PURPOSE.

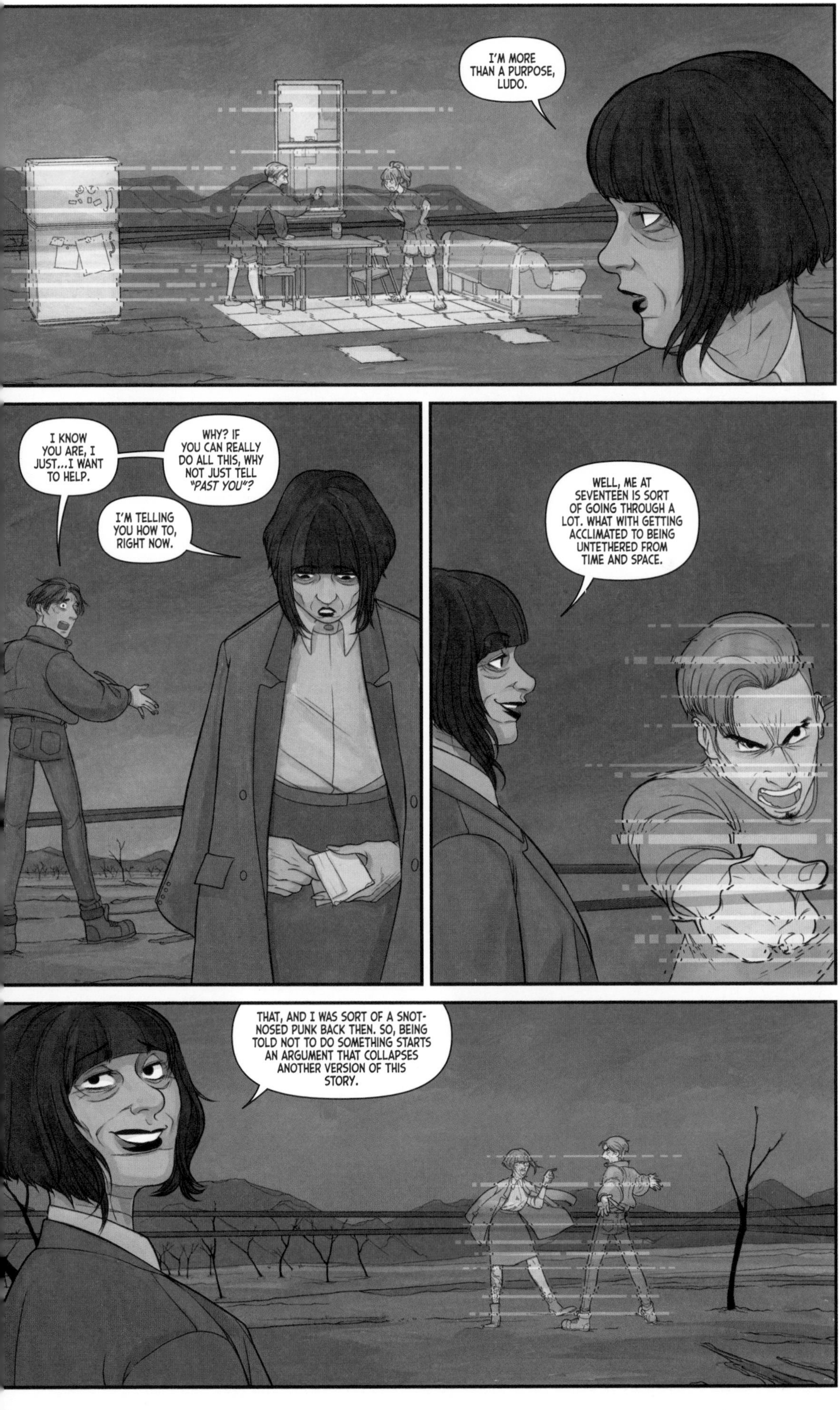
I'M MORE THAN A PURPOSE, LUDO.
I KNOW YOU ARE, I JUST...I WANT TO HELP.
WHY? IF YOU CAN REALLY DO ALL THIS, WHY NOT JUST TELL "PAST YOU"?
I'M TELLING YOU HOW TO, RIGHT NOW.
WELL, ME AT SEVENTEEN IS SORT OF GOING THROUGH A LOT. WHAT WITH GETTING ACCLIMATED TO BEING UNTETHERED FROM TIME AND SPACE.
THAT, AND I WAS SORT OF A SNOT-NOSED PUNK BACK THEN. SO, BEING TOLD NOT TO DO SOMETHING STARTS AN ARGUMENT THAT COLLAPSES ANOTHER VERSION OF THIS STORY.

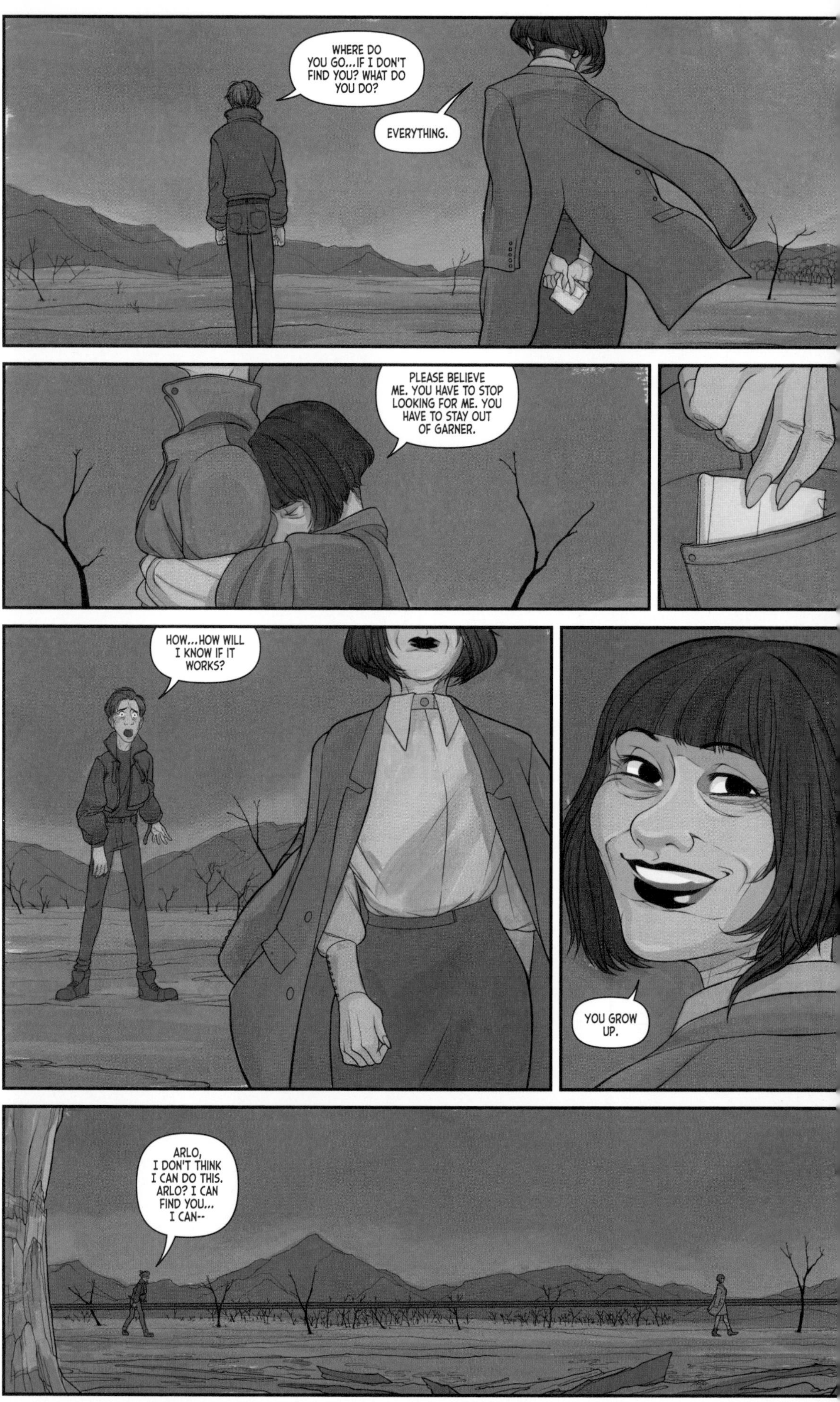
WHERE DO YOU GO...IF I DON'T FIND YOU? WHAT DO YOU DO?
EVERYTHING.
PLEASE BELIEVE ME. YOU HAVE TO STOP LOOKING FOR ME. YOU HAVE TO STAY OUT OF GARNER.
HOW...HOW WILL I KNOW IF IT WORKS?
YOU GROW UP.
ARLO, I DON'T THINK I CAN DO THIS. ARLO? I CAN FIND YOU... I CAN--

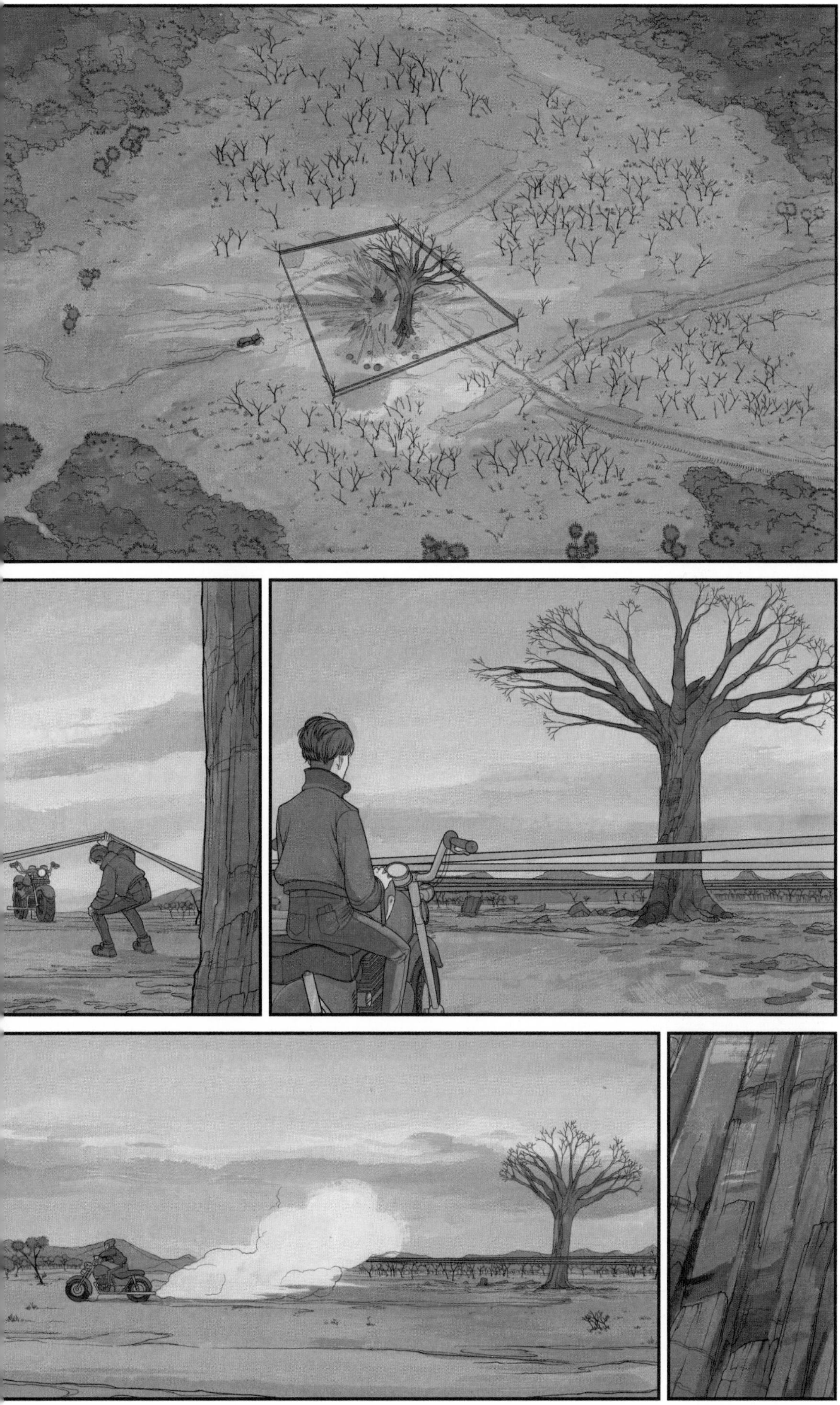

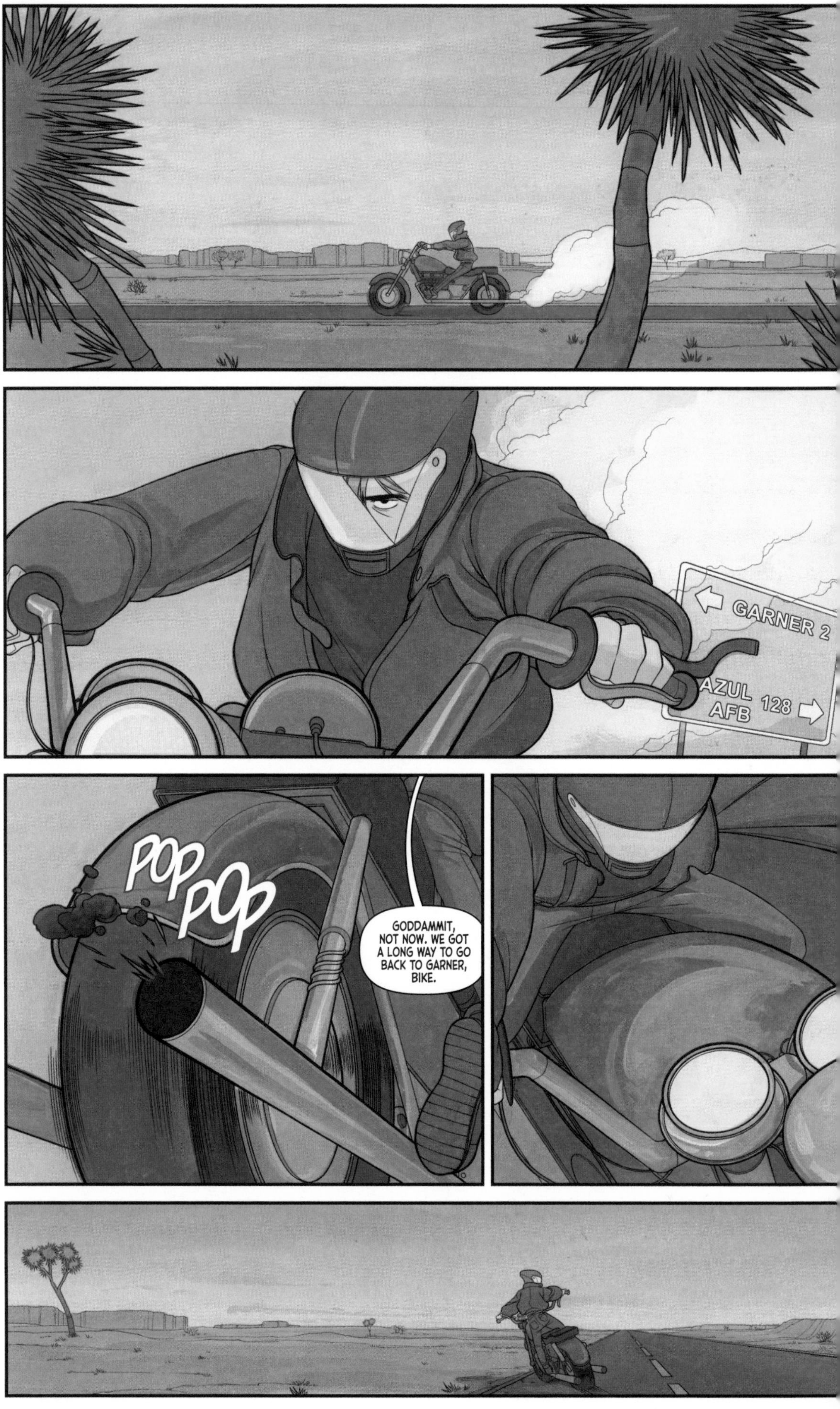
GARNER 2
AZUL AFB 128
POP POP
GODDAMMIT, NOT NOW. WE GOT A LONG WAY TO GO BACK TO GARNER, BIKE.

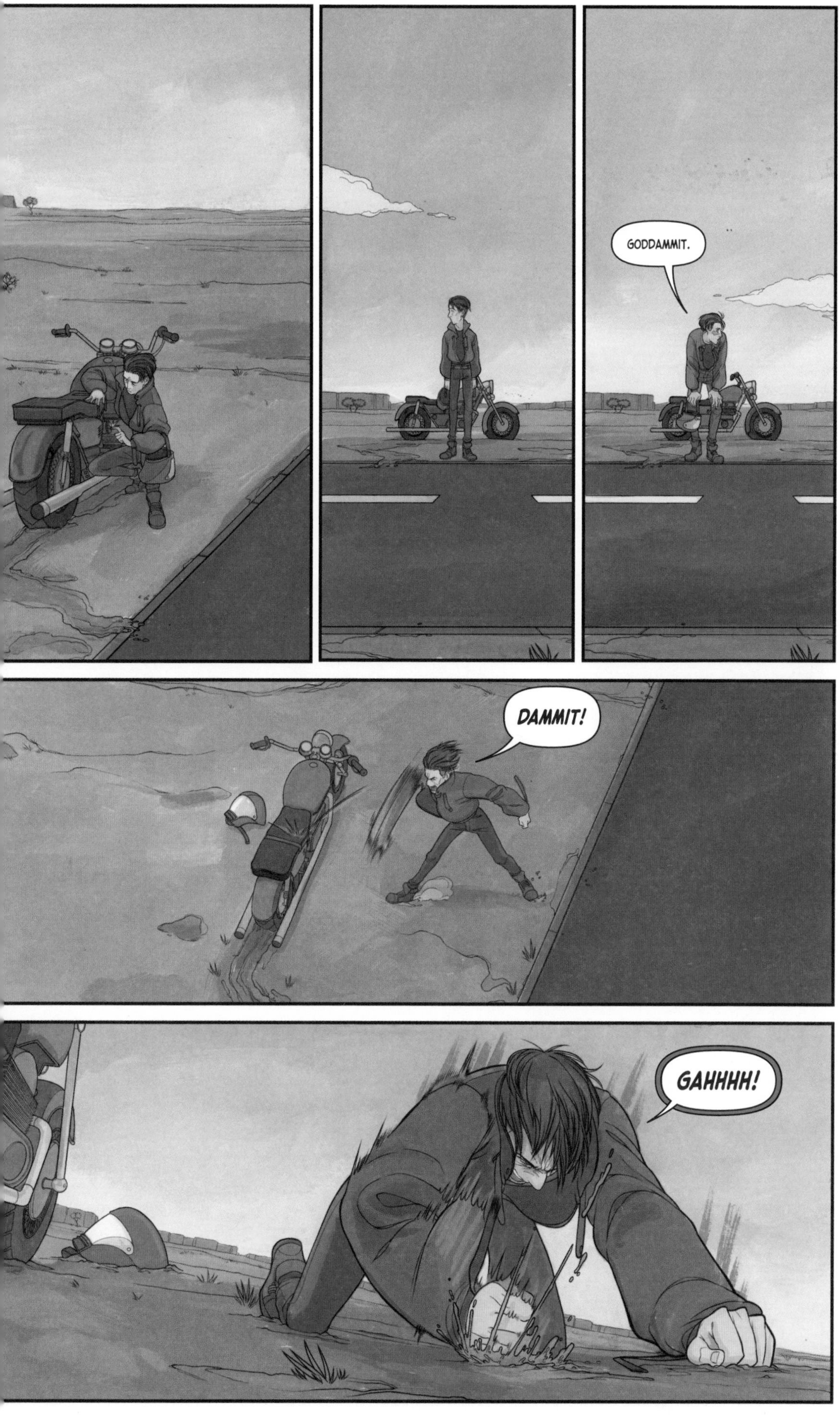
GODDAMMIT.
DAMMIT!
GAHHHH!

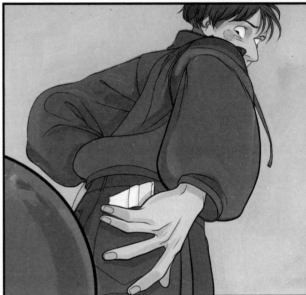

There's a world where this doesn't happen.

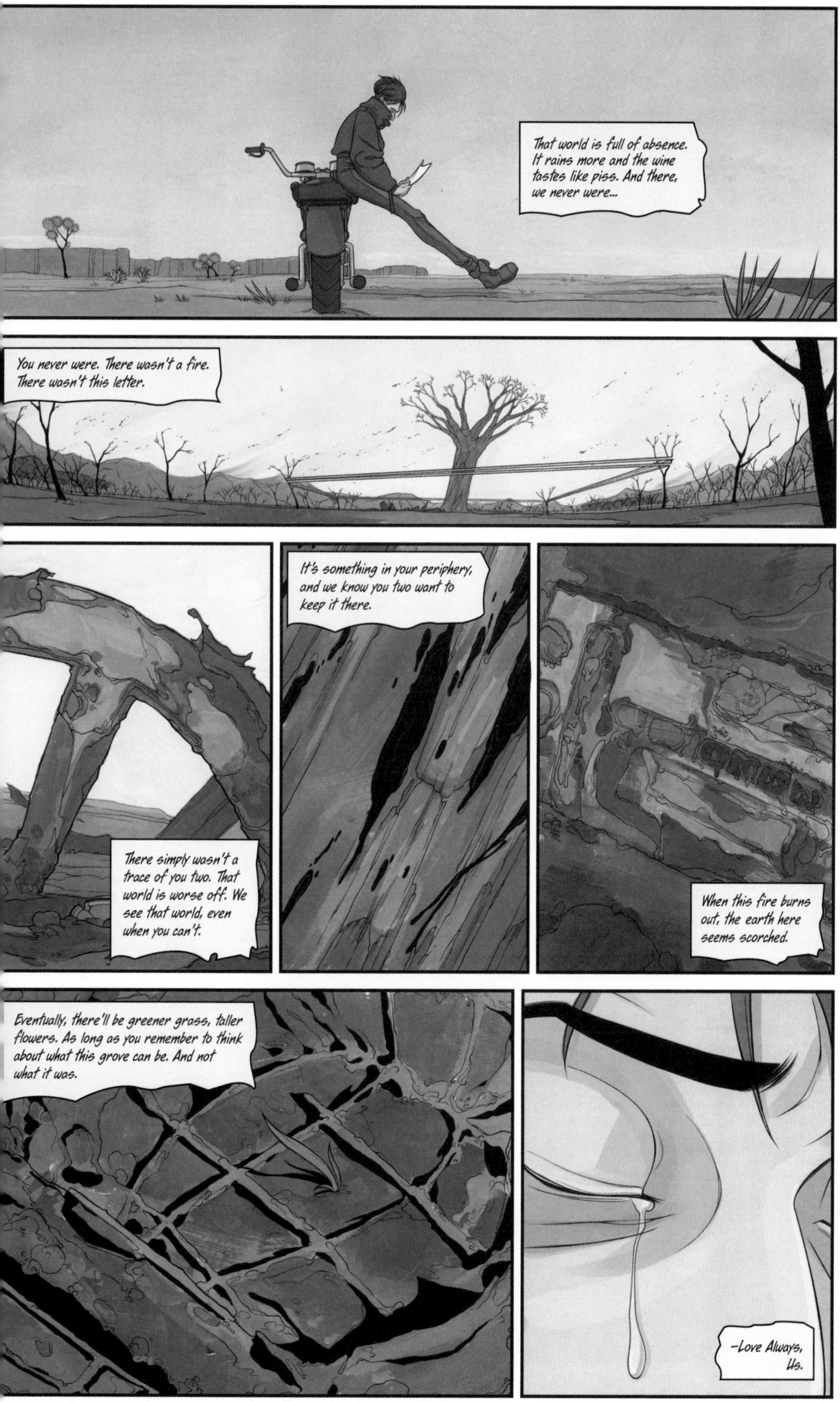
That world is full of absence. It rains more and the wine tastes like piss. And there, we never were...
You never were. There wasn't a fire. There wasn't this letter.
There simply wasn't a trace of you two. That world is worse off. We see that world, even when you can't.
It's something in your periphery, and we know you two want to keep it there.
When this fire burns out, the earth here seems scorched.
Eventually, there'll be greener grass, taller flowers. As long as you remember to think about what this grove can be. And not what it was.
–Love Always, Us.

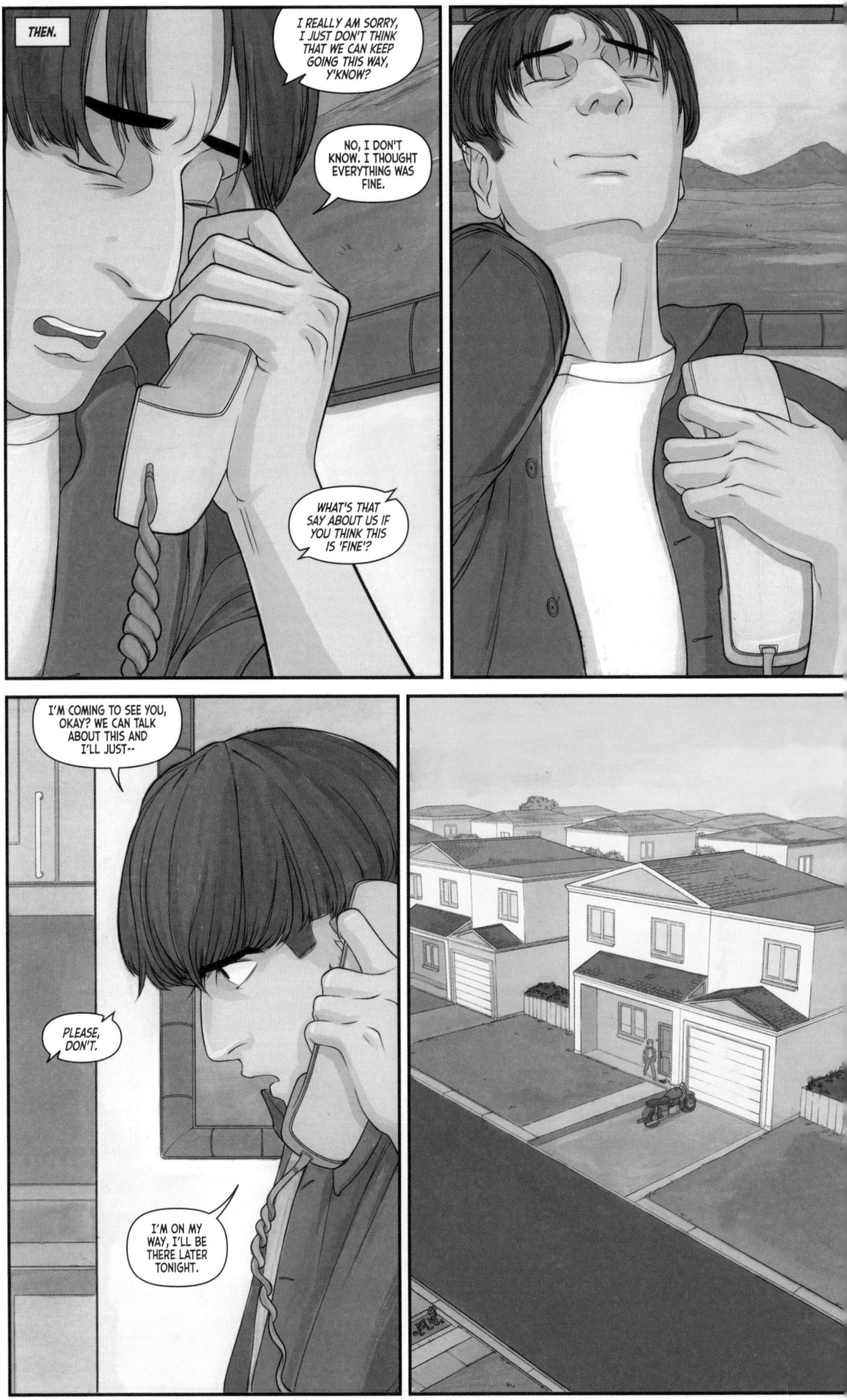
THEN.
I REALLY AM SORRY, I JUST DON'T THINK THAT WE CAN KEEP GOING THIS WAY, Y'KNOW?
NO, I DON'T KNOW. I THOUGHT EVERYTHING WAS FINE.
WHAT'S THAT SAY ABOUT US IF YOU THINK THIS IS 'FINE'?
I'M COMING TO SEE YOU, OKAY? WE CAN TALK ABOUT THIS AND I'LL JUST--
PLEASE, DON'T.
I'M ON MY WAY, I'LL BE THERE LATER TONIGHT.

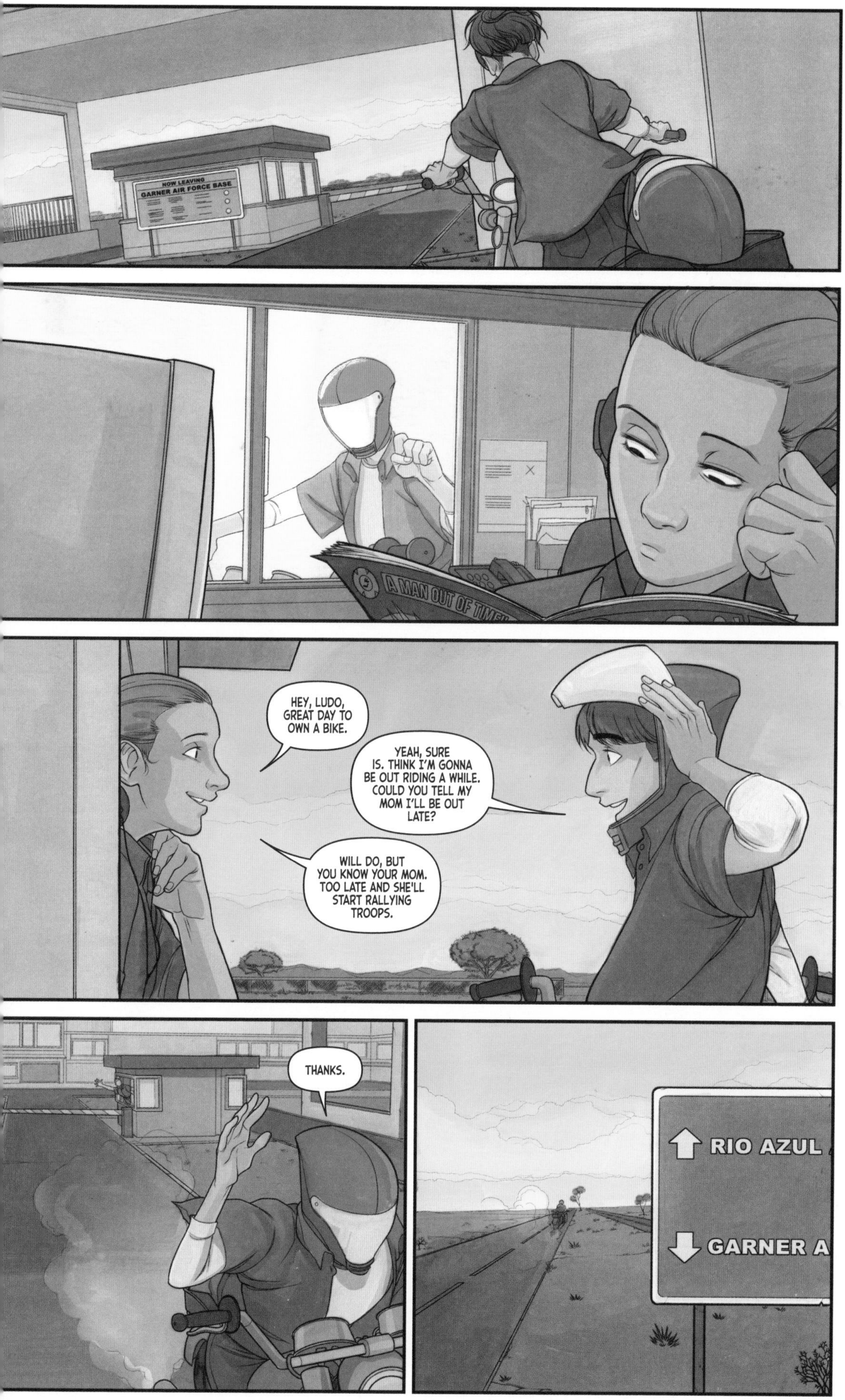
NOW LEAVING
GARNER AIR FORCE BASE
A MAN OUT OF TIME
HEY, LUDO, GREAT DAY TO OWN A BIKE.
YEAH, SURE IS. THINK I'M GONNA BE OUT RIDING A WHILE. COULD YOU TELL MY MOM I'LL BE OUT LATE?
WILL DO, BUT YOU KNOW YOUR MOM. TOO LATE AND SHE'LL START RALLYING TROOPS.
THANKS.
RIO AZUL
GARNER A

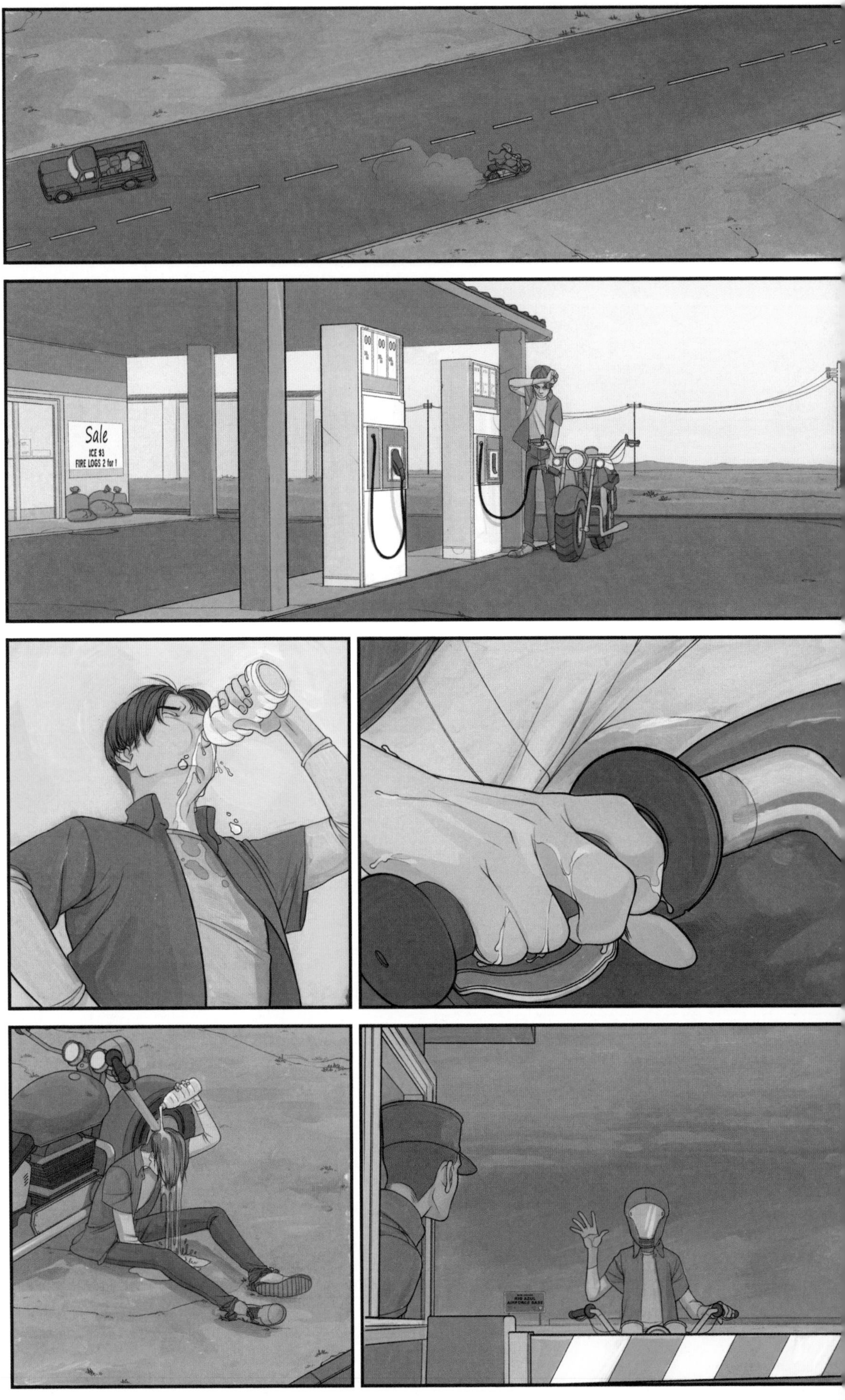
Sale
ICE $3
FIRE LOGS 2 for 1
RIO AZUL
AIRFORCE BASE

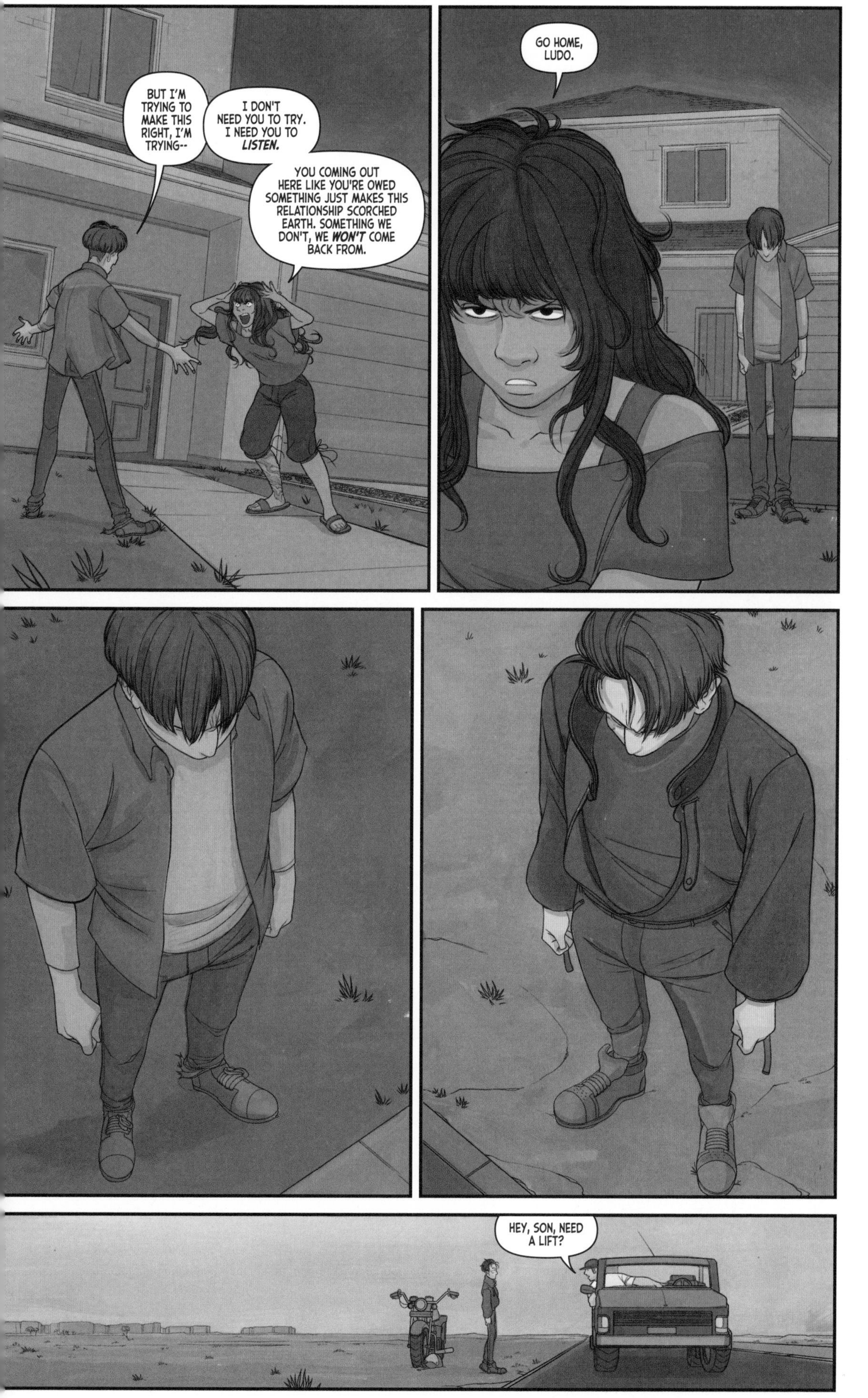
BUT I'M TRYING TO MAKE THIS RIGHT, I'M TRYING--
I DON'T NEED YOU TO TRY. I NEED YOU TO ***LISTEN.***
YOU COMING OUT HERE LIKE YOU'RE OWED SOMETHING JUST MAKES THIS RELATIONSHIP SCORCHED EARTH. SOMETHING WE DON'T, WE ***WON'T*** COME BACK FROM.
GO HOME, LUDO.
HEY, SON, NEED A LIFT?

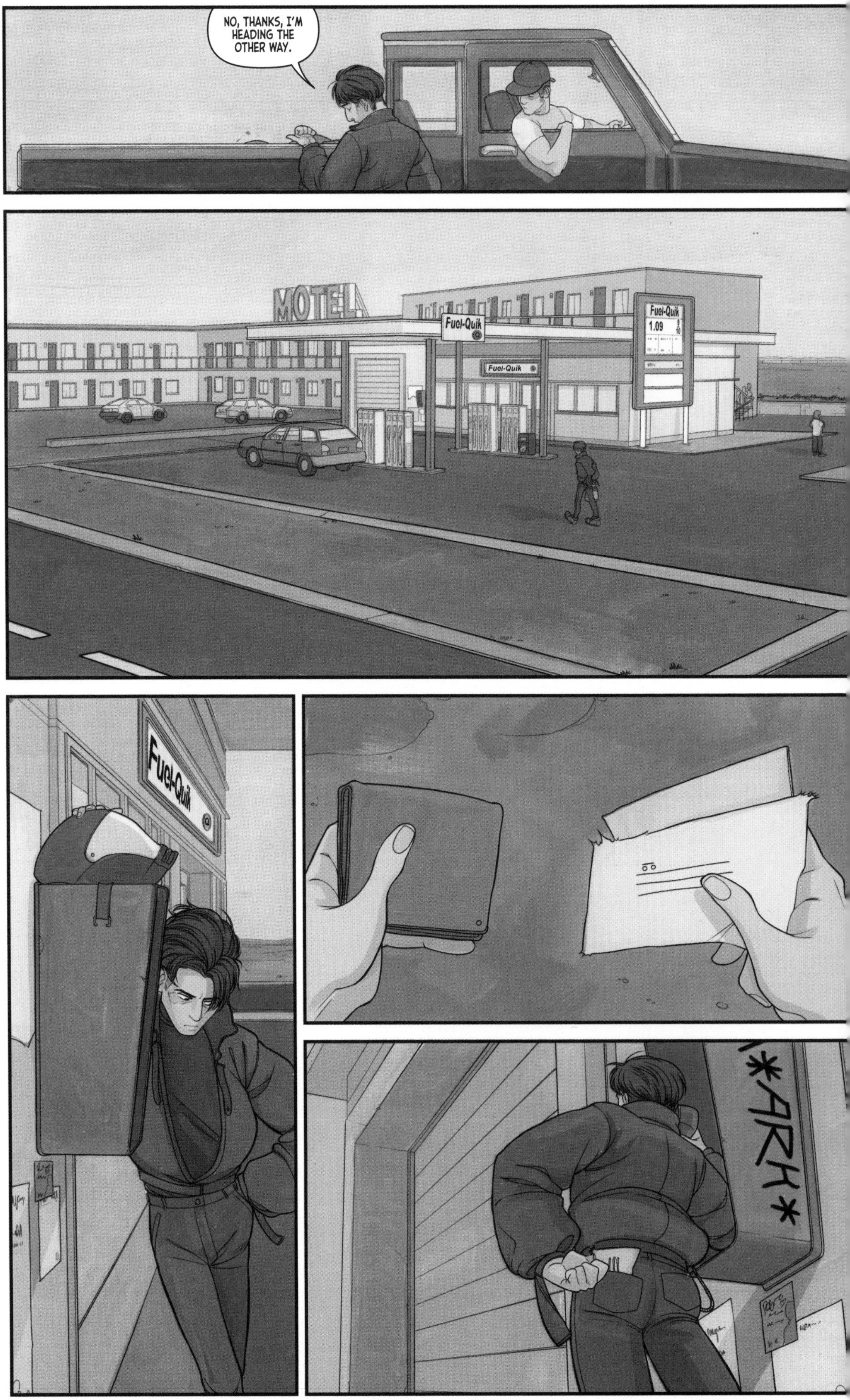
NO, THANKS, I'M HEADING THE OTHER WAY.
MOTEL
Fuel-Quik
Fuel-Quik
1.09
Fuel-Quik
Fuel-Quik

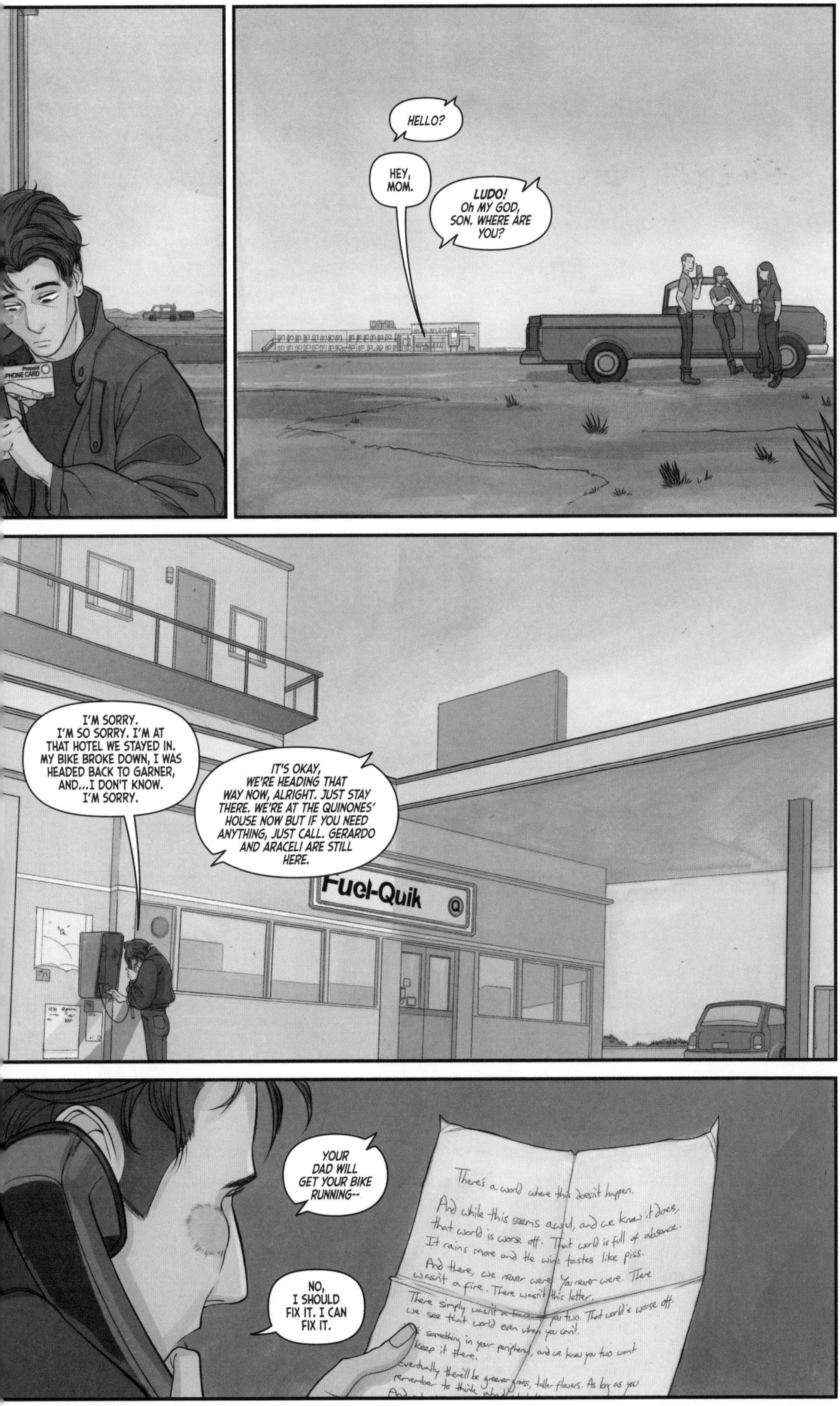

Prepaid PHONE CARD
HELLO?
HEY, MOM.
LUDO! Oh MY GOD, SON. WHERE ARE YOU?
MOTEL
I'M SORRY. I'M SO SORRY. I'M AT THAT HOTEL WE STAYED IN. MY BIKE BROKE DOWN, I WAS HEADED BACK TO GARNER, AND...I DON'T KNOW. I'M SORRY.
IT'S OKAY, WE'RE HEADING THAT WAY NOW, ALRIGHT. JUST STAY THERE. WE'RE AT THE QUINONES' HOUSE NOW BUT IF YOU NEED ANYTHING, JUST CALL. GERARDO AND ARACELI ARE STILL HERE.
Fuel-Quik
YOUR DAD WILL GET YOUR BIKE RUNNING--
There's a world where this doesn't happen.
And while this seems awful, and we know it does, that world is worse off. That world is full of absence.
It rains more and the wine tastes like piss.
And there, we never were. You never were. There wasn't a fire. There wasn't this letter.
There simply wasn't
you two. That world's worse off.
we see that world even when you can't.
something in your peripheral, and we know you two won't
keep it there.
Eventually there'll be greener grass, taller flowers. As long as you
remember to think
NO, I SHOULD FIX IT. I CAN FIX IT.

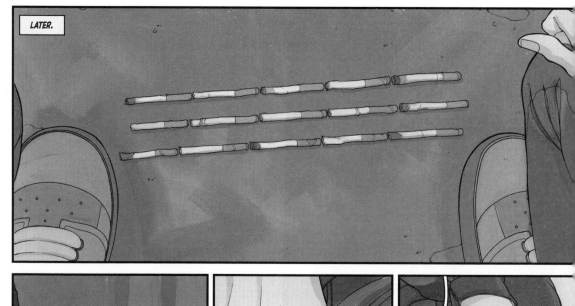

LATER.
$10 Prepaid PHONE CARD can be used with any public phone
HELLO?
ARLO?
YEAH, WHO'S THIS?
Um, IT'S LUDO.
$10 Prepaid PHONE CARD can be used with any public phone
Oh, FROM THE COOKOUT. THAT WAS QUICK, YOU GUYS JUST LEFT A FEW HOURS AGO.
YEAH, I uh, COULDN'T WAIT TO SEE IF YOU GOT PAST THAT MINE CART STAGE.

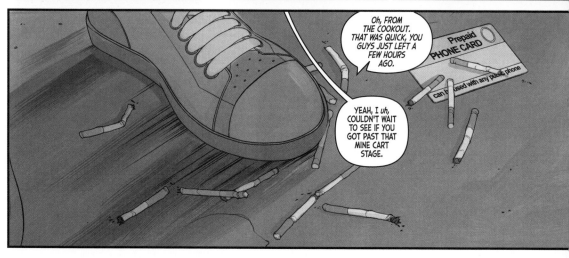

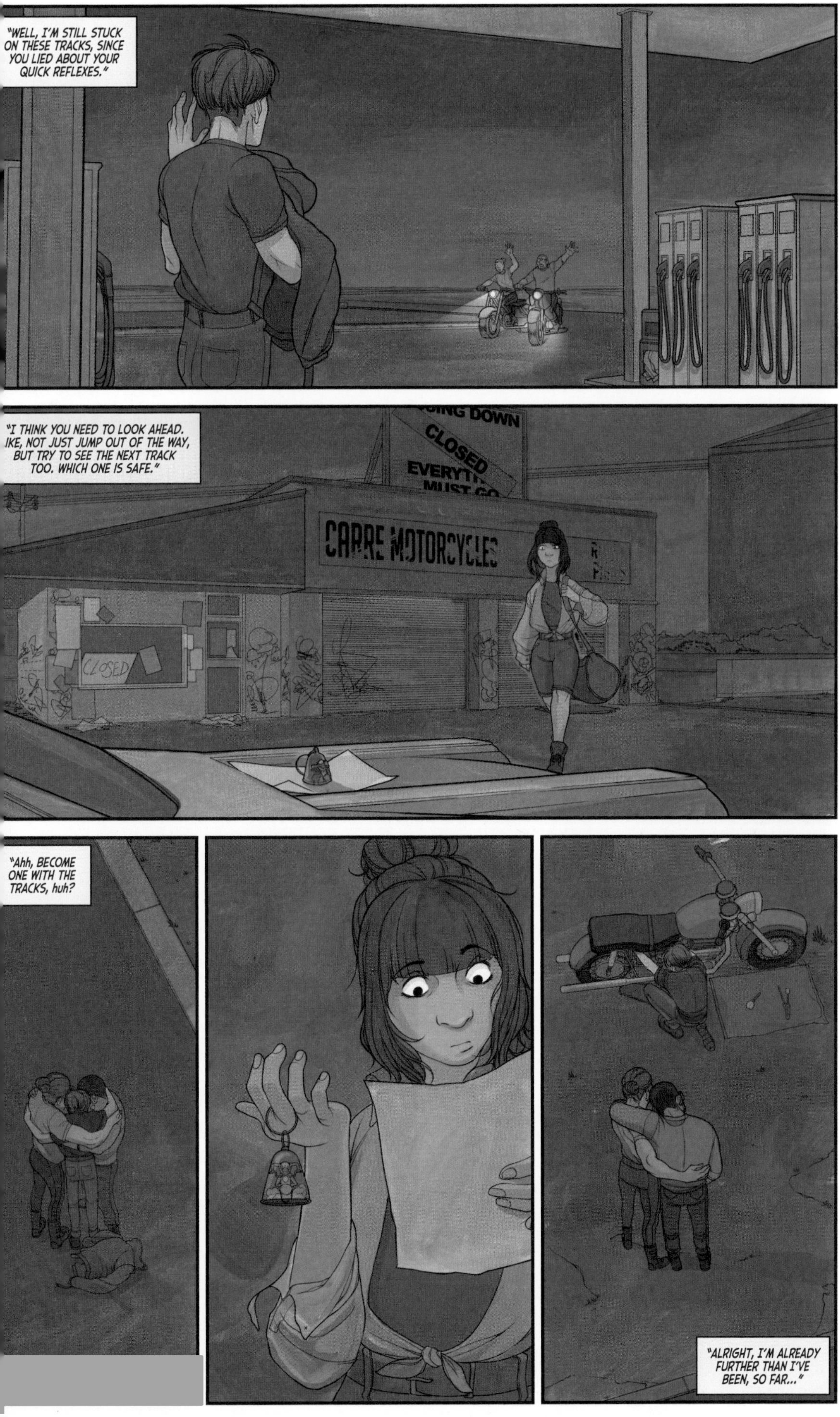
"WELL, I'M STILL STUCK ON THESE TRACKS, SINCE YOU LIED ABOUT YOUR QUICK REFLEXES."
"I THINK YOU NEED TO LOOK AHEAD. IKE, NOT JUST JUMP OUT OF THE WAY, BUT TRY TO SEE THE NEXT TRACK TOO. WHICH ONE IS SAFE."
CLOSED
CARRE MOTORCYCLES
CLOSED
"Ahh, BECOME ONE WITH THE TRACKS, huh?
"ALRIGHT, I'M ALREADY FURTHER THAN I'VE BEEN, SO FAR..."

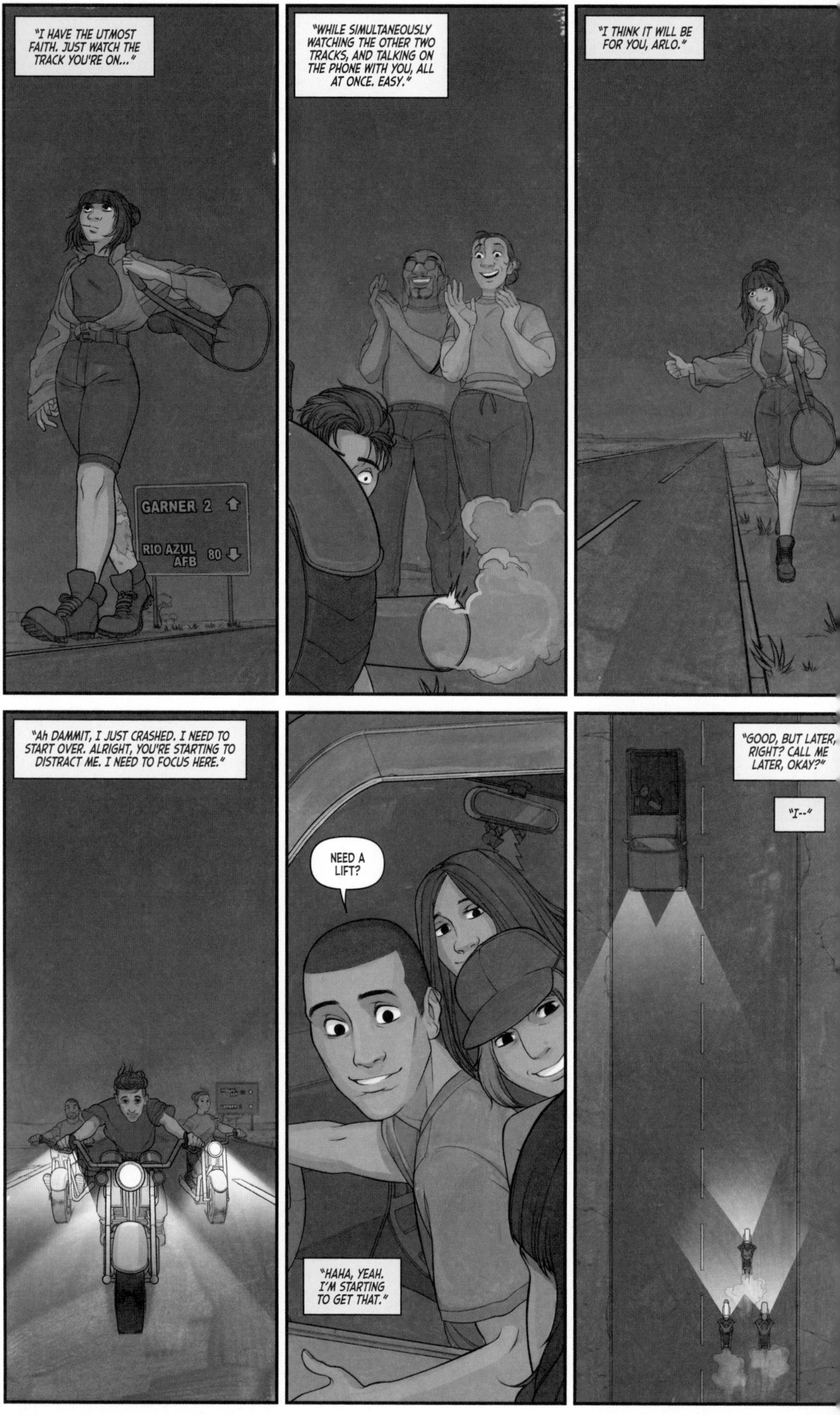
"I HAVE THE UTMOST FAITH. JUST WATCH THE TRACK YOU'RE ON..."
GARNER 2
RIO AZUL AFB 80
"WHILE SIMULTANEOUSLY WATCHING THE OTHER TWO TRACKS, AND TALKING ON THE PHONE WITH YOU, ALL AT ONCE. EASY."
"I THINK IT WILL BE FOR YOU, ARLO."
"Ah DAMMIT, I JUST CRASHED. I NEED TO START OVER. ALRIGHT, YOU'RE STARTING TO DISTRACT ME. I NEED TO FOCUS HERE."
NEED A LIFT?
"HAHA, YEAH. I'M STARTING TO GET THAT."
"GOOD, BUT LATER, RIGHT? CALL ME LATER, OKAY?"
"I--"

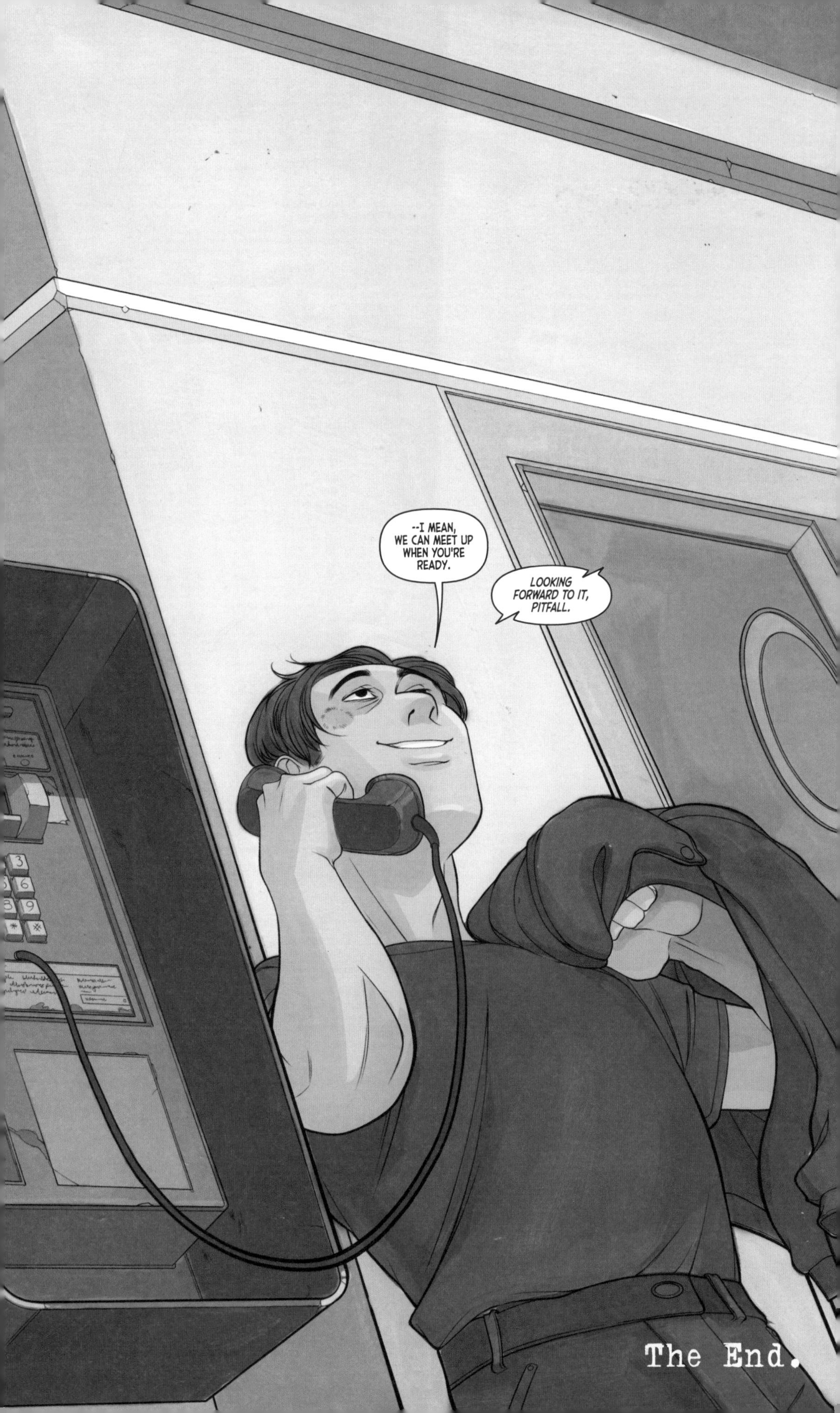
--I MEAN, WE CAN MEET UP WHEN YOU'RE READY.
LOOKING FORWARD TO IT, PITFALL.
The End.

COVER GALLERY

ISSUE #1 COVER by DEENA SO'OTEH

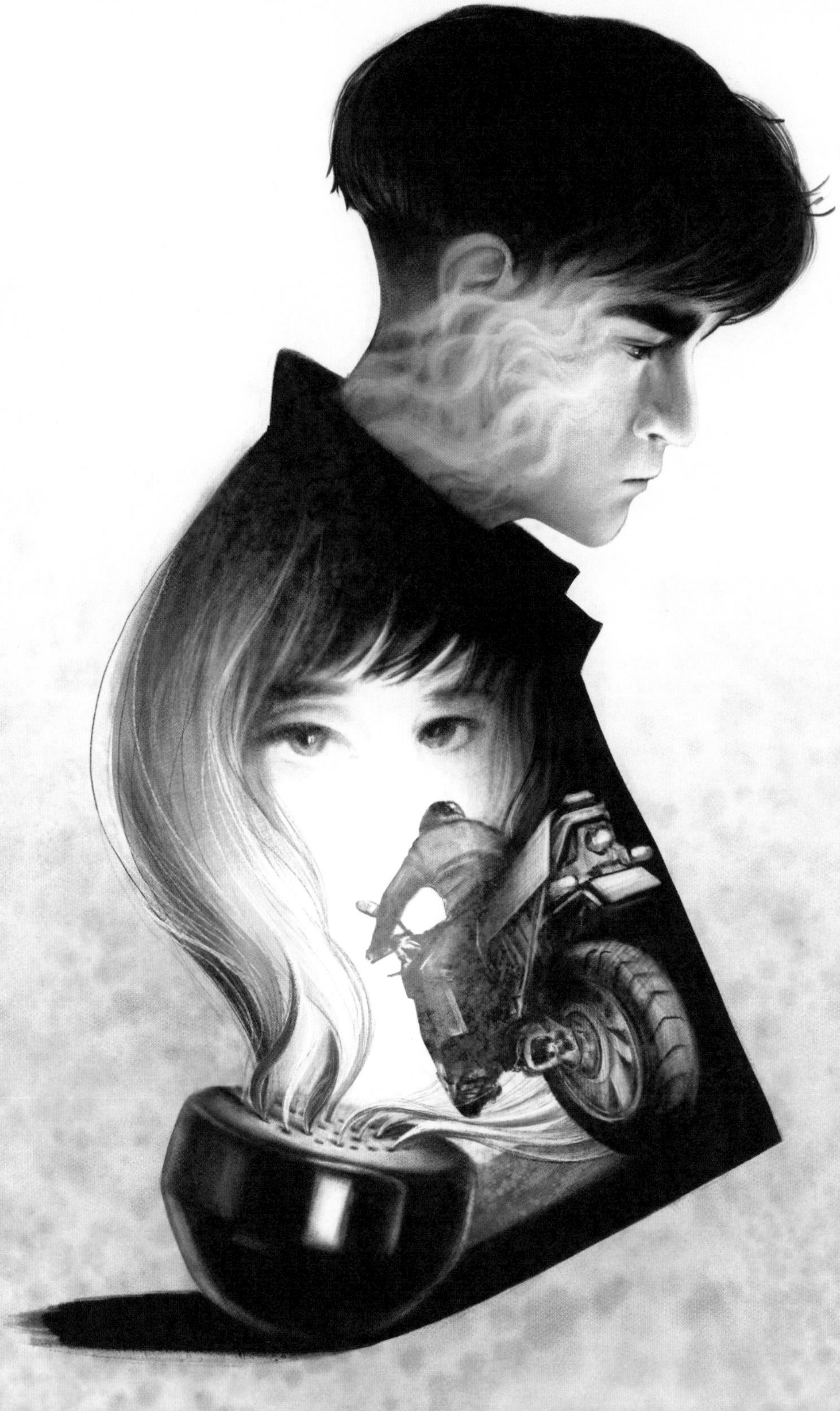

ISSUE #1 COVER CONCEPTS

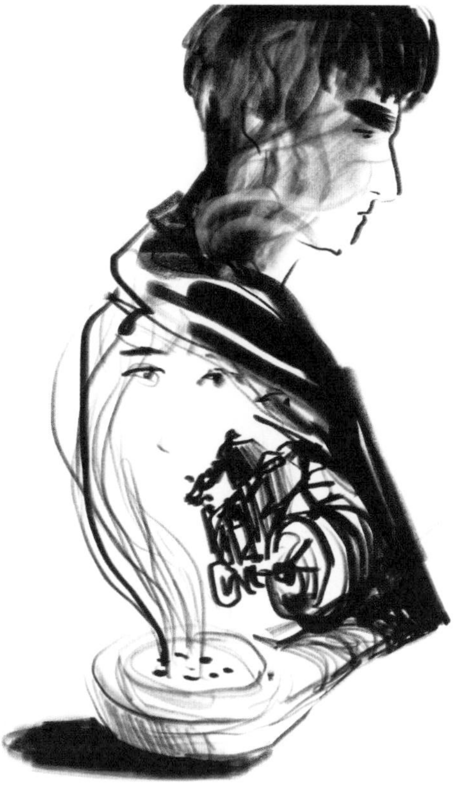

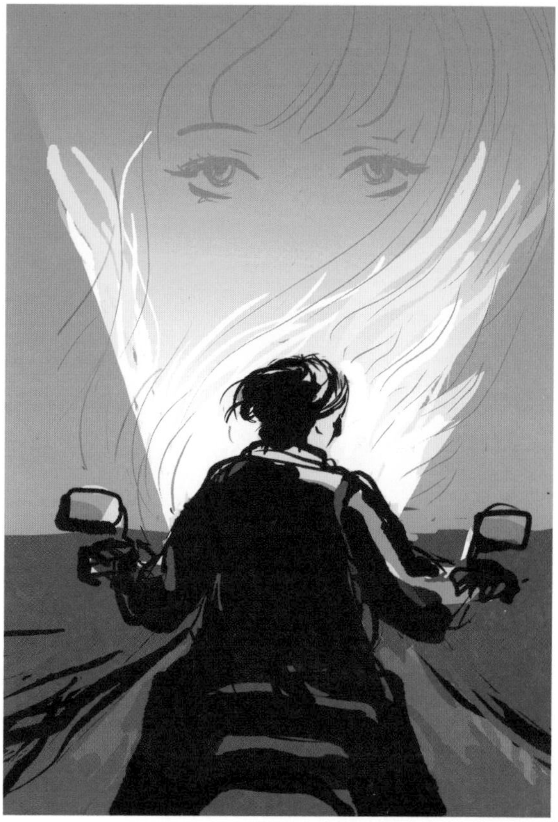

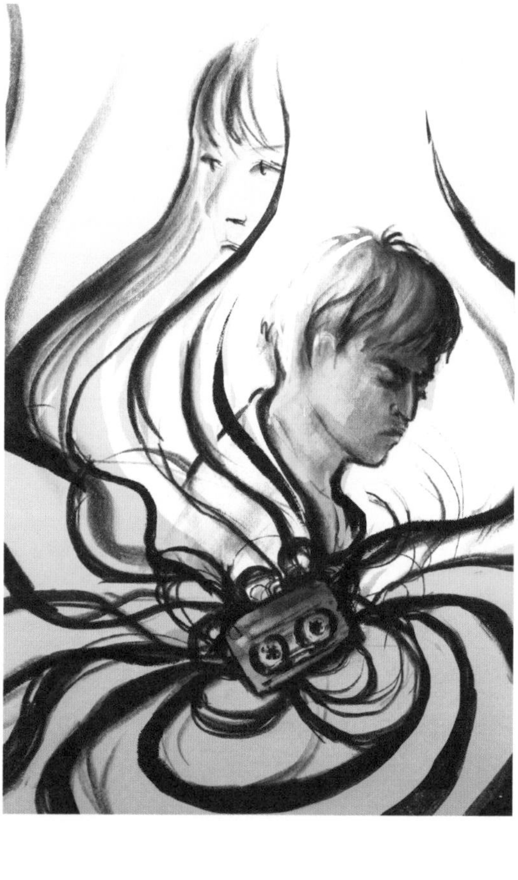

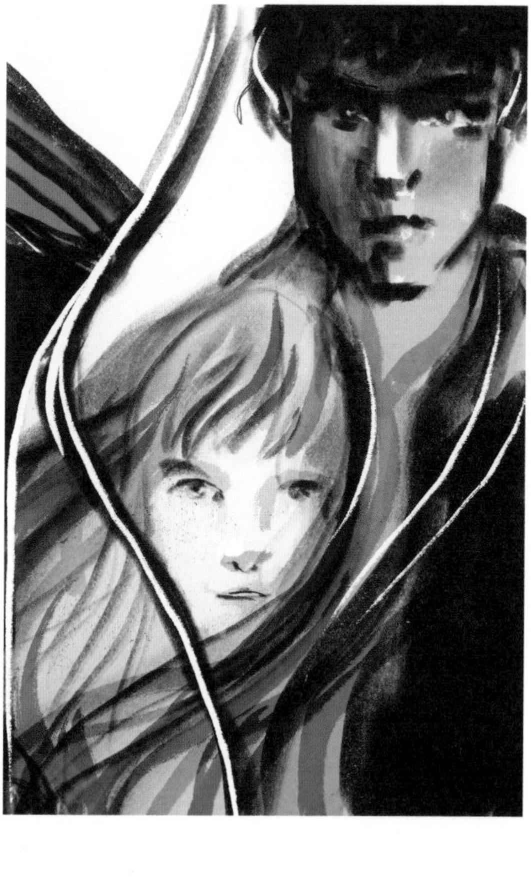

ISSUE #2 COVER by DEENA SO'OTEH

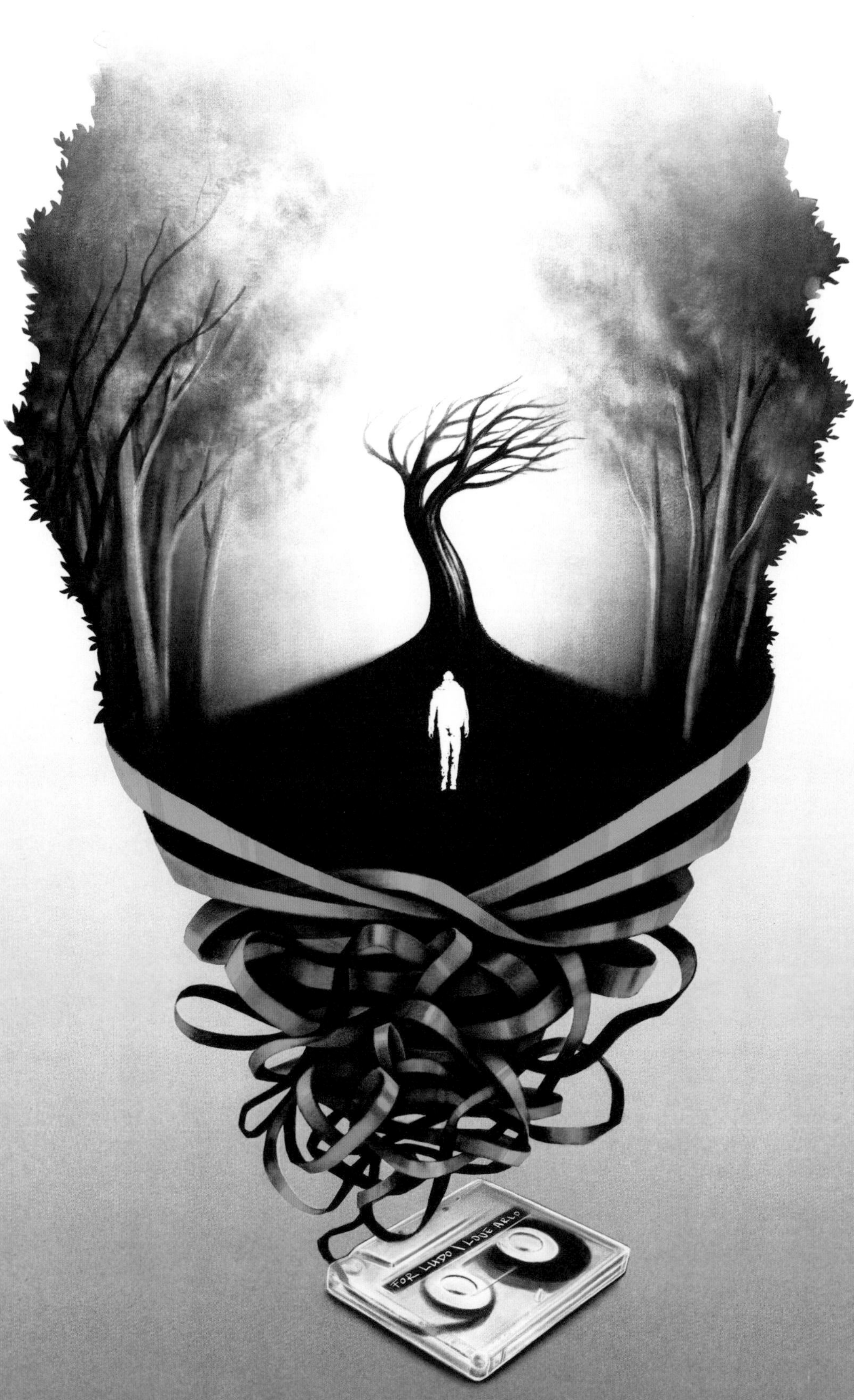
FOR LUDO \ LOVE ARLO

ISSUE #2 COVER CONCEPTS

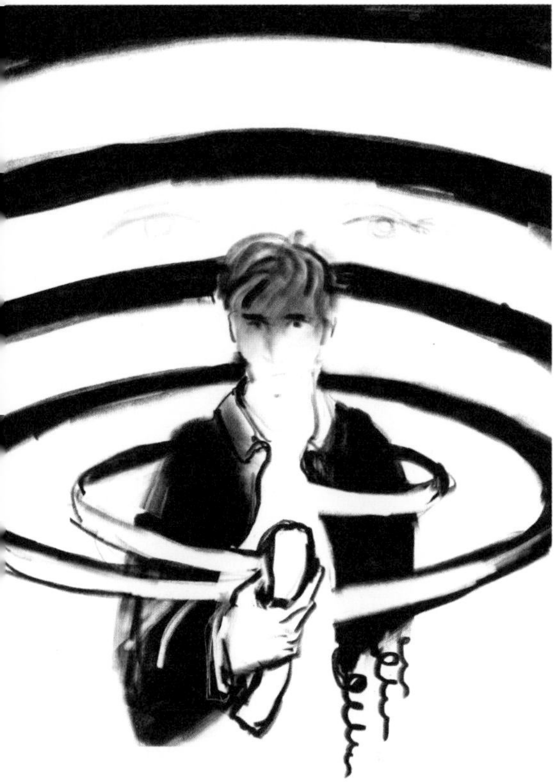

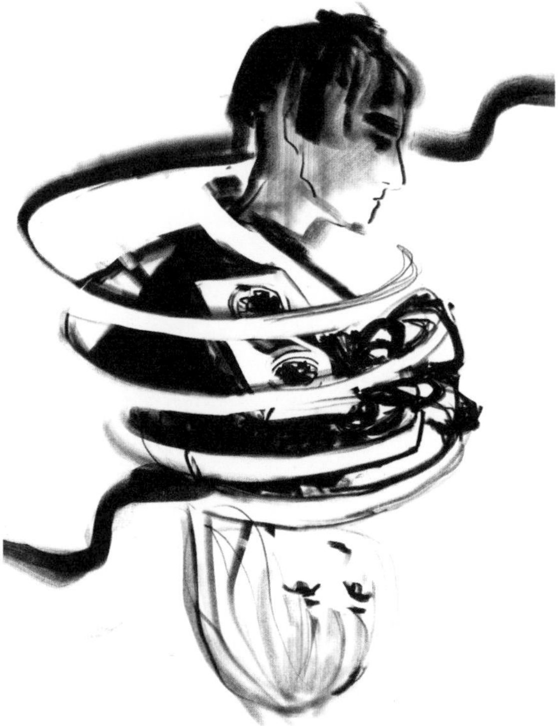

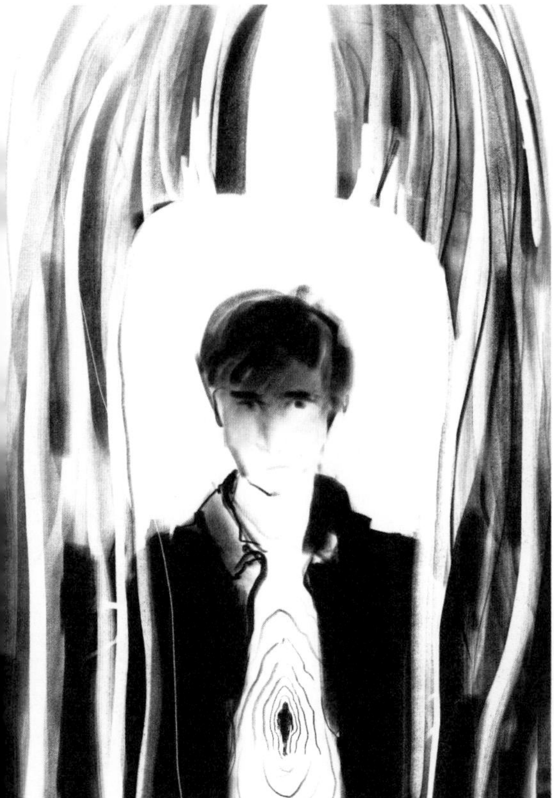

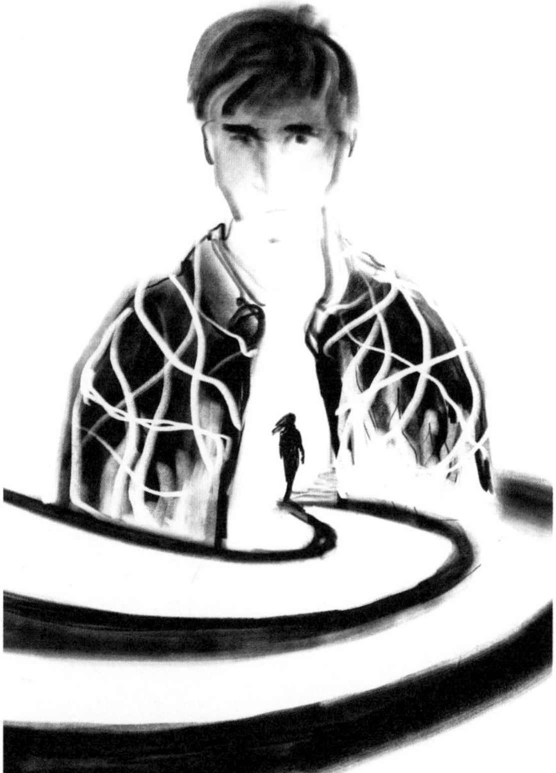

ISSUE #3 COVER by DEENA SO'OTEH

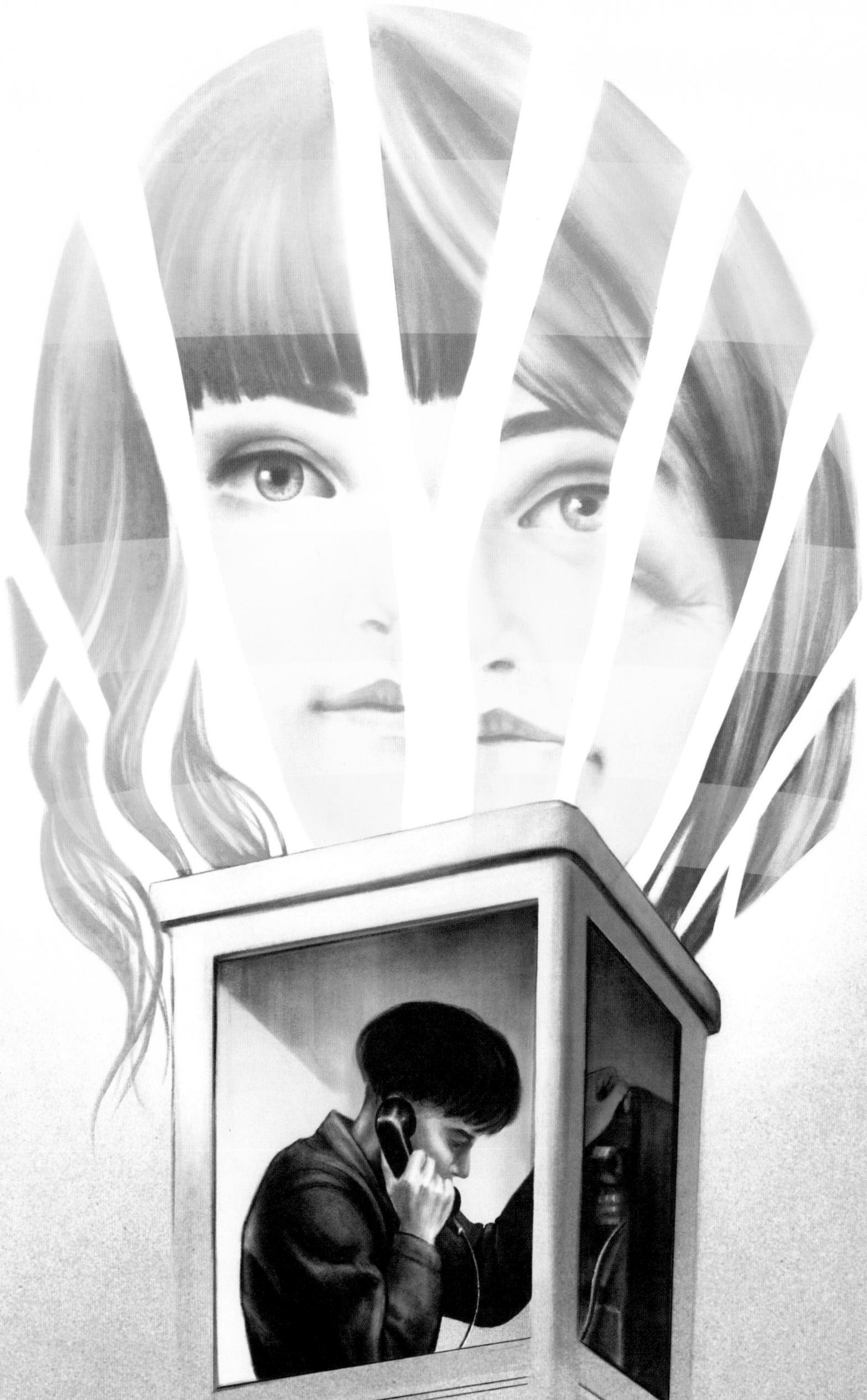

ISSUE #3 COVER CONCEPTS

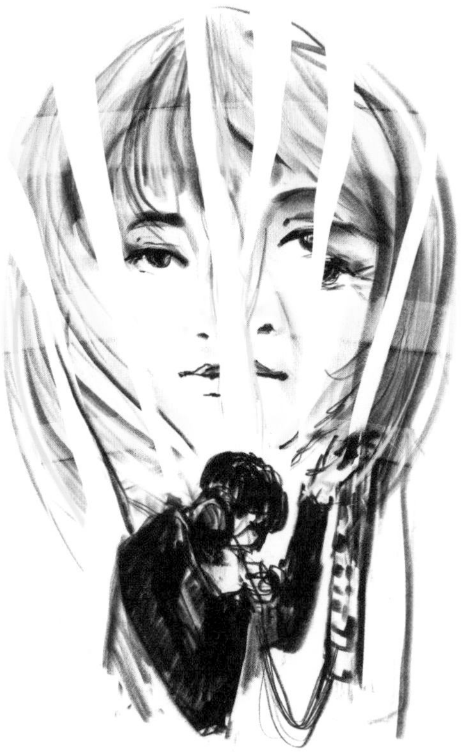

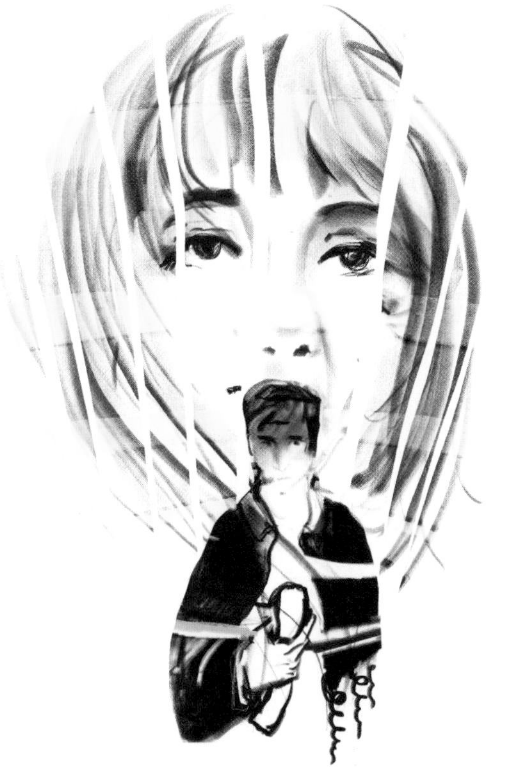

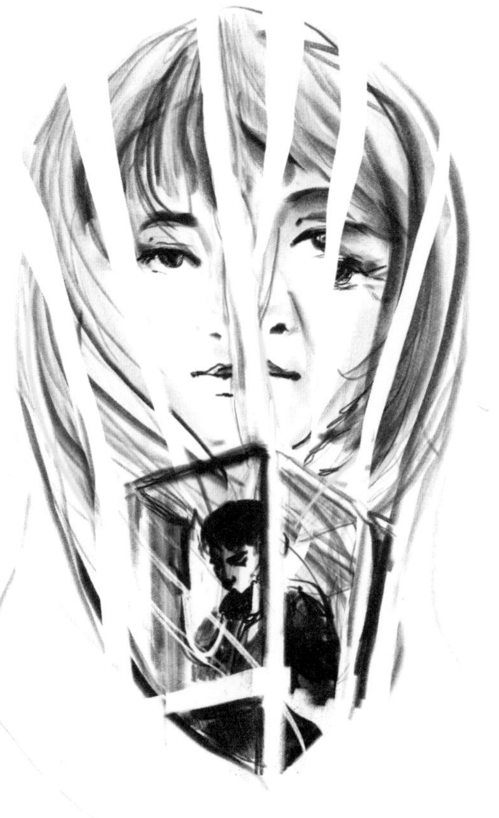

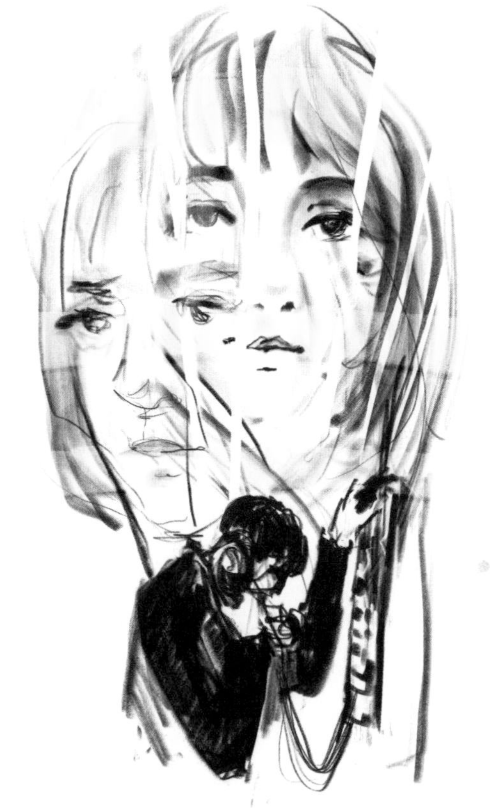

CHARACTER DESIGNS

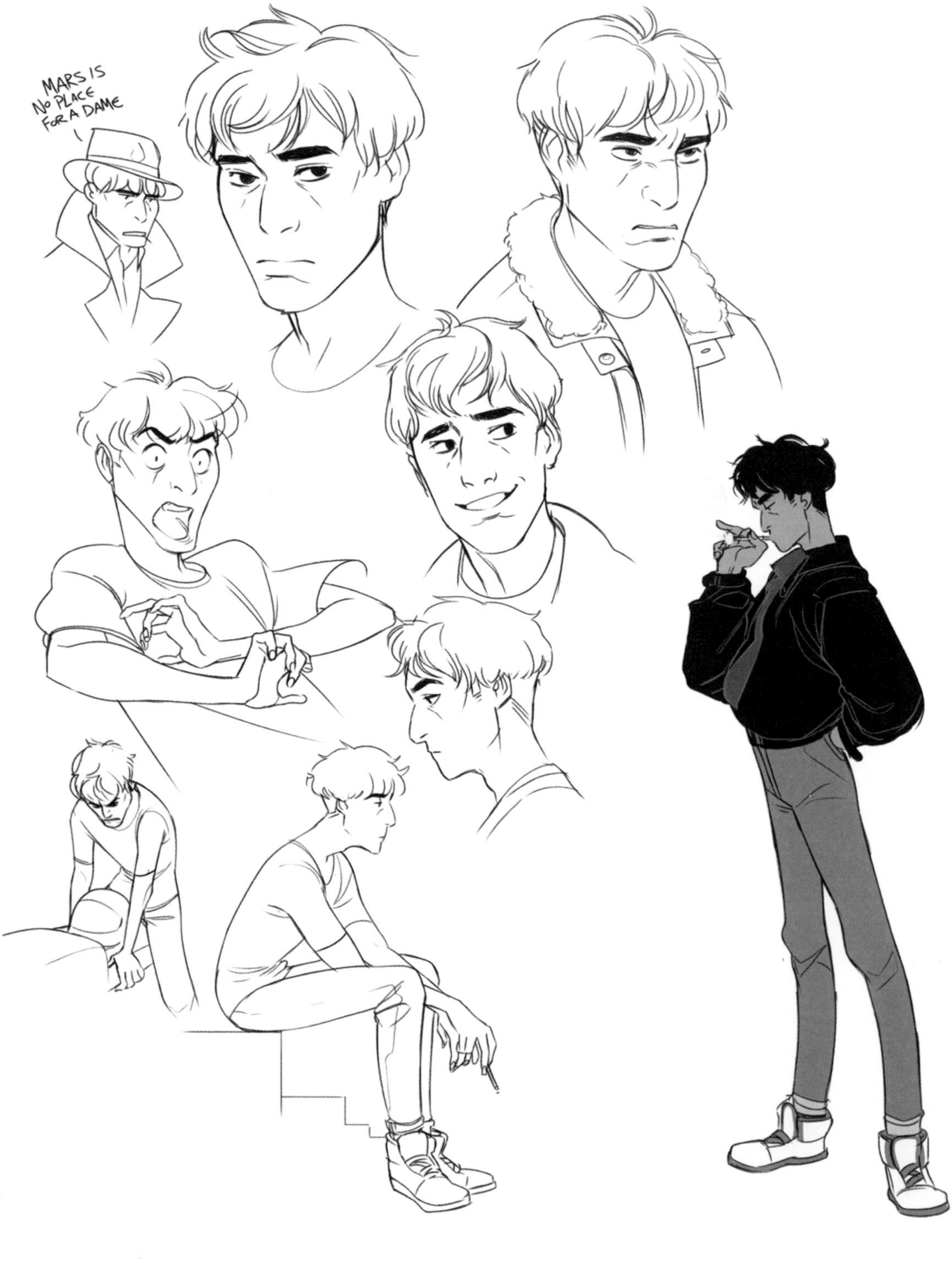
MARS IS NO PLACE FOR A DAME

LUDO CARRE

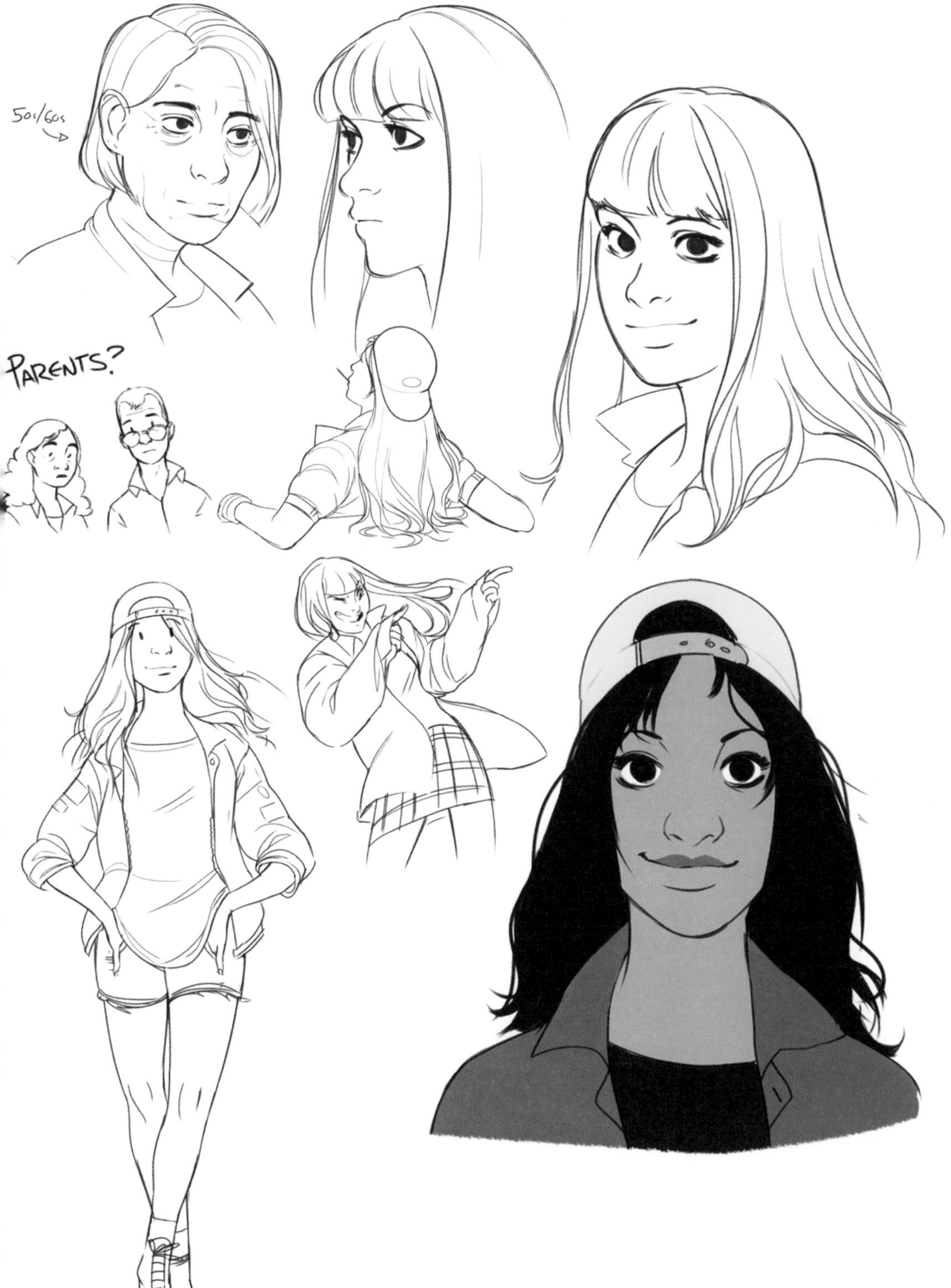
50s/60s
PARENTS?

ARLO QUINONES

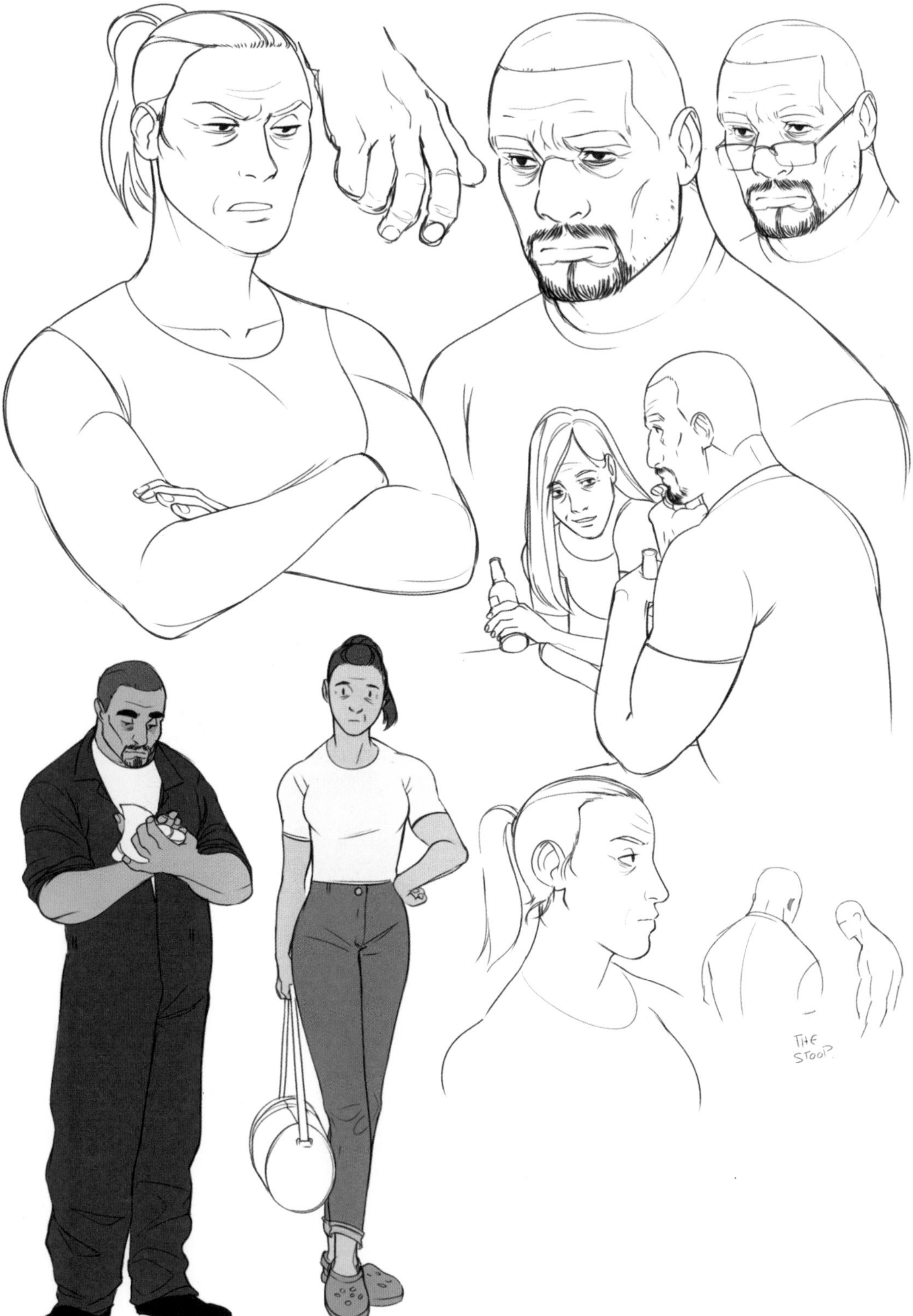
THE STOOP.

MYRIAM AND BENNY

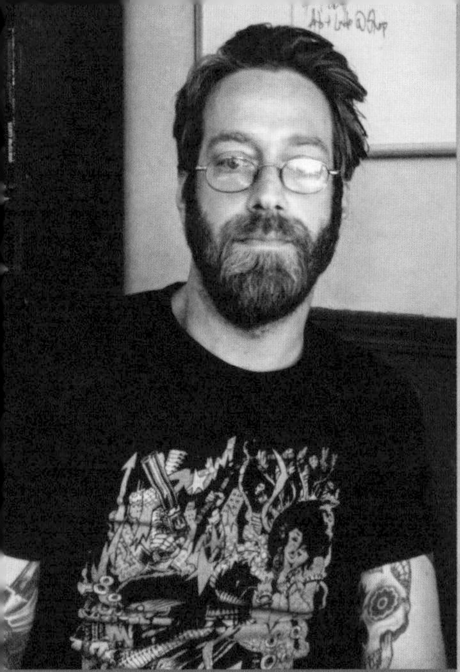

ADAM SMITH

Adam Smith is the writer of Eisner and Harvey-nominated *Long Walk to Valhalla* for Archaia Comics. He also co-created and wrote *LoveRunRiot* for Stella Comics. He was featured in DC's New Talent Showcase and has written various *Labyrinth* shorts as well as *Beneath the Dark Crystal* for The Jim Henson Company and Archaia Comics. He lives and works in Kansas City, Missouri.

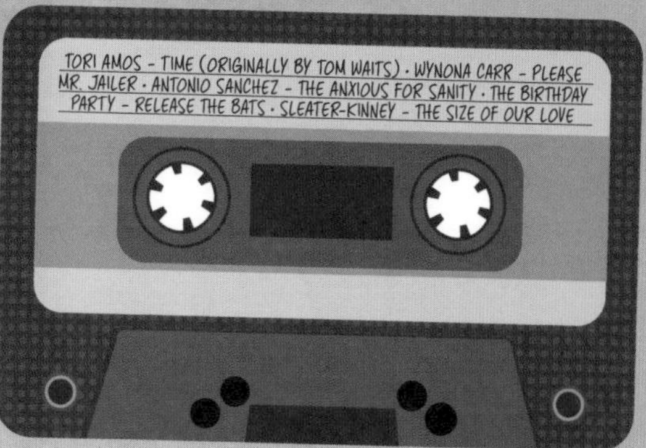
TORI AMOS - TIME (ORIGINALLY BY TOM WAITS) · WYNONA CARR - PLEASE
MR. JAILER · ANTONIO SANCHEZ - THE ANXIOUS FOR SANITY · THE BIRTHDAY
PARTY - RELEASE THE BATS · SLEATER-KINNEY - THE SIZE OF OUR LOVE

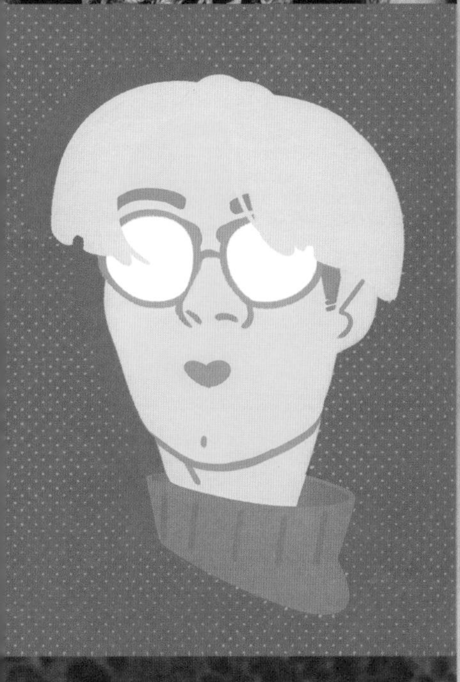

V.V. GLASS

V.V. Glass is an illustrator and cover artist specializing in digital painting techniques in comics. They have worked with Titan, 2000AD, Twisted Dark, and MTV, as well as producing game assets and concepts.

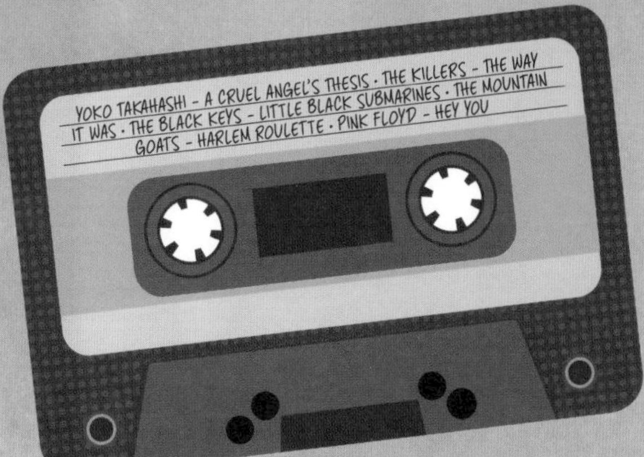
YOKO TAKAHASHI - A CRUEL ANGEL'S THESIS · THE KILLERS - THE WAY
IT WAS · THE BLACK KEYS - LITTLE BLACK SUBMARINES · THE MOUNTAIN
GOATS - HARLEM ROULETTE · PINK FLOYD - HEY YOU

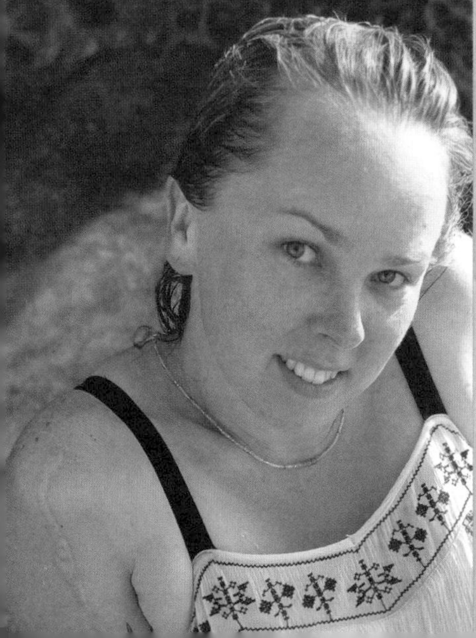

HILARY JENKINS

Hilary Jenkins' love for painting has helped create the unconventional process which she uses to colour comics. Gouache, a highly opaque medium, has allowed for the painterly style found in this book. Raised on a tiny little island, off the coast of Vancouver, she was mentored by artist David Barker. Most everything she knows about painting can be attributed to his guidance and her own unshakable wonder of the world.

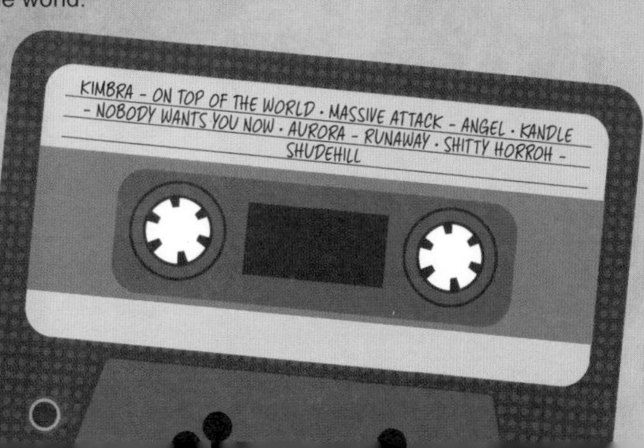
KIMBRA - ON TOP OF THE WORLD · MASSIVE ATTACK - ANGEL · KANDLE
- NOBODY WANTS YOU NOW · AURORA - RUNAWAY · SHITTY HORROH -
SHUDEHILL